WANDERING WOMEN

To my wandering grandchildren

WANDERING WOMEN

Two centuries of travel out of Ireland

A.A. Kelly

WOLFHOUND PRESS

First published 1995 by
WOLFHOUND PRESS Ltd
68 Mountjoy Square
Dublin 1

British Library Cataloguing in Publication Data
A catalogue record for this book is available from the British Library

ISBN 0-86327-445-5

Cover illustration: Katharine White, based on Helen Selina Blackwood's illustration, 'Miss Gushington experiences a new sensation,' from *Lispings from Low Latitudes: Extracts from the Journal of The Hon Impulsia Gushington*, London: John Murray, 1863. (See page 58)
Cover design: Joe Gervin
Maps: Aileen Caffrey
Typesetting: Wolfhound Press
Printed by the Guernsey Press Co Ltd, Guernsey, Channel Isles

CONTENTS
The Wanderers

PREFACE

Ireland has always been an island of wanderers, so that the Irish, like the Jewish race, now possess a diaspora. Racial and emotional attachments to the heartland remain immensely strong.

Looking back over two centuries of travel for women of Ireland, the reader travels in time as well as space, entering the minds of women who write from lives led at a pace slower than our own, a pace which gradually increases as we reach our hectic age of global communication. It is also true, as Mary Russell pointed out in her book about women travellers and their world, *The Blessings of a Good Thick Skirt* (1986), that the history of the woman traveller and her journey towards self-identification mirrors the development of female consciousness as a whole. Reading the actual words of Irish women travellers written over two centuries we are aware of the time dimension within geographical space, but also of a growing self-awareness and a changing attitude within women themselves. We are caught up in the web of a social history which brings us to our own times, an era when though in some countries women may safely hitch-hike alone, as Rosita Boland recently did round Ireland, in many parts of the world, including the so-called most civilised countries, this has either never been possible, or is today more dangerous than it was a generation ago.

Many of these women are Anglo-Irish, and all from before Ireland's independence were also perforce British. Among a similar group of women drawn from Britain but excluding Ireland there would be more empire builders and missionaries' wives, fewer single religious. Yet the latter, so numerous from Ireland, were reticent and are thus under-represented in this volume. There is a strong sense, when assessing the writings of Irish women, that a crowd of travelling emigrants, self-effacing nuns, many simple, unsung women, must be hovering, silent and shadowy, in the background.

Eleanor Cavanagh and Maureen Hamish represent those who worked as servants in houses abroad or accompanied travellers as ladies' maids, but what of the thousands who might or might not travel on once they reached America, South Africa, or Australia? Somewhere, hidden in attics and boxes there must be letters from this unrepresented multitude.

In the main, women from Ireland who wrote about travel were well educated and determined. As the nineteenth century advanced social restrictions upon women shrank, though they have still not disappeared. For early nineteenth century women two-way travel was confined to 'proper' destinations. Women went as companions or governesses, with relatives, to stay with friends. It was only after the introduction of mass travel, initiated by Thomas Cook, that single women could find suitably escorted groups within which they were respectably secure. Tourism now began, though the word 'tourist' had been in use since 1800 or so, used originally to describe those touring round museums and local places of interest.

An objectionably conceited Dr Abraham Eldon wrote *The Continental Traveller's Oracle: Maxims for Foreign Locomotion*, edited by his nephew after his death and published in 1828. Italy was then a dangerous country 'infested with robbers of all hues'. Young women travellers should be taught that the Continent is a lion's den, Frenchmen and Italians little better than two-legged beasts, said he. In fact Eldon is so protective of single women that he believes they should avoid travel, stay at home and read the Bible. He is also sarcastic about young women who travel on the Continent and then become 'lady oracles' upon their return, 'holding forth in loud voices'.

Sixty years later things have changed, and the writing of Lillias Campbell Davidson in her *Hints to Lady Travellers at home and abroad* (1889) reflects the growth of organised travel. She does not recommend taking a maid, for they are usually a great nuisance, 'weak and impotent things'. 'Now and then one alights upon a brilliant exception who looks after one's luggage and one's personal comfort and takes one's tickets and the care of one's belongings in a way which allows one to dismiss all care from one's mind'!

Davidson writes euphemistically that: 'Southall's inventions are highly to be recommended and will be found most convenient and handy.' She also recommends taking wedges for doors to prevent 'outside tampering' when the lock is poor or missing. She adds: 'There is perhaps no better medicine than a course of foreign travel,' and 'if you confine yourself to the beaten track, to hotels frequented by English and American travellers, your own language will be enough to trust to.' Porters were to be found 'in flocks everywhere'. Passports were not necessary on the Continent, though it was safer to have one, and tea being in general contraband, only a small amount should be carried. Yet only forty years before this Murray's *Handbook for Northern Europe* (1849) had considered it indispensable to take letters of introduction and speak fluent French!

Dorothy Middleton in *Victorian Lady Travellers* (1965) has interesting opinions about travel for the house-bound, male-dominated Victorian woman: 'Trained from birth to an almost impossible ideal of womanly submission and self-discipline, of obligation to class and devotion to religion, she had need of an emotional as well as of an intellectual outlet. This she found, often late in life, in travel, and though her dignity never wavered, and she seems to have imposed her severe moral standards on the very rough company in which she often found herself, she was able to enjoy a freedom of action unthinkable at home. Fortified by a kind of innocent valour, convinced of the civilizing mission of woman, clothed in long skirts and armed with an umbrella or sunshade according to the climate, the nineteenth century woman traveller covered thousands of miles – writing, painting, observing, botanizing, missionizing, collecting and, latterly, photographing. They deplored the necessity of riding astride and could rarely bring themselves to wear trousers.'

At the end of the nineteenth century W. Fraser Rae wrote the significantly titled *The Business of Travel* (1891) to celebrate the silver jubilee of Messrs Thomas Cook & Son, whose first organised trip was the 1841 Leicester to Loughborough twelve mile train journey, when 570 passengers travelled for one shilling each plus band and fanfare, ending with tea and buns in the park. Cook's Holy Land tours began in 1868 and tours down the Nile followed. Such travellers were no longer at the mercy of 'savage chiefs' who had made earlier travellers pay for protection, and the element of danger had been almost entirely removed. In 1872 Thomas Cook, aged sixty-four, and a group of nine men from England, Scotland, Russia, America and Greece set off by sea and land on an exploratory world tour, which took them 222 days, so that by the time Fraser Rae's book came out a tour of the globe 'was a matter of everyday occurrence'. It was these would-be travellers who read Beatrice

Grimshaw's books.

By the 1890s mass travel was established. Thomas Cook & Son now sold some 30,000 guide books per annum, their monthly journal, *Excursionist*, had a circulation of 120,000, while their staff employed in Egypt and Palestine alone numbered 978.

And what of the twentieth century? Sybille Bedford remarks in *A Visit to Don Otavio* (1960) that since travel has become more commonplace 'the foreigner in some countries has lost much of her curiosity value.' Reading through the accounts these earlier Irish women give, they are frequently regarded with awe, disbelief, sometimes even terror, and in other cultures usually given the honorary status of a male, a situation which Dervla Murphy has had upon occasions to disprove, even quite recently, by baring her breasts.

Women who are able to travel and write about it today have lost their status as 'civilisers' in return for more equality with men. They are no longer expected to be subservient to the male, yet there remain extensive areas of the world where a woman still may not travel alone easily by daylight, let alone after dark.

Written just after the second world war, Dorothy Carrington's introduction to her travel anthology *The Traveller's Eye* (1949) could not have foreseen the travel explosion which was to come in the latter part of the twentieth century: 'At the time I write this, travel has become difficult, perhaps more difficult than at any time in the last two centuries. Since the many left at home are greedy for news, the few privileged travellers must all be reporters; roaring over continents at unparalleled speed and in no great comfort, they recognise their duty to jot down their impressions of the dislocated world. The few who stay long in one place are zealous observers resembling the travellers of the seventeenth century, save that their study is no longer nature but man ... A new conception of the world is being formed in our time.'

The purposes of travel of the women in this book are manifold, as are the unforeseen fruits their experience brings. Some of the finer ladies went to acquire taste and learning, most sought greater opportunity for new and wider lives. Through travel increased wealth might follow, but its acquisition was not the prime purpose, for even Sarah Heckford when she set off to South Africa did not originally intend to become a trader.

Of all the women considered here only Daisy Bates and Beatrice Grimshaw remained permanently overseas, locally integrated, with Ireland a memory. Some, such as the Countess of Blessington, Louise Costello and Emily de

Burgh Daly, lived for years in one country. Others went abroad perforce with husbands and fathers, for work or experience. More than half of these women also wrote fiction or poetry in which their travel experience was used, and several of them were artists or photographers. Then there are the nuns whose travel was involuntary, undertaken as part of their vocation.

John Julius Norwich in his anthology, *A Taste for Travel* (1985), analyses the difference between the traveller and the tourist, and suggests that nowadays the difference between the two lies less in the places we go to than in the way we go to them. This criterion would certainly apply to women such as Flora Shaw, Daisy Bates, Beatrice Grimshaw, Dervla Murphy and Mary Russell, all exploratory travellers.

There are many opinions about the reasons for and the benefits of travel. For Albert Camus fear gave value to travel. Deprived of normal routine, often unable to communicate adequately, stripped of our social underpinning, we are exposed at our face value. For Lawrence Durrell travel formed a reward-ing form of introspection. Salman Rushdie, in 'On Adventure' (1985), writes that the best travel adventures have 'some inner journey, some adventure in the self'. Dervla Murphy believes one motive for her travel is escape, espe-cially from modern cities. She would agree with Daisy Bates: 'The natural nomad [is] the man who all at once feels he must abandon home and friends and wander somewhere, anywhere away from the interminable sameness of houses and streets and people'.

There are those who travel from curiosity, to study nature or humankind, and those who go initially for health reasons, or to find their true selves in a strange environment. Some go to run away from responsibilities, others to confront fresh ones. All travel enriches in some way. Freya Stark, when aged eighty-three, expresses this well:

'When the years of travel came they justified everything that the coloured maps, and especially their emptier patches, had promised; and, now that I find actual journeys not so easy, they still feed me with their Ariel voices and make my world feel wider than it is.' (*A Peak in Darien*, 1976)

During the period covered by this volume travel has passed through two transformations: first the beginning of organised travel for the middle classes, started by Thomas Cook, which spread so rapidly in the nineteenth century, and secondly the late twentieth-century explosion of mass tourism with the introduction of cheap charter flights.

At the end of the twentieth century solo woman travellers are still rare. Few men and fewer woman will tolerate the discomfort and uncertainty of exploratory travel off the beaten track. Those women who do are mostly young, as we can see from an advisory anthology such as *Women travel – adventures, advice and experience* (editors, Miranda Davies & Natania Jansz (1990), one of the Rough Guide series. It contains a number of essays by lone women travelling round China or hitch-hiking to Tibet, together with notes on accommodation, transport, special problems, the status of women in each area, and reading lists. Some of these women were working in volunteer organisations, some travelled alone for the first time, some were journalists, students, or worked as educators, etc. One cycled solo across the Nubian desert as part of a journey through Africa. The recent Virago series of woman's travel guides to big cities includes notes on sexual harassment and what to do about it.

Travel has made us conscious of our global responsibility. Not only has mass tourism, now the world's largest industry, ruined certain populous areas of the world, but it has latterly made many decide that they should travel with a conscience. Such an awareness has spawned books such as *The Good Tourist* (1991), by Katie Wood & Syd House, a worldwide guide for the green traveller. There is John Gormley's *The Green Guide for Ireland* (Wolfhound Press, 1990) and *The Handbook for Women Travellers*, by Maggie & Gemma Ross. Tourism Concern (London) produces school teaching packs on the global effects of tourism, and there is now a Third World European Network on Tourism (TEN) in Germany and a centre for responsible travelling in California.

Mary Russell, in *The Blessings of a Good Thick Skirt*, divides travellers into two types, those who set out for a distant destination on a quest for a specific goal, and those who 'weave in and out among the lives of people they encounter on the way'. She notes that most women fall into the latter category.

Some of these women from Ireland travelled only when impelled, or employed, to do so, Charlotte O'Brien to improve conditions on emigrant ships, Edith Somerville to write magazine articles, Flora Shaw as a political correspondent. Many of the earlier women went anywhere opportunity, marriage or family took them, some unwillingly like Clarissa Trant. Of them all only a few such as Grimshaw, Bates, Murphy and Connell fall into the category of those who enjoy weaving in and out of the lives of people, the Papuans, the Australian aborigines, the Tibetans, the Nepalese, to whom each becomes attached by sharing their working lives.

The excerpts from each participant in this volume have been chosen for their variety, and at sufficient length to give an idea of each writer's voice. Except for the modern writers most of their books are out of print, which is why the fascinating Beatrice Grimshaw, who deserves a book to herself, has been treated at some length.

The fruits of mass travel are related to those of mass communication, the other phenomenon of our age, for never in the course of human history have so many individuals met or viewed so many others. The results must have both positive and negative results. Positive is a growing awareness of our globe as an entity, with its immense variety. Negative could be a callousness to the problems of population growth and poverty in less fortunate areas. For even as in 1800 only the prosperous few amongst Europeans travelled in style with carriages and servants, so today a minority of the world's population can afford to travel by air, cushioned by tour leaders, staying in ghettos of relative comfort, where water comes in bottles and a stray mosquito under the bed is regarded with horror. The scale has changed, distances have shrunk, but the principle has remained the same, except that those early travellers in their carriages put up with more discomfort than most of us.

~

Unless you were a nun or an emigrant, travel for Irish women before the nineteenth century, and indeed for most women at that time, was restricted to excursions into Europe, accompanied by the appropriate retinue or with a husband, father or brother in tow. We know from the well-known diaries of writers such as William Beckford, James Boswell or Charles Burney that when the Grand Tour was at its height in the eighteeenth century, roads were often poor and accommodation patchy.

Travel beyond Europe was most often as a wife accompanying her husband, sometimes as a daughter with her father, or as a companion, so that the earlier records of Irish women travel writers are journals, letters and memoirs, written in the leisured style of the day, either published by such women upon their return, or by relatives years later.

MELASINA TRENCH

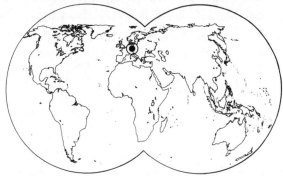

A European traveller struggling with social class in Germany and Austria.

Melasina (1768-1827) (née Chenevix) was brought up by her grandfather the Bishop of Waterford, then in 1786 married Colonel Richard St George who died in Portugal two years later. As a young widow she kept a journal on her visit to Germany in 1799/1800. In 1803 she married Richard Trench of County Galway. Her youthful journal was eventually edited and published by her son in 1861.

Melasina evidently found social restrictions impeded her as a traveller. From Vienna she writes: 'It grieves me to find travelling contribute so little to the improvement of my mind. A variety of causes operates to prevent the possibility of a woman reaping *much* benefit from a journey through Germany, unless she totally gives up the world. A certain enlargement of ideas must imperceptibly follow, and she corrects some erroneous notions; but she finds infinite difficulty in making any new acquirements. The multiplicity of visits, not confined to leaving a card, as in London, but real substantial, bodily visits, and the impossibility, without overstepping all the bounds of custom, of associating with any but *noblesse*, may be reckoned among the greatest obstacles. To make travelling subservient to improvement, it must be undertaken on a different plan from my present journey.'

This then was why she wished to travel, for 'improvement', but alas 'the world', that is her own social class, to which she was restricted, often proved frustratingly conventional.

Letters of introduction were then indispensable, so was a good knowledge of French. *Murray's Handbook for Northern Europe* (1849) also recommends an ability 'to foot it on the light fantastic' as 'an accomplishment highly prized and likely to be constantly in requisition', dancing then being the only occasion upon which the sexes could draw close to one another.

Although writers such as Melasina Trench give us useful glimpses of contemporary life – Vienna, for example, then contained 53,000 inhabitants and one could walk round the walls in an hour – such writings were chiefly of interest to readers for anecdotes about famous persons met at receptions or dinners, such as the following extract from Melasina written in Dresden:

— Dined at Mr Elliot's with only the Nelson party. It is plain that Lord Nelson thinks of nothing but Lady Hamilton, who is totally occupied by the same object. She is bold, forward, coarse, assuming, and vain. Her figure is colossal, but, excepting her feet, which are hideous, well shaped. Her bones are large, and she is exceedingly *enbonpoint*. She resembles the bust of Ariadne; the shape of all her features is fine, as is the form of her head, and particularly her ears; her teeth are a little irregular, but tolerably white; her eyes light blue, with a brown spot in one, which, though a defect, takes nothing away from her beauty and expression. Her eyebrows and hair are dark, and her complexion coarse. Her expression is strongly marked, variable, and interesting; her movements in common life ungraceful; her voice loud, yet not disagreeable. Lord Nelson is a little man, without any dignity... Lady Hamilton takes possession of him, and he is a willing captive, the most submissive and devoted I have seen. —

It is interesting to compare Melasina's impression with that of J.B.S. Morritt (1772-1843) whose almost contemporary diary records that Lady Hamilton is '*most* elegant' with 'the finest hair in the world, flowing loose over her shoulders. These set off a tall, beautiful figure, and a face that varies for ever, and is always lovely.'

The following day Melasina went to the Opera with the Nelson party and the next day, at Lady Hamilton's invitation, went to see Lord Nelson dressed for Court. The third day she dined with Lord Nelson and went on to a concert. Such detail would be of interest to the curious reader at a time when there were no gossip columns or popular Press.

KATHERINE AND MARTHA WILMOT

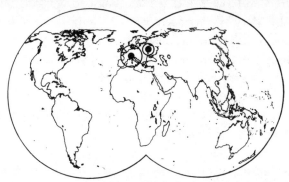

Sisters whose journeys ranged from the exigencies of the Grand Tour, to the depths of Russia

Almost contemporary with Melasina are the journals of the Wilmot sisters, whose original letters and diaries are in the library of the Royal Irish Academy. Edited extracts from their various journals were not published until 1920 and 1934 respectively. A further volume, *The Grand Tours of Katherine Wilmot: France 1801-3 and Russia 1805-7*, compiled and edited by Elizabeth Mavor, has recently been published (1992). The Wilmots also show evidence of impatience with social restrictions.

Katherine Wilmot (1773-1824), eldest of six daughters and three sons, was born in Drogheda where her father, Captain Edward Wilmot, originally from Derbyshire, was then port surveyor. Martha (1775-1873) was born in County Cork where her mother came from. After the Peace of Amiens (1802) Katherine, who had just inherited a legacy from her grandmother, went with Lord Mount Cashell's party on a Grand Tour of the Continent.

Katherine gives a lively account of this tour, edited by Thomas U. Sadleir, and published in 1920 as *An Irish Peer on the Continent 1801-1803, being a narrative of the tour of Stephen 2nd Earl Mountcashell through France, Italy, etc. as related by Catherine Wilmot*.

It is extraordinary that such a party should have set off into a still turbulent Continent, relying upon what turned out to be the hollow Treaty of Amiens, but travel had been impossible since 1789. The Mount Cashells, their two small daughters and Katherine were 'packed into the family coach, with two valets and two maids in another carriage'. Katherine calls them 'nine Irish adventurers'. On the cross-channel boat Lady Mount Cashell, aged thirty and three months pregnant with her seventh child, smuggled a Monsieur Amoulin in her suite because he could not get a passport.

Margaret Mount Cashell (daughter of Lord Kingsborough), the second of twelve children, and a very independent-minded woman, had been tutored in her teens by Mary Wollstonecraft. To the annoyance of her husband she was interested in Irish republican politics.

Many English and Irish tourers had flocked over the Channel after so many years of not being able to travel. The Mount Cashells stayed in Paris for nine months, dining with Talleyrand, Napoleon and socialising with many friends. When they left Paris they made quite a party. A governess had arrived for the girls, and an Irish tutor for their young sons, Robert and Edward, who joined them. Mary Smith, a maid, travelled separately with Lady Mount Cashell and her newborn son, who had been helped into the world by Katherine. Para, the avant courier, rode in front to arrange accommodation.

They stayed six months in Italy. Katherine caught cold in the Alps and spent most of their two weeks in Turin in bed. Their ten days in Milan was in 'uninterrupted rain'.

Katherine writes thus from the Albergo Pio, Florence, 28 November, 1802:

— It is a fortnight since I wrote last from Milan, which we quitted that day. We have since been loitering at Pavia, Plaisance, Parma, Modena, Bologna and yesterday arrived at Florence. The distance from Milan to this place is 219 English miles which we performed with voituriers, the slowest and most sleepy mode of travelling in the world.

On quitting Milan we travelled on for about fifteen miles, where we turned a little out of our road to see the famous Chartreuse, which is reckoned the finest [sic] in Europe. It has entirely escaped the devastations of the French, though they have deprived the Carthusian monks of their revenues, and reduced them to twenty-five from an establishment of five hundred. It is formed on the model of the Cathedral of Milan and built by Visconti. It stands in an open country, and you see it at the end of an enormous long avenue made of cypress; it is wrought as beautifully almost upon the outside as the ivory work of a fan, and the sculpture is perfection itself. The collection of precious stones and pillars of the finest marble, together with the paintings in fresco, surpass belief. The monks in their black robes, wandering through the aisles give a peculiarly picturesque appearance to the character of the place.

Just before we entered Pavia we saw the spot celebrated for the victory of Charles 5th over Francis 1st. On driving into the town we saw the equestrian status of Marcus Aurelius Antoninus, the Lance of Orlando, etc., and the next day were disabled from going any farther than a few miles by the torrents of rain that fell, and therefore were obliged to put up at a miserable, wild, dismantled looking house, with all the air in the world of being haunted, either with spirits or banditti. Bands of robbers infest this part of the country, and we heard of the horrid assassination of five men when we were in Milan, which ... must not only have been in this spot, but their murderers harboured precisely in this very house, from the description answering so exactly to everything we saw.

On these occasions whenever Lady Mount Cashell and my courage began to give way, we consulted the expression of Para's countenance, the courier who knew every inch of the ground, and had served in that public capacity in the French army during all the campaigns in Italy. He had more address and intrepidity of nature than any man I ever knew; bore hunger, cold and sleeplessness absolutely without the consciousness of their being evils, and quite with the distinguished air of a cavalier, possessed a cheerfulness of humour and courtesy of manner that in the life of adventure we were rendered in Para a person of the highest moment.

On our going therefore upstairs, and (from the cracked panes of the trickling windows) seeing that the rains had swelled the water so as to moat round the Inn like an island, and perceiving everything inside in frightful disorder, the long deal table overturned and cut and slashed with dinner knives upon the surface, a picture of Jesus Christ reversed upon its peg and warnings scrawled with blood and charcoal against the wall, we trembled like a pair of arch cowards, and with one accord and at the same moment, asked each other what Para thought of the situation we were in?

We instantly went flying in pursuit of him and found him with a parcel of faggots in his arms, coming to light our fire on a flat expanse of hearth, and followed by two black hideous looking men, with torn mattresses on their backs, which they flumpt down in a passion in the middle of the floor, and went off growling like a pair of demons. This did not add much to our composure, nor did Para's face, which was set exactly in that resolute way which augured perfect hopelessness on our part of expounding his thoughts, by any questions we could put to him, and therefore we let him follow his inventions, which were these.

For the mattresses of straw to be laid round the fire, on which Lady Mount Cashell, the child and I were to repose covered over with our greatcoats. Candles to burn on the tables throughout the night and the fire to be eternally replenished, for which bundles of wood were unwillingly brought into the room. Lord Mount Cashell to be in the little closet within side of us.

For our supper they brought us up a patriarchal cock with stiff black legs, which seemed to have died of gout a month before, and macaroni in a bowl writhing into a hundred serpents. The door was then locked and we were to await our doom till morning.

You can imagine the kind of night we spent. The wind was roaring a hurricane, and the rain pattering frightfully against the windows. There were no shutters to prevent our seeing bright blue flashes of lightning fork across the room, or hearing the crashes of thunder breaking in hollow echoes amongst the Apennines, which eternally reminded us of these mountains being the resort of legions of banditti, who always find in their recesses a sanctuary from the pursuits of justice. —

The following morning as they drove away Para rode up to the carriage window and congratulated them from escaping from the 'most complete cut-throat spot in Italy'. He had armed himself with pistols, the two voituriers with stilettos, and they had all sat up with the people of the inn all night, drinking, and found out that the inn was indeed 'a harbour for assassins', aided by the innkeeper and his sons.

Later on the journey, they have a private audience with the Pope:

— At four o'clock on Good Friday Lady Mount Cashell and I, accompanied the Princess Borghese to the gardens of the Vatican where at the end of a long avenue, we beheld Pius VII encircled by his righteous conclave. He was dressed in a scarlet large flowing mantle trimmed with gold, scarlet beaver hat bound with gold, scarlet shoes with gold crosses embroidered on each, and a friar's dress underneath his mantle. The Princess, as we approached his holiness, stepped forward and throwing herself on her knees kissed his toe. Lady Mount Cashell and I advanced and were half bent to perform the like operation when I am grieved to say the Pope, by a motion of his hand, dispensed us from this tribute, which we would most gladly have paid, and sincerely disappointed at the compliment, we walked with him towards the pavilion into which he walked first, though this prerogative he made appear as much the effect of accident as possible. Here we sat an hour, extremely pleasant and utterly free from the slightest form of ceremony. He is more than sixty years of age apparently, with sincere, simple and gentleman-like manners. —

Evidently Katherine spoke reasonable Italian as well as French. They later get permission to visit the Convent of the Capucines, where the monks came out to meet them 'in full grin', showed them their cells, and then the underground cemetery where the monks were left to dry naturally after death. 'In each compartment, erect against the wall, stood six skeletons in the capuchin habit with their skins dried tight upon their bones, and their long beards flowing grizzly to their girdles .... The live monks who conducted us told us all their names, pointed out who and who were their friends, showed us the vacant niches they expected they should fill, and altogether appeared as little appalled at the idea of becoming like those horrid grim skeletons, as if the transformation was not to be acquired through the ordeal of death.'

Shortly after this the activities of Napoleon made it imperative for foreigners, even from Ireland, to return home. The four Mount Cashell children had been left behind in Nîmes with their tutor and governess, and were taken to Geneva for safety, though Mr Egan, the tutor, was imprisoned by the French. The Mount Cashells later united their scattered flock in Rome where the following year Margaret Mount Cashell gave birth to her eighth child, and shortly afterwards fell in love with George William Tighe. Leaving her family she settled in Pisa with Tighe under the name of Mrs Mason (from a character in a Mary Wollstonecraft short story!) She had two daughters by Tighe and is said to have inspired Shelley's 'The Sensitive Plant'. She died in 1835.

Katherine, meantime, had left the Mount Cashells and joined a friend, Mrs Clifford, on a long barouche journey home through Vienna, Prague, Berlin and Denmark.

While Katherine travelled with the Mount Cashells Martha Wilmot, who edited a monthly magazine and wrote plays, had been invited, through the introduction of a cousin, to visit Princess Daschkov (1744-1810), president of the Academy of Sciences at St Petersburg and largely instrumental in putting Catherine II on the throne. Martha, depressed by the recent death of her favourite brother, and envious of her sister Katherine's travel, persuaded her father to let her go. This was her first time out of Ireland and it took her four months to reach Troitskoe, the Princess's estate east of Moscow. She travelled by road to Dublin, took the Holyhead packet, then the stagecoach to London, and a ship from Gravesend. In the end Martha stayed with the Princess, who became infatuated with her, for five years, then left hurriedly in 1808 when war broke out.

By 1805 Martha had already been with the Princess for two years and Katherine was instructed by her parents to go to Russia and bring her home. In her journal Katherine gives a witty account of her journey to Russia and of life with Princess Dashkov.

After almost two years in Russia, failing to persuade the Princess to part with Martha, Katherine returned to Ireland bringing with her a copy of the

Princess's memoirs as dictated to Martha. She took ship home and from Elsinore, spent five weeks tacking into head winds and passed through the British fleet the day before the bombardment of Copenhagen. She later picked up a trading steamer Bristol-Cork in Autumn 1807. Katherine was more delicate than Martha. She afterwards lived in Paris, and died there of tuberculosis.

Martha published the memoirs of Princess Daschkov, translated into English, in 1840, waiting as requested for thirty years after their author's death. Martha was by then married to the Reverend William Bradford, chaplain to the British Embassy in Vienna. In 1857, when he died, she returned to Dublin and lived with a married daughter. Her first child was named Catherine Anne Dashkov after the Princess.

When Martha eventually left Russia for Ireland in 1808 she had trouble with the Customs. She was then shipwrecked off Finland and eventually got back home, much delayed. She gives a good account of the uncertainties of travel during that stormy Napoleonic year. She also describes the simple Finnish family on an island with whom she took refuge after the shipwreck:

— The Mamma was my delight. I tried to find out from her everything that I could relative to the state of a society in which she appeared to take the lead. She told me the population of the place was fifty-two souls, including men, women and children. All their habits, manners, customs and their religious, were such as had existed when they belonged to Sweden; at present they were Russian subjects. She had another son, it appeared, at Fredericksham, learning to read, which they all could do without exception. A clergyman came to the island twice a year, to instruct them in their religion, of which they appeared to understand the principles, and which, as well as I could judge, was Lutheran ...

Nature has been bountiful to these dear islanders in the gifts of strength and rustic beauty; the women in particular are well formed, and, thanks to their industry, remarkably well clothed. Their costume is Swedish. They labour at the oar, and manage the boats quite as well as the men; and I have seen them, after braving death in the rough blast, and exerting admirable courage and dexterity, haul their boats on shore, return to the cottage, refresh themselves slightly, and, with the utmost simplicity, sit down to their spinning or knitting as if nothing had happened, whilst I, at a humble distance, looked upon them as heroines. —

This glimpse of life outside her normally restricted social circle was evidently fascinating to Martha.

The Wilmot journals certainly illustrate some of the vicissitudes of travel in those days!

ELEANOR CAVANAGH

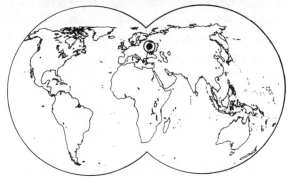

One of the few surviving records made by a servant

Eleanor Cavanagh, Katherine's maid, also from County Cork, accompanied her mistress to Russia. Eleanor's long letters to her father from Troitskoe seem to have survived because they were shown to the Wilmot parents. Eleanor gives a lively description of the carriage journey, eight days and eight nights long, which took herself and Katherine from St Petersburg to Troitskoe, and of the warm welcome when they arrived at the 'Country Palace' eighty miles from Moscow.

— October 4th, 1805: ...'From Moscow to the Country Palace where we now are & where we have been 3 weeks is more than 80 mile. 'Twas like an army when we left Moscow! Such loads of coaches & sarvants! I druve with the Princess's first maid Natasia. At night the devil an inn we came to, but a big palace belonging to a Count! We sat very warm & pleasant, & then a sight of maids belonging to the palace came in & kissed us all round. I counted eleven of them, handsome looking girls enough, mighty civil & nice. They made signs to us & we followed them out of doors across a garden to a darling place, & up we went upstairs... till we got into a playhouse. May I never stir but I believe it was! There was an auld man with a trumpet in his mouth & his two eyes looking at me. 'Come here,' says Miss Anna Petrovna, the Pss niece (a fine young lady who lives with her always). 'Come here,' sais she. 'I'm frightened Ma'am,' says....I looked thro' a little hole & faith there I seen London & Petersburg & cartloads of grand towns, but 'twas very quair Cork did not come anyhow. There was voices of live people talking out of little small trumpets & singing & doing everything like Christians. 'Well to be sure,' sais I, 'Russia! & good luck to you, you are a comical place, & you'll give me something to talk of many a long day!'...

— There is 16 Villages all belonging to the Princess here, & them that lives in them comes to the number of 3000 men and women, all her subjects and loving her as if she was their Mother. There is 200 servants that lives in & out of the house. She one morning sent for me, & she was sitting in her own room about 7 o'clock in the morning. 'Ellen,' sais she, 'I believe you have none of the money of my country'. 'No Ma'am,' sais I. 'Well then,' sais she (looking as good humour'd as anything) 'you ought to know how to reckon, & so here are 20 roubles for you (each rouble is more than half a crown), & they are in different kinds of coin, you will learn to understand the value'. 'Ma'am,' sais I, 'I'm much oblig'd to you,' & with that I kiss'd her hand. —

At the end of the letter Eleanor writes:

— We'll all be laiving this the 13th of December for Moscow again where we are to stay three months in the same palace of the Princess I talk'd to you about. And God knows I never seen such a good lady since ever I was born, nor so kind, nor so generous I've reason to say dear knows! Once every week there is a play acted here in a nice little play house belonging to the Princess. We are all given laive to go. 'Tis the sarvents who act just for her amusement. —

In an establishment where even the servants 'live like Queens', as Eleanor tells us, no wonder Martha could not be dragged away, for the Princess depended upon her. Princess Dashkov died two years after Martha left her. Troitskoe was looted and destroyed by the French in 1812.

ANNA BROWNELL JAMESON

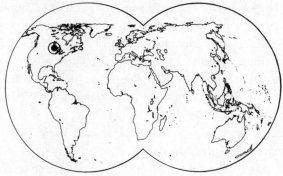

An artist's view of Canada

Anna (1794-1860) née Murphy, was the eldest of five daughters of a United Irishman miniature painter and no mean artist herself. As an art historian she wrote her *Companion to the Public Picture Galleries of London* (1842), thus being the first woman claiming to be a specialist in the history of art. Anna believed that there was a specific form of female art, equal but different from that of men. She outlined her theories in *Sacred and Legendary Art* (1848), pointing out how much women had contributed to the Christian tradition in art, and her opinions had a good deal of influence at the time. Anna also wrote memoirs of Italian painters, and legends of the Madonna as represented in the fine arts. She was concerned about the social employment of women, lecturing and writing another book about the work of the Sisters of Charity amongst the poor, aged and insane in Paris, Vienna, Turin, Genoa, Montreal, Quebec, Detroit and in Ireland during cholera and famine, though 'I am no friend to nunneries'.

Anna travelled to the Continent and North America. She was one of a circle that included Lady Byron, Elizabeth B. Browning, Fanny Kemble and Ottiline van Goethe. Her travel books are laced with critical discussion.

Anna first supported herself as a governess, and to make her 1821 continental tour with the family she worked for more interesting, she created a fictional invalid travelling to escape some tragedy. This successful travel book was entitled *The Diary of an Ennuyée* (1826). The Preface states that the diary was found by the Ennuyée's side where she lay dead of a broken heart in Autun, and was therefore published anonymously, but an 1834 reprint revealed the true author. In reality Anna, before leaving as a governess, had broken off with Robert Jameson whom she then married the following year.

Anna's marriage was unhappy and she lived apart from her husband except when she visited him in Canada in 1837 to support his candidature as vice-chancellor. While in North America she made two tours, one via Toronto, Hamilton, Niagara and Buffalo to Detroit using a public stagecoach and taking no servants, and the other north to Mackinaw and Chippewa Indian territory. Her diary records that Hamilton then had a population of 3,000. Detroit was 'a beautiful little city' with some excellent shops, a theatre and many taverns and gaming houses. To her chagrin she missed hearing Daniel Webster speak there on the 'money transactions of the government'.

At Lake Huron she travelled in a canoe and a native bateau with five Indian oarsmen. This was a unique adventure 'such as few European women of refined and civilised habits have ever risked, and none have recorded.' She is interesting on the subject of Indian customs. While in North Michigan she began by staying with Schoolcraft, American agent with the Indians. His wife was granddaughter of a Chippewa chief. This passage comes from her *Winter Studies and Summer Rambles in Canada* (1838):

— I was sitting last Friday, at sultry noon-tide, under the shadow of a schooner which had just anchored alongside the little pier – sketching and dreaming – when up came a messenger, breathless, to say that a boat was going off for the Sault-Sainte-Marie, in which I could be accommodated with a passage. Now this was precisely what I had been wishing and waiting for, and yet I heard the information with an emotion of regret. I had become every day more attached to the society of Mrs Schoolcraft, more interested about her, and the idea of parting, and parting suddenly, took me by surprise and was anything but agreeable. On reaching the house I found all in movement, and learned to my inexpressible delight, that my friend would take the opportunity of paying a visit to her mother and family and, with her children, was to accompany me on my voyage.

We had but one hour to prepare packages, provisions, everything – and in one hour all was ready.

This voyage of two days was to be made in a little Canadian bateau, rowed by five *voyageurs* from the Sault. The boat might have carried fifteen persons, hardly more, and was rather clumsy in form. The two ends were appropriated to the rowers, baggage and provisions. In the centre there was a clear space, with a locker on each side, on which we sat or reclined, having stowed away in them our smaller and more valuable packages. This was the internal arrangement.

The distance to the Sault, or as the Americans call it, the Sou, is not more than thirty miles overland as the bird flies, but the whole region being one mass of tangled forest and swamp, infested with bears and mosquitoes, it is seldom crossed but in winter, and in snow-shoes. The usual route by water is ninety-four miles.

At three o'clock in the afternoon, with a favourable breeze, we launched forth on the lake, and having rowed about a mile from the shore, the little square sail was hoisted and away we went merrily over the waves.

...the voyageurs in our boat were not favourable specimens of their very amusing and peculiar class. They were fatigued with rowing for three days previous, and had only two helpless women to deal with. As soon, therefore, as the sail was hoisted two began to play cards on top of a keg, the other two went to sleep. The youngest and most intelligent of the set, a lively half-breed boy of eighteen, took the helm. He told us with great self-complacency that he was captain, and that it was already the third time that he had been elected by his comrades to this dignity, but I cannot say he had a very obedient crew.

About seven o'clock we landed to cook our supper on an island which [was once named] Isle des Outardes, and is now Goose Island. Mrs Schoolcraft undertook the general management with all the alertness of one accustomed to these impromptu arrangements, and I did my best in my new vocation – dragged one or two blasted boughs to the fire, the least of them twice as big as myself, and laid the cloth upon the pebbly beach. The enormous fire was to keep off the mosquitoes, in which we succeeded pretty well, swallowing, however, as much smoke as would have dried us externally into hams or red herrings. We then returned to the boat, spread a bed for the children (who were my delight) in the bottom of it with mats and blankets, and disposed our own, on the lockers on each side, with buffalo skins, blankets, shawls, cloaks and whatever was available, with my writing case for a pillow...

We remained in conversation till long after midnight, then the boat was moored to a tree, but kept offshore, for fear of the mosquitoes, and we addressed ourselves to sleep ...

I slept, however, uneasily, not being yet accustomed to a board and a blanket, ça viendra avec le temps. About dawn I awoke in a sort of stupor, but after bathing my face and hands over the boat side, I felt refreshed. The voyageurs, after a good night's rest, were in better humour, and took manfully to their oars. Soon after sunrise, we passed round that very conspicuous cape, famous in the history of northwest adventure, called the 'Grand Détour', halfway between Mackinaw and the Sault. Now, if you look at the map, you will see that our course was henceforth quite altered. We had been running down the coast of the mainland towards the east, we had now to turn short round the point and steer almost due west, hence its most fitting name. The wind, hitherto favourable, was now dead against us. This part of Lake Huron is studded with little islands which, as well as the neighbouring mainland, are all uninhabited yet clothed with the richest, loveliest, most fantastic vegetation, no doubt swarming with animal life.

I cannot attempt to describe to you the strange sensation one had thus thrown for a time beyond the bounds of civilised humanity, or indeed any humanity, nor the wild yet solemn reveries which come over one in the midst of this wilderness of woods and water. All was so solitary, so grand in its solitude, as if nature unviolated sufficed to herself. Two days and nights the solitude was unbroken, not a trace of social life, not a human being, not a canoe, not even a deserted wigwam, met our view. Our little boat held on its way over the placid lake, and among the green tufted islands, and we, its inmates, differing in clime, nation, complexion, strangers to each other but a few days ago, might have fancied ourselves alone in a newborn world.

We landed to boil our kettle and breakfast on a point of the island of St Joseph's. This most beautiful island is between thirty and forty miles in length, and nearly a hundred miles in circumference, and towards the centre the land is high and picturesque. They tell me that on the other side of the island there is a settlement of whites and Indians ...

By the time breakfast was over the children had gathered some fine strawberries. The heat had now become almost intolerable and unluckily we had no awning. The men rowed languidly and we made but little way.... The sky was without a cloud, a speck – except when the great fish eagle was descried sailing over its blue depths – the water without a wave. We were too hot and too languid to converse. Nothing disturbed the deep noontide stillness but the dip of the oars, or the spring and plash of a sturgeon as he leapt from the surface of the lake, leaving a circle of little wavelets spreading around. All the islands we passed were so woody, and so infested with mosquitoes that we could not land and light our fire till we reached the entrance of St Mary's River, between Nebish island and the mainland.

Here was a well known spot, a sort of little opening on a flat shore, called the Encampment, because a party of boatmen coming down from Lake Superior and camping here for the night, were surprised by frost and obliged to remain the whole winter till the opening of the ice in spring. After rowing all this hot day till seven o'clock against the wind (what there was of it), and against the current coming rapidly and strongly down from Lake Superior, we did at length reach this promised harbour of rest and refreshment. Alas! there was neither for us. The moment our boat touched the shore we were enveloped in a cloud of mosquitoes. Fires were lighted instantly, six were burning in a circle at once. We were well nigh suffocated and smoke-dried – all in vain. At last we left the voyageurs to boil the kettle and retreated to our boat, desiring them to make us fast to a tree by a long rope. Then, each of us taking an oar, I only wish you could have seen us, we pushed off from the land while the children were sweeping away the enemy with green boughs. This being done we commenced supper, really half-famished, with which we were too much engrossed to look about us. Suddenly we were again surrounded by our adversaries. They came upon us in swarms, in clouds, in myriads, entering our eyes, our noses, our mouths, stinging till the blood followed .... The dear children cried with agony and impatience, and but for the shame I could almost have cried too ....

Well, we left this most detestable and inhospitable shore as soon as possible, but the enemy followed us, and we did not soon get rid of them. Night came on and we were still twenty miles below the Sault.

I offered an extra gratuity to the men, if they would keep to their oars without interruption, and then, fairly exhausted, laid down on my locker and blanket. But whenever I woke from uneasy, restless slumbers, there was Mrs Schoolcraft, bending over her sleeping children, and waving off the mosquitoes, singing all the time a low, melancholy Indian song, while the northern lights were streaming and dancing in the sky, and the fitful moaning of the wind, the gathering clouds and chilly atmosphere foretold a change of weather. This would have been the *comble de malheur*. When daylight came we passed Sugar Island, where immense quantities of maple sugar are made every spring, and just as the rain began to fall in earnest we arrived at the Sault-Sainte-Marie. On one side of the river Mrs Schoolcraft was welcomed by her mother, and on the other my friends, the MacMurrays, received me with delighted and delightful hospitality. I went to bed – oh the luxury! – and slept for six hours. —

It is probable that most of the mosquitoes were in fact, black fly. Mr MacMurray was an Anglican missionary with an Indian wife, sister to Mrs Schoolcraft from whom Anna learns a great deal about Indian traditions and customs, which then causes her to reflect:

— God forbid that I should think to disparage the blessings of civilisation! I am a woman, and to the progress of civilisation alone can we women look for release from many pains and penalties and liabilities which now lie heavily upon us. Neither am I greatly in love with savage life, with all its picturesque accompaniments and lofty virtues. I see no reason why these virtues should be necessarily connected with dirt, ignorance and barbarism. I am thankful to live in a land of literature and steam-engines. Chatsworth is better than a wigwam and a seventy-four is a finer thing than a bark canoe. I do not positively assert that soap and water are preferable as cosmetics to tallow and charcoal, for these are matters of taste and mine may be disputed. But I do say that if our advantages of intellect and refinement are not to lead on to farther moral superiority, I prefer the Indians on the score of consistency. They are what they profess to be, and we are *not* what we profess to be. They profess to be warriors and hunters and are so. We profess to be Christians and civilised — are we so? —

Anna longs to shoot the rapids of St Mary's Fall which had a two mile portage, so she hires a ten foot canoe with a steersman. The canoe is launched from the top of the portage:

— light, elegant and buoyant as a bird on the waters. I reclined on a mat at the bottom, Indian fashion (there are no seats in a genuine Indian canoe). In a minute we were within the verge of the rapids and down we went, with a whirl and a splash! The white surge leaping around me, over me. The Indian, with astonishing dexterity, kept the head of the canoe to the breakers and somehow or other we danced through them. I could see, as I looked over the edge of the canoe, that the passage between the rocks was sometimes not more than two feet in width and we had to turn sharp angles, a touch of which would have sent us to destruction. All this I could see through the transparent eddying waters, but I can truly say I had not even a momentary sensation of fear, but rather of giddy, breathless, delicious excitement. I could even admire the beautiful attitude of a fisher, past whom we swept as we came to the bottom. The whole affair, from the moment I entered the canoe till I reached the landing place, occupied seven minutes and the distance is about three quarters of a mile. —

Anna almost certainly could not swim and there were no life-jackets for white-water trips in those days! She goes on to tell us:

— My Indians were enchanted and when I reached home my good friends were not less delighted at my exploit. They told me I was the first European female who had ever performed it and assuredly I shall not be the last. I recommend it as an exercise before breakfast. As for my Neengai [Mrs MacMurray], she laughed, clapped her hands and embraced me several times. I was declared duly initiated and adopted into the family by the name of Wahsahgewahnoqua, which signifies 'the woman of the bright foam'. —

Adopted as a member of the Chippewas, Anna leaves the MacMurrays after her stay of several weeks, and sets off by canoe for Toronto, in a larger party this time. The following passages come from her account of this seven day journey.

— We landed at sunset on a flat ledge of rock, free from bushes, which we avoided as much as possible, from fear of mosquitoes and rattlesnakes, and while the men pitched the marquees and cooked supper, I walked and mused.

I wish I could give you the least idea of the beauty of this evening, but while I try to put in words what was before me, the sense of its ineffable loveliness overpowers me now even as it did then. The sun had set in that cloudless splendour and that peculiar blending of rose and amber light that belongs only to these climes and Italy. The lake lay weltering under the western sky like a bath of molten gold. The rocky islands that studded its surface were of a dense purple, except where their edges seemed fringed with fire. They assumed, to the visionary eye, strange forms. Some were like great horned beetles and some like turtles, others like crocodiles, sleeping whales or winged fish, while the foliage upon the islands ressembled dorsal fins or feathery tufts. Then, as the purple shadows came darkening from the east, the young crescent moon showed herself, flinging a paly splendour over the water ...

They pitched my tent at a respectful distance from the rest and made me a delicious elastic bed of some boughs, over which was spread a bearskin and then blankets, but the night was hot and feverish. The voyageurs, after rowing since daylight, were dancing and singing on the shores till near midnight.

Next morning we were off again at early dawn, paddled 'trois pipes' before breakfast, over an open space which they call a 'traverse', caught eleven bass fish and shot two pigeons. The island on which we breakfasted was in great part white marble, and in the clefts and hollows grew quantities of goose-berries and raspberries, wild roses, crimson columbine, a large species of harebell, a sort of willow, juniper, birch and stunted pine. Such was the usual vegetation ...

We landed today on the Island of Skulls, an ancient sepulchre of the Hurons. Some skulls and bones were scattered about, with the rough stones which had once been heaped over them. The spot was most wild and desolate, rising from the water edge in successive ledges of rock to a considerable height, with a few blasted gray pines here and there, round which several pair of hawks were wheeling and uttering their shrill cry. We all declared we would not dine on this ominous island and proceeded ....

We again came upon lovely groups of Elysian islands, channels winding among rocks and foliage, with more fields of waterlilies. In passing through a beautiful channel I had an opportunity of seeing the manner in which an Indian communicates with his friends when en route. A branch was so ar-ranged as to project far across the water and catch the eye. In a cleft at the extremity a piece of birch bark was stuck with some hieroglyphic marks scratched with red ochre, of which we could make nothing. One figure, I thought, represented a fish ...

I wonder how it is that some of those gentry whom I used to see in London, looking as though they would give an empire for a new pleasure or a new sensation, do not come here? If epicures, they should come to eat white fish and beavers' tails; if sportsmen, here is a very paradise for bear hunting, deer hunting, otter hunting and wild fowl in thousands, fish in shoals. If they be contemplative lovers of the picturesque, *blasés* with Italy and elbowed out of Switzerland, let them come here and find the true philosopher's stone, or rather the true elixir of life – novelty!

At sunset we encamped on a rocky island of most fantastic form, like a Z. They pitched my tent on a height, and close to the door was a precipitous descent into a hollow, where they lighted vast fires and thus kept off the mosquitoes, which were in great force. I slept well but towards morning some creature crept into my tent and over my bed, a snake, as I supposed. After this I slept no more.

We started at half past four. Hitherto the weather had been glorious, but this morning the sun rose among red and black clouds, fearfully ominous. As we were turning a point under some lofty rocks we heard the crack of a rifle and saw an Indian leaping along the rocks and down towards the shore. We rowed in, not knowing what it meant and came upon a night camp of Indians, part of the Aisence tribe (the Clam). They had only hailed us to make some trifling enquiries and I heard Louis, sotto voce, send them *au diable*, for now the weather lowered darker and darker and every moment was precious.

We breakfasted on an island almost covered with flowers, some gorgeous, strange and unknown, others sweet and familiar, plenty of wild pea, for instance, and wild roses of which I had many offerings. I made my toilette in a recess among some rocks, but just as I was emerging from my primitive dressing room I felt a few drops of rain, and saw too clearly that our good fortune was at an end.

We swallowed a hasty breakfast and had just time to arrange ourselves in the canoe with all available defences of cloaks and umbrellas, when the rain came down heavily and hopelessly.... These are called the Bear Islands, from the number of those animals found upon them. Old Solomon told me that an Indian whom he knew had shot nine bears in the course of a single day. We found three bears' heads stuck upon the boughs of a dead pine, probably as offerings to the souls of the slaughtered animals, or to the 'Great Spirit', both being usual. —

LADY MORGAN

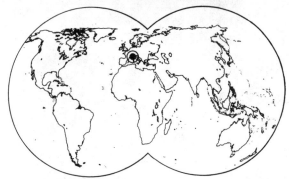

A view of French high society, by a radical hostess

Even better known than Anna Jameson in her day was Sydney, Lady Morgan (née Owenson) (c.1776-1859), daughter of Robert Owenson (or MacOwen) from Connaught, a failed actor-manager, and his English wife, Jane Hill. Sydney and her sister went to a Huguenot school in Clontarf and learned good French.

By 1798 her father was bankrupt and her mother dead. Sydney, an admirer of Fanny Burney, had begun to write novels but to earn her living became governess to the Featherstones of Bracklin Castle, Westmeath, then moved to a Tipperary family, where she played the harp and taught them Irish jigs. She published some poems, then two novels in 1803 and 1805, but made her name with *The Wild Irish Girl* (1806), a novel promoting Irish emancipation; the following year she wrote a comic opera.

Sydney held liberal and anti-clerical views. She deplored absentee land-lords and the 1800 Union. In 1812 she married a young widowed doctor Sir Charles Morgan, a quiet scholarly man in contrast to her volatile and ener-getic personality. After marriage she created Dublin's only literary salon and *O'Donnel* (1814) added to her reputation as a novelist.

The Continent had been closed to travellers since 1803, but in April 1816 the Morgans left for Paris where Lady Morgan, already known as a novelist, made her mark on Parisian society. She found soulmates there with similar progressive views, among them Voltaire's adopted daughter Madame de Villette and supporters of the revolution such as La Fayette.

Her book *France* (1817) tried to give a personal impression of all aspects of French society, but she was already biased against despotic secular government and a powerful priesthood and contemptuous of the restored monarchy. Her book, which went into four editions in two years and caused

Lady Morgan (Sydney Owenson, 1776-1859)

an uproar on both sides of the channel, was at once translated into French with some modifications and suppressions. Her publisher, Henry Colburn, then offered her £2,000 for a book on Italy and in August 1818 she returned to Paris and began an intensive course of reading for this.

In May 1819 the Morgans crossed the Alps to Italy where friends lent them a villa on Lake Como. She travelled widely in Italy and returned to Dublin the following year. In 1821 her Italian book came out in two volumes, revealing strong opinions about Papal misrule and Austrian tyranny. She also criticised the Italian prevalence of corruption and superstition. This book also pro-voked violent reaction both for and against her opinions. *Italy* was banned by the Pope, the King of Sardinia and the Emperor of Austria, but Lord Byron found it 'fearless and excellent'. Lady Morgan's work after this is less notable, though she produced the first book in English on the artist Salvador Rosa.

Lady Morgan became a celebrated Dublin hostess. She is said to have helped the passing of the Emancipation of Catholics Act (1829) through her influence in society and by the themes of her much-praised novels.

The following passage from *France* shows her being sarcastic about the restored monarchy:

— There appears, indeed, among these ardent royalists a resolute determination to see every object through the medium of their wishes. It is vain to talk to them of the past, or to lead them to the future; they exist but for the present, in the persuasion that change can never come, almost forgetting that it did occur, and believing that the *beau siécle de Louis XIV* is about to be restored in all its splendour and extent of despotism. Everything that is said or done by every member of the royal family, is repeated with interest and detailed with delight, and if the infirmities of the monarch allowed him the innocent amusement of pulling the chairs from under the ladies of the court, like his great predecessor, there would be scarcely one amongst them who would not canvas the distinction of a *culbute* [tumble], like the former subservient Duchesses of Versailles ...

Personal devotion to the king is not, however, exclusively confined to the elders of the privileged classes. It was a profane maxim of a profane French wit, that *'les vieilles et les laides sont toujours pour Dieu,'* and his present Majesty of France seems to enjoy a similar devotion, as part of his divine right. Many of the aged members of the middle classes of the capital have remained true to the good old cause. The *petits rentiers*, or stockholders of the fauxbourg St Germain (that centre of all antiquity and royalism), assemble morning and evening before the windows of the Tuileries in the hope of seeing the king pass and repass to and from his morning's drive .... These venerable votaries of loyalty, who have so long 'owed heaven a death' that they seem to have been forgotten by their creditor, are chiefly females ....

The daily course of patience, to which these veteran dames submit, is relieved by the employment of knitting and netting, and by a *causerie* in all the set phrase and jargon of better times. The speculations are endless, whether the king will, or will not drive out ...

These phalanxes of antiquarian loyalty, male and female, were however daily thinning when I left France, from the total inability of the 'best of kings' to provide for his venerable adherents in a manner suitable to their spirited ambition and sanguine hopes. All who can furbish up an old claim to the distinction of a *gentil-homme né*, call for restitution of lands, rights and privileges; and though they, many of them, return to their country at the end of twenty-five years, neither more indigent nor more insignificant than when they left it, they raise the outcry against royal ingratitude, mount a *crois de St Louis*, talk most pathetically of the ancient splendour of their *château* and their *terres*, and exclaim against the impolicy of the king in neglecting his *fidéle noblesse*, who would alone form a fence round his throne! —

Later in the book Lady Morgan relates the following anecdote:

— I was one morning, in the summer of 1816, walking under the venerable towers of Château la Grange, and leaning on the arm of its illustrious master, general the marquis de la Fayette (and who would not boast of being supported by that arm, which raised the standard of independence in America, and placed her banner above the dungeons of France?). The figure of a labourer, who was working on the moat which nearly surrounded the chateau, struck me as being both distinguished and singular. He was a tall athletic man, something advanced in life. As we approached, he touched the little embroidered cap, which did not conceal his grey locks, and drawing up into an erect posture, gave the military salute, which M. de la Fayette most punctiliously returned. As the labourer resumed his spade, I asked the general, in English, whether this was not one of the disbanded soldiers of the Loire. 'I should suppose,' he replied, 'a distinguished one; for I find he is a member of the legion of honour, and you may perceive the ensign of his order glittering through the rents in his jacket'.... 'That brave fellow,' said M. la Fayette, as we pursued our walk, 'has passed twenty years in the service of his country. He is covered with scars. He had already obtained the subaltern distinctions of his profession, and in another year was to have been appointed a commissioned officer; *en attendant*, he received the cross of the legion of honour, and thought himself amply recompensed for all his services ... He labours through the week in his tattered fustian jacket, and gratifies all that is left of his military pride, by exposing his badge of honour to the admiration of the rustic crowd, with which he mingles at mass on Sundays.' —

In *France* Lady Morgan also draws extended and unflattering comparisons between French and English society, unlikely to be welcome in England so soon after the protracted Napoleonic wars, such as in the following passage:

— Frauds of address and petty thefts of all sorts are less frequent in Paris, than in almost any of the best governed towns in England. The streets of Paris at all hours of the night, and I do not only speak on the testimony of some veteran Parisians, but on individual experience, (for I have returned from English and French balls at very late hours) are perfectly safe and quiet ....

In France, and its capital, the extremes of poverty and wealth are less distant, the habits of life are more regular and abstemious than in England; and the mildness, equality, and proportionate infliction of the penal code, require neither temperament from royal clemency, nor forbearance from individual prosecutors. Its punishments fall with certainty upon the offender, and are formidable, because they are not severe. Atrocities against nature, parricide, infanticide, &c. are rarely committed in France, and that brutal and rapacious violence exercised by those, to whom popular language in England has given the name of '*monsters*', who stab with wanton fury, the helpless female exposed to their horrible and unaccountable attacks, is so unknown in France, and when an anecdote of this nature was read before me, in a French society from an English paper, it not only excited emotions of horror and disgust, but was denied credibility by the greater number present, as being out of nature and possibility. —

The irony of the bloody French revolution lurks behind this latter passage.

Lady Morgan was evidently a Francophile, as she was also a supporter of Irish liberty and independence. Even so in 1837 she accepted a £300 a year pension from Lord Melbourne, in recognition of her literary achievements, and the Morgans left Dublin for London. Her husband died in 1843. Her autobiography was published in the year of her death.

MARGUERITE, COUNTESS OF BLESSINGTON

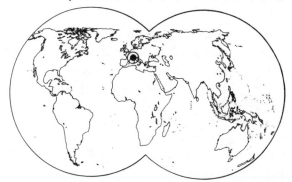

A romantic aristocrat with a penchant for Lord Byron

Another woman from this early nineteenth-century period who wrote about Europe was the glamorous Marguerite (née Power) (1789-1849), born in Clonmel, whose father Edmund, won over to the English side after 1798, was a hated magistrate and a drunken bully. Marguerite was first married, against her will, aged fifteen, but soon fled her husband to live with another army officer for ten years, educating herself during this time. Luckily her husband was killed in a fight in the debtors' prison, after which, aged twenty-eight, she was free to marry the widower Earl of Blessington, seven years older, whom she had charmed. Now, though still considered somewhat scandalous, she became a leading London hostess and started to travel extensively with her husband in Europe where she met Byron and published some poetry.

When Marguerite was thirty-nine Lord Blessington died of a stroke and her income was reduced from over £20,000 to £2,000 per annum, still a respectable sum in those days. Marguerite then started to live with Alfred, Count D'Orsay, the estranged husband of her stepdaughter whom D'Orsay had married, aged fifteen, in exchange for her fortune. D'Orsay had, almost at once, separated from the girl in exchange for £100,000 and relinquished his claim on the Blessington estates. Lady Blessington and D'Orsay, who was twelve years her junior, lived together for the rest of her life. Marguerite ran a London salon and did not care what people thought.

While married to Blessington, Marguerite had been based in France for ten years. She was the fashionable tourist par excellence and her books *The Idler in Italy* (1839/40) and *The Idler in France* (1841) did much to popularise the Grand Tour amongst the quality. Continental travel now became fashionable, and it was no coincidence that Thomas Cook started organised travel in 1841.

Lady Blessington also wrote a number of 'silver fork' novels, initiated by the publisher Henry Colburn, and memoirs of Lord Byron, to whom she was devoted.

In 1849, her income cut by the Irish famine, she fled to Paris to escape her debts, and died of apoplexy a month later leaving a heartbroken D'Orsay.

To us Lady Blessington now appears a self-regarding and extravagantly romantic person. The following, from *The Idler in Italy*, illustrates her discursive style:

— *Genoa* – Once more at Genoa. How many recollections come crowding on memory at the sight of this place, and the well-known objects that everywhere meet my view! In each and all Byron bears a prominent part, and everything around me looks so exactly as when he used to be present that I feel my regret for his loss renewed afresh. Strange and powerful effect of association! On the balcony near which I now write *he* has stood conversing with me; the same scene spread out before us, the same blue clouds floating over our heads. So distinctly does the spot recall him to my memory that I seem to see again his face, that expressive and intelligent countenance, and to hear the sound of that clear, low and musical voice, never more to be heard on earth ...

When I last visited Genoa it was on our route to Nice in 1826. Snow was then on the ground, and everything was so dark and dreary that Genoa no longer appeared as I had been accustomed to behold it, but now, with a blue sky and sunshine, a genial air and everything around wearing the aspect of summer, it

Marguerite, Countess of Blessington, (engraved by Henry T. Ryall)

looks so precisely as it was wont to do, when in 1823 I first sojourned here, that all my recollections of that happy period are awakened.

Our kind friend Mr Barry has been already here to greet us, and we have promised to dine with him tomorrow at Albaro, in the Palazzo Saluzzi, the house where I first saw Byron ...

The public walks, the Acqua Verde and the Acqua Sola, are much improved since I left them. Walking in the latter, I saw, attended by a lady, an English girl whose countenance struck me as resembling in an extraordinary degree that of Lord Byron, and on approaching nearer to her, the likeness became still more evident. Our *laquais-de-place*, observing that the young lady excited our curiosity, advanced and in a low tone of voice informed us that she was the daughter of the great poet, Lord Byron.

It was indeed 'Ada, sole daughter of my house and heart'. We had not previously heard that Lady Byron was in Genoa, so that we were little conscious when remarking the family resemblance how natural it was ...

We went early today to our dinner engagement at Mr Barry's and felt a mournful interest in inspecting the apartments occupied by Lord Byron. They are very nearly in the same state as when he resided here, for Mr and Mrs Barry entertain a lively recollection of him, and like to leave undisturbed everything that identifies the place with his memory ...

We sat for some time in the chamber in which Byron always wrote. Into this no one was permitted to enter while he occupied it; his door was locked and a perfect stillness reigned around. Here he completed the 'Age of Bronze' and the last cantos of 'Don Juan'. Here also he wrote all the letters and the poems addressed to me, now in my possession. —

Lord Byron was the Elvis Presley of that generation!

SELINA BUNBURY

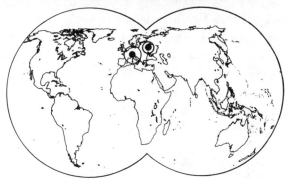

The excitement of a visit to Vesuvius, from a late-developing traveller

Selina (1802-1882) is a person of a more sympathetic stamp. She became a writer to subsidise her family's finances. One of fifteen children of a Co. Louth Methodist minister, Selina had a distant family connection with Fanny Burney upon whom she may have modelled herself. When her father became bankrupt in 1819 the family moved to Dublin, where Selina taught in a primary school and began writing in secret because her mother disapproved. In 1830 the Bunburys moved to Liverpool, and Selina kept house for her twin brother, supporting them both by her writing until he married in 1845.

Selina's first book, *A Visit to My Birthplace* (Dublin, 1821), which showed Ireland before the Famine, ran into twelve editions and launched her career. She began to travel after her parents died and eventually visited every country in Europe except Greece and Portugal. A prolific writer, her romantic novels were very popular in their day. Her travel writing outside Ireland covers Russia, Italy, Scandinavia, and the Pyrenees. She also wrote evangelical short fiction. Selina died in Cheltenham.

In her account of a midnight visit to Vesuvius, published 1849, Selina said she was writing 'for the less learned class of reader'.

— The beautiful aspect of Mount Vesuvius by night, as well as the intense heat of the weather, determined us to choose that time for its ascent; indeed, we could have attempted it at no other. That night was one which I shall not forget, and I bless God, who gave me the capacity in mind, as well as in body, to enjoy it.

The form of Vesuvius is remarkable; it has two summits, and rises in a gentle swell from the seashore. The lower region, or base of the mountain, presents a strong contrast to the upper. At five o'clock on a charming afternoon we left Naples in a carriage, hoping to traverse this lower region in time to see the sunset from the more elevated one. We engaged the carriage to convey us to the Hermitage, situated at that part of the mountain from whence the real difficulty of the ascent commences; for it is an instance of the rare facilities which our times afford to exploring travellers, that a carriage road, rather difficult but perfectly practicable, has been made upon Mount Vesuvius, a circumstance which causes much indignation and meets with much opposition from the numerous guides and conductors whose business it has been to supply mules, ponies or asses for that purpose. The road, however, has not been formed solely for the convenience of curious travellers; an observatory has been erected on Mount Vesuvius, and a carriage road on this account has been made up to the Hermitage, which may be said to terminate the first of the two distinct regions into which the mountain is divided.

The lower region, which we traversed in the carriage, is one of the most fertile, populous and lovely that can be conceived: the higher is the most awful, stern and singular that is commonly to be beheld. The first region, both on the side of the sea and inland, is covered with towns and villages, the sites of which have been swept over by the devastating lava and re-edified by their persevering inhabitants....

We left our carriage at the Hermitage and mounted mules which took us along a path about three quarters of a mile farther on. The guides were provided with immense torches, perhaps eight feet long. At the spot where I dismounted these were lighted and the glare they flung around revealed the most singular scene I ever beheld.

A field of blocks of lava, of that grey dark colour it assumes when cold, lay beside us. Ashes, cinders and these sharp hard masses, covered the whole space up to the cone – a bare and savage looking scene, while from the red summit the pillar of flame shot out in fitful splendour and fiery pumice stones of a great size descended again from the night-shadowed skies towards which they had been flung, and fell, sometimes back into the burning centre, some-times on the outside of the glowing crater....

It was over this lava field we had to walk. Our guide said it was impossible I could do it, and wanted to remain with me while the stouter members of our society visited the lava river, but as I saw the man would be glad of any excuse to get off the toil of an expedition he was obliged to make often, I would not yield to him ...

I set out over the blocks of lava with a good heart, for I firmly believed a path had been tracked out through them, and would shortly be found. A delusion which probably enabled me to effect my purpose, for had I known that I was really to walk for more than a mile on these sharp, hard, unsteady blocks, almost like pointed irons to the feet – up ridges and into furrows, guided only by the fitful light of torches, for the moon had not yet fully risen – I fear I should not have continued my way, but turned back with the less reluctant guide, as I had promised to do if weary ...

Weary indeed I was, and several times ready to give up, but some little assistance... again impelled me onward. In ascending Vesuvius I am aware that ladies, and even gentlemen, need not unless they wish it undergo any fatigue, or make any exertion. A little money obviates all that. They may be carried up in a chair, or pulled up by the guides and satisfy their own curiosity at the expense only of other men's labours ...

At last the increasing heat told of our approach to the region of fire. The air was sulphurous and gave a choking sensation. It was loaded also with smoke. The ground grew hot and hotter. We mounted a ridge of cinders and there, at the other side, I beheld the lava stream, stood beside it on the brink of the bed it had tracked for itself! It was quite a river of fire, about thirty feet broad slowly moving on; over the top was heard a slight fizzing sound, such as cinders make when cooling...The ground was so hot, and my feet so sore, having never found a single resting place from the sharp lava during our entire progress, that I found it impossible to stand for an instant on one spot. My shoes were almost literally burned off, and while the gentlemen were burning the ends of their sticks, as the customary souvenir of Vesuvius, I very undes-ignedly brought away its memorial in a burned dress. —

The heat and fumes make Selina feel faint, but she manages to conceal this from the others by sitting on a block of lava out of sight until she regains her equilibrium. They then walk one hour down the mountain back to their mules. Only the men in the party climbed to the cone, though some of the other women were carried up in chairs. For Selina it was on foot or not at all.

Much of Selina's travel writing is interwoven with storytelling. Her book *Evenings in the Pyrenees* (1845) is subtitled *Stories of wanderers from many lands*. In her writing about a journey from Stockholm to the Austrian Tyrol (1847-8), she introduces a bevy of characters and their romantic attachments, with stories about their past lives. Her last travel book was written when she visited Russia just after the Crimean war.

LOUISE STUART COSTELLO

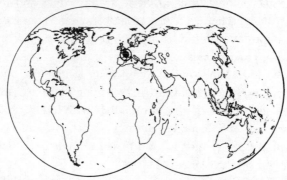

An intrepid travel adviser, who blazed many trails for the inexperienced

Louise (1799-1870) was born in Ireland, the daughter of an Irish officer in the British army. She was taken to France in childhood and studied painting in Paris. Her father died when she was sixteen so she helped to support the family by painting miniatures, making it possible for her brother Dudley to stay at Sandhurst. After Dudley left the army in 1828 they illustrated books together, and also specialised in the copying of medieval manuscripts. Dudley became foreign correspondent for the *Daily News* and wrote popular travel books, as did Louise, who also wrote poetry, novels and history.

Louise's travels on the Continent, illustrated by herself, were published in the 1840's, and she became the first professional woman travel writer by recommending simple itineraries with the historical and topographical interest sought by Victorian tourists. She was one of the early Continental travel advisers aiding the budding Thomas Cook who, after arranging many excursions in Britain, launched his first Continental tour in 1855 at the time of the Paris Exhibition.

Advertisements in Cook's *The Excursionist* give us clues to the travellers' worries of this time. They range from Keating's insect powder to Seymour's Magnetic Amnyterion Appliances against seasickness, and Dr Collis Browne's chlorodyne against diarrhoea. There is a portable door fastener and a Gladstone bag which incorporates a rope and pulley to fix to a window frame and use as a fire escape. Ladies could also buy a metal pail, disguised as a bonnet box, with removable polished mahogany rim, to avoid using immodest unisex lavatories in France, where they might come upon a man with his braces down seated with the door open. Ladies felt protected travelling with Cook, and his tours opened the door to those many middle class women who had previously not dared, nor had the means, to travel alone.

Louise obtained a civil list pension in 1852. She died of mouth cancer, probably the result of licking paint brushes.

This description of the Puy de Dôme comes from her *A Pilgrimage to Auvergne from Picardy to Le Velay* (1842):

— From Clermont to la Baraque, the village from which guides are procured, the drive is about two hours by a very fine broad road, extremely steep in parts, but by no means difficult. The views are splendid during the whole journey and become bolder and grander as the great Puy is approached, which stands upwards of 1400 metres above the level of the sea and more than 1100 above the plain of La Limagne ...

At La Baraque we stopped at the cottage where we hoped to find the guide recommended to us. His wife informed us that he had ascended the mountain with some travellers a few hours before, but that she was ready to accompany us. As she spoke in Auvergnat, we were uneasy, thinking she would be unable to answer any of our questions if we took her, but she soon quieted our fears by assuring us she could speak French as well as us, or any other Paris ladies – all strangers being considered Parisians.

She accordingly got into the carriage, which conveyed us in about half an hour to the part of the plain where the lava begins its irregular formations. Further than this we could not go, and it was only then we found that the ascent could only be made on foot, as it was not considered safe for animals of any sort. The way seemed long and the attempt perilous, but we would not give it up. Therefore, abandoning ourselves to the guidance of the old woman who was to show us the way, we began our march.

The day was bright and warm in the plains below, but we had felt the wind increasing as we mounted, till it now became sensibly violent. There are few days in the year when the blasts from the Puy de Dôme are not severe, but we were not prepared for the hurricane we had to brave. Long before we had reached the first ascent we were nearly exhausted with our struggles, but after resting at every convenient opportunity we recovered our strength and went on. Nothing could be worse than the path strewn with masses of rock and ploughed by the torrents which come rushing down from the summit. Now we were ankle-deep in sand, now wading through slippery mud, now sliding over short turf, now struggling through tangled bushes. In short, buffeted as we were by the wind, which swept in eddies round us, we had the utmost difficulty to keep our feet.

We had not reached a quarter of the way when we met a party of ladies who had found the ascent too difficult and were returning. The gentlemen of their party had continued their journey to the top with the guide. They earnestly recommended us to abandon the attempt, but we were obstinate and though our companion seemed half inclined to dissuade us too, we resumed our endeavours.

We were now a little sheltered by a projection of the huge mountain and sat down for some time to share our welcome refreshments with our guide, who appeared more exhausted than ourselves, though accustomed to the ascent....

While we were conversing a loud shout was heard above us and she started up, imagining that her husband was coming down. She hurried before us, smiling and looking quite delighted, but called out in an altered voice that it was not him, only a mountaineer with his cows.

Presently we reached the spot where the pair stood, and a more savage-looking apparition I never beheld than the herdsman before me. He was sunburnt, with black, bright eyes and a quantity of long wild black hair flying about his face from under his large broad-edged beaver hat. His shaggy cloak was hanging in drapery round him. He held a long staff and was throwing his arms about with vehement gestures. When I approached he rushed towards me and, casting himself down on the grass nearly at my feet, began talking in a very high key, using forcible gesticulations....

He could speak a few words of French, from which I gathered he was desirous of affording us assistance and would with the greatest pleasure carry us in his arms up the remainder of the mountain. I felt afraid of being seized upon and borne away in spite of myself by my Orson-like champion, and with grateful acknowledgements declined his offer ...

We soon after met [our guide's] husband with his party of three gentleman, one of whom had a handkerchief tied round his head, as the wind had carried off his hat on the summit of the Puy. They were amazed at our intending to go further, but though we required a hand at this moment to help us over a difficult pass, in the usual style of modern French gallantry they seemed resolved to take care of themselves only and hurried away, while the husband called after us many *bon courages* to encourage our attempt.

Just where we met them a magnificent point of view opened before us. We were on a level with the Petit Puy, and beheld a panorama of the greatest beauty stretched out as far as we could gaze, rocks on rocks, mountains on mountains, plains, valleys and forest at our feet, peaks whose craters seemed still yawning, with all their chasms, unseen in the distance, clearly visible and opening their huge jaws like some antediluvian monsters. The Nid de la Poule is the most conspicuous and presents a large hollow crater of most singular appearance.

We had now arrived at the part from whence the ascent is the most difficult.

To the crest of the mountain it appeared almost perpendicular and all the way was strewn with the white ashes of its ancient eruption. We had now a very difficult task and were obliged to exert all our energies to reach the summit, which after great exertion we at length accomplished. The wind roared round us and was icy cold. We hurried to throw ourselves down in a hollow of the irregular plateau which crowns the Puy, at the foot of an erection placed there for observations.

In a few minutes we were able to look about us and magnificent was the prospect which burst upon our sight. All the wide extent of La Marche and Le Limousin was beneath us as in a map. The first elevations of the chain of the Monts Dômes running far into the distance and those of the Monts Dores, the expanse of Lake Aydat and the vast basin of La Limagne, through which runs the silver line of the Allier which the eye may follow into the Bourbonnais. All this and much more which we were assured we could see, we were not permitted long to gaze on, for almost in an instant clouds gathered over the mountain, spreading in all directions as if attracted towards it. The blast howled furiously and a dense vapour closed us in, shutting the landscape from us entirely. There was no hope of its clearing again but some chance of a storm, which we had little inclination to witness. Therefore, hastily gathering up some pieces of calcined rock and a few leaves as souvenirs of the wondrous volcano, we began our descent ...

The descent was even more fatiguing than we found it mounting, and we were obliged to rest as many times.

I asked our guide if there were wolves here, or if there was any tradition of the *loup-garou* [werewolf]. She answered gravely that neither were to be found on the Puy de Dôme, and as for fairies, they were never seen here. 'Because,' said she, 'they are fond of woods and we have no trees. In Le Forez, over yonder, there are plenty, for there they find the shade they love' ...

We had been joined by a traveller who, in spite of her assurances that he would find no path in any other direction, persisted in attempting to descend on the opposite side from that we took. She warned him that he might share the fate of a party who would not be persuaded and had met with an adventure, comic enough but not very agreeable.

Four priests had mounted to the top of the Puy and, after enjoying a repast in the hollow crater, resolved to try the descent in the direction which pleased them most. They attempted it but had not got far when the evil spirits, evidently jealous of their daring, came forth in the form of a furious wind. All four were thrown down, their feet slipped, for the ground was perpendicular and as smooth as glass. One of them was sent flying down the side, pieces of his habit resting on every bush. His priest's hat was borne away, the sport of the mischievous imps who were gamboling in the air. After much struggling, screaming and panting, the discomfited party were fain to crawl on hands and knees back to the summit and submit to descend by the usual route, which is certainly precipitous enough to satisfy the most adventurous.

On St John's Eve this solitary mountain presents a curious spectacle. Crowds from every village and town in the district flock hither and climb to the summit, where a great fire is lighted in honour of the saint....It must be a grand sight from the Petit Puy or any of the lower hills and revive the traditionary aspect of the country when the Puy de Dôme sent forth flames from its centre into the clouds. Then every peak of Auvergne and Velay was on fire and shot up tongues of lurid light to heaven. Surely the great mastodon and megalosaurus were then grazing in the plains beneath and giants and ogres were their herdsmen! —

Nowadays a road climbs to the summit of Puy de Dôme where the modern traveller will find a restaurant, observatory and TV transmitter. Until comparatively recently the Auvergne, with poor roads and harsh winters, was a little-known, somewhat secretive province, and belief in fairies and such things as werewolves may well have existed there until the middle of this century!

CLARISSA TRANT

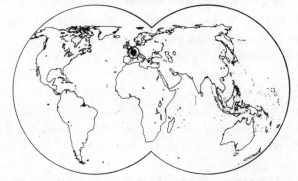

Accompanying her father on endless journeys, full of discomfort and irritations

Clarissa (1800-1844) was another army officer's daughter. Her father came from Cork and attended a French military college before joining the Irish Brigade in France, but in the French revolution he served as a lieutenant in the

British 84th Foot. Clarissa was born in Lisbon of an English mother who died five years later. Her father retired after the 1802 Peace of Amiens, then rejoined in the Peninsula Wars and as a Brigadier-General captured Coimbra at the head of Portuguese troops. He then became governor of Oporto as Sir Nicholas Trant, and sent for his two children aged ten and six. As a result of the Penal Code in Ireland Clarissa's uncle Dominick, called 'The Irish La-fayette', fought against George III in the American war of independence, while Uncle Eduardo was a cadet in the Spanish army. Until the end of the eighteenth century no Roman Catholic could serve in the British army.

Clarissa and her brother Tom led a peripatetic childhood. After her father left Oporto to rent a house in London he became restless and Clarissa contin-ued, reluctantly, to accompany him. Her 1800-1832 journal, edited by C.G. Luard, was not published until 1925, and the following extract, written when she was sixteen, comes from this:

— 1816, Jan. This winter was one of the coldest which has ever been known in England. To me it was a drear one in many respects. My Father's health and spirits were at that time at their lowest ebb and he was oppressed by pecuni-ary cares. I had no one to comfort me and yet I felt I must exert myself to comfort him. My Father determined upon leaving England for the purpose of living in some cheap town in France. Mr Lawlor happened to be in London. I described his sister Anty whom I had met in Ireland to my Father as one whom I was very sure would consent to share our exile, in case he would allow me to make her the proposal. He consented with his usual kindness as he was anxious that I should not be thrown without a female friend into the society of foreigners at my early age and it was settled that Mr Lawlor should escort his sister in the Spring to some seaport where my Father would meet her and convey her to our temporary home.

On 17th January, after parting with the few old friends who continued their affectionate attentions to the last moment of our stay in London, my Father and I bid adieu to Seymour Street and commenced our cold and dreary journey to Weymouth. At five o'clock on the evening of the 18th we embarked on board the Jersey packet [Steamers were not yet established]. The wind and weather proving equally favourable we landed the mail at Guernsey at eight o'clock on the 19th and reached Jersey the same evening. We were detained some days in Jersey by contrary winds. My Father's patience was at length exhausted and finding that the regular packet would not sail, he determined to hire a small French Coasting Vessel bound for Granville, in which we embarked on the 24th.

I had risen before daybreak and dressed myself by candlelight, but finding that the wind was very high, and the weather wet and stormy I hoped to the last moment that something might occur to prevent our embarking. My Father kindly offered to forfeit the passage money if I was *very* averse to sailing and I would have gladly taken him at his word but I felt ashamed of my selfish cowardice. I walked with a heavy heart and a tearful eye to the dismal scene of our embarkation. It was scarcely daylight when we reached the end of the pier and saw our little vessel rocking to and fro amidst the white surf, which was dashing over it. The hollow sound of the wind, the roaring of the waves, the pattering of the rain – all was in character with the visions of shipwrecks and horrors of every kind which had haunted me during the past night. It was with some difficulty our little boat reached the vessel and here a new scene of misery awaited us. On entering the little dark hole which was dignified with the name of cabin and had been secured for my accommodation, I was startled at the sight of two dirty, grim-visag'd men, whose faces were half-concealed by their greasy red night-caps – one of whom proceeded very quietly to dress himself in my presence, whilst the other whom I had roused out of a sound sleep, saluted my astonished ears with a loud yawn followed by; 'Ah, ma petite, te voila arrivée!' I called to my Father who was engaged with the baggage on deck, and gave him an account of my strange reception but I was comforted for all by hearing the Captain declare that it would be impossible to venture to sea in such a storm! With a lighter heart I jumped into the boat which had not yet left the vessel and after a short but rough voyage we landed at St Helier.

On the 28th we embarked on a little vessel of 20 tons on board of which were literally *stuffed* twenty-two passengers, six sailors and a dog. Amongst the former were two Englishwomen and their attendant 'John Bull', six fat Norman peasant girls, one sabreur who, if we might believe his own report of his exploits, had slaughtered half a hundred English soldiers in battle, and ten drunken men whose dreadful oaths were fortunately expressed in patois and therefore almost unintelligible to me.

The cabin! Oh, what a scene was there. The Black Hole of Calcutta could scarcely have been a more horrible dungeon. The cries of the children, the groans of the sick, the fumes of Tobacco, the combination of every offensive smell all added to its horrors. To complete the picture, John Bull entered with a dish of cold pork, of which he generously invited his fellow passengers to partake.

The coast of Brittany is a very dangerous one and many shipwrecks occur on the chain of rocks which extend to a considerable distance between Jersey and St Malo. We were becalmed for two hours within a league of the harbour, and it was eight o'clock when we found ourselves sailing beneath the ramparts. I now ventured upon deck, and was struck with the singular appearance of the ancient town of St Malo, with its tall many windowed old houses peeping above the fortifications; the night was lovely as my Father and I glided over the water in the little boat which conveyed us to the Hotel des Voyageurs. The Equinoctial gales which had detained us at Jersey continued after our arrival and we heard that the first packet which left St Malo for Guernsey after our arrival struck upon a rock and went to pieces. We remained at St Malo until March.

My thoughts often wandered to our cheerful house in Seymour Street, but still more often to the Leander frigate in which my beloved Brother was ploughing the wide ocean.

The little town of Avranches had been recommended to my Father as a cheap and quiet residence, well adapted to our half pay finances. On our arrival, we settled ourselves in private lodgings. It was not a cheerful time. The little knowledge I had of Religion was not deeply enough rooted in my heart to fill it with 'that peace which the world cannot give'. We had no clergyman, no opportunity of hearing God's Holy Word; no friends to cheer our spirit; no books; no pianoforte to beguile the length of the lonely evenings.

In this little Town, as in every other part of France, the English were cordially detested, and in order to procure common civility we found it necessary to put forward our Irish extraction. 'Ah, Monsieur est Irlandais! et M'amselle aussi! Oh, my foi, c'est bien différent! Qu'est ce qu'il y a pour votre service?' —

Five years later they are in Baden and Clarissa is much more self-confident:

— Aug. 28th. 1821. This morning I went out with Lisette my little maid in quest of lodging where we are to remain while my Father goes to spend a week at Baden for the benefit of the Baths. My first attempt at independence!

I was fortunate in finding three rooms at Dr G's, and as his wife offered to take us en pension during that interval for 18 fcs. each per week, we have agreed.

Aug. 31st. Our hosts took us to see the Institut des Aveugles, where we passed a most interesting morning – 15 years established. Every young person remains about 4 or 5 years and on leaving they are presented with a complete set of all the necessary implements for writing, reading and working in order to provide them with employment in their families...Letter from my dear Father giving me permission to join him at Baden with Lisette.

Sept. 2nd. At seven o'clock I embarked in the Wasser Diligence for Baden; Lisette was to have been my companion but as the Doctor recommended me to the care of two old Zurich ladies, I thought I might dispense with this piece of heavy baggage. Me voila donc seule amidst a variety of honest, stupid, Swiss phizzes. The prospect of meeting my dear Father on landing gave me courage. The navigation of the Limmath is extremely dangerous, and in one passage the torrent was so strong that the waves actually dashed over the boat, altho' the weather was perfectly calm. My Father had strongly urged me not to come by water, as he thought it would be too great a trial for my nerves, but I wished to prove myself a heroine....

Sept. 3rd. This day I had a dose of the Parisian couple and most heartily wished for their departure. Madame is une petite Française dans toute la force du term, legère, inconséquente, agaçante avec les Messieurs, et parlant morale avec moi. Monsieur, one of the most decided Republicans, who invents lies sooner than another could repeat them. I thought my Father's patience held out a long time, but at length it was exhausted and before our evening walk was ended we parted company. Went to the convent of Wellingstein; heard the monks singing vespers in the choir, the stillness of the church and the gloom of the evening made the scene imposing.

Sept. 4th. Took a civil leave of M. and Mme. Gendrin, most devoutly wishing never to see them again. After prayers enjoyed a quiet walk with my Father. The environs of Baden are pretty and romantic, but the place itself is very *triste*, chiefly frequented by bourgeois from Zurich. My room at the Stadt Hof looks out upon the river and the noise of the Torrent is not unpleasing. Directly underneath my window is the sulphurous source which Tacitus sought in vain to discover. Montaigne visited Baden in '16, and complained of bugs, fleas, dirt and mauvaise chère, all of which inconveniences still exist. —

Clarissa was devoted to her brother Tom, serving in India, but he died aged twenty-seven. Clarissa married another army officer when aged thirty-two, the point at which her journal ends. After this she lived for twelve years in a succession of lonely European billets and then died of pleurisy. All the involuntary travel to which Clarissa was subjected held no glamour for her, but this reluctant traveller left us some interesting descriptions of her journeys such as one over Mount Cenis in winter during which, after progressing one mile in five and a half hours with eight horses, they took refuge at the Hospice.

ANNA JANE THORNTON

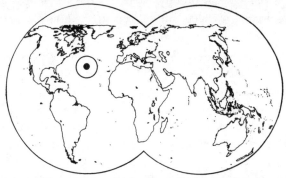

The extraordinary tale of a 'sailor' discovered to be a girl

Another motherless girl was the courageous Anna Jane Thornton, born c.1818 in Gloucester, who from 1821 lived in Donegal. Aged sixteen she achieved fame by masquerading as a sailor in order to get to New York and find Alexander Burke, with whom she had fallen in love in Ireland three years before. When she gets there Alexander's father tells her his son has just died.

Her adventures as a female sailor, reported in the *Weekly Dispatch* on 8th February, 1835, caused a sensation when she arrived back at London's Fresh Wharf aboard the 'Sarah' from St John's, Newfoundland. One of the sailors had glimpsed her breasts while she was washing. The Lord Mayor of London invited her to the Mansion House and a pamphlet was subsequently published by J. Thompson (1835) which created quite a sensation. This contradicted reports that she had been jeered at and treated disrespectfully by sailors and dock workers on the wharf. Anna's story was reprinted in Providence, Rhode Island accompanied by a ballad 'The Female Sailor':

— A few days ago a tide-waiter, who was doing duty on board a vessel called the *Belfast*, from Belfast, lying at Fresh Wharf, near Billingsgate, saw a sailor strike another of the crew, who appeared to be a mere lad, a violent blow, without cause. The lad, who was called James, began to cry, and the tide-waiter, after having called the assailant a cowardly rascal for beating the boy, turned round and said to the latter, 'Don't cry – why you are like a great girl'. 'Girl,' roared out the seaman, 'you may say that; she is a girl, the d-d bitch; and blow me, if she makes any fuss about it, I'll let everybody know all about it'.

Surprised at this information, which issued from the brute with a savage sincerity of manner, the tide-waiter did not delay inquiry, and he soon learned that the charge against the poor insulted person of being a female was correct.

News of this kind could not be long confined to few persons in such a neighbourhood as Billingsgate, and the captain of the vessel finding that a general
interest was excited, invited some gentlemen to see his phenomenon fly up the
shrouds.

Amongst those who went to witness the exhibition were two gentlemen,
who, perceiving the reluctance with which the order of the captain was com-
plied with, and judging that such an unfeeling master was not the sort of
person under whose guidance a child of misfortune was likely to be benefited,
asked the object of their interests to accompany them ashore, and let them
know the history of so strange a metamorphosis, and point out to them in what
manner they could render service in such an exigency. The girl, who was at this
time dressed in a red worsted jacket and duck trowsers, consented to leave the
vessel, although she appeared very anxious to receive a five months' pay,
which was due to her from the captain, at the rate of £2.10s. a month, but which
he was just as anxious to retain, expecting that by holding this menace of
exposure over her she might be induced to abandon the money.

The history she gave was indeed a romantic one. Having stated her name,
of which we are in possession, but which, from motives the reader will admit
to be cogent as he peruses the history, we conceal, she said that some years ago
her father left Gloucestershire for Ireland, where, in a northern county, he
carried on the business of a cornfactor, and lived respectably. Upwards of three
years ago she became acquainted with, and soon after attached to, the captain
of a vessel which traded to the next port. The attachment was mutual. The
captain was, however, obliged to sail for America, and thither, after having
waited in vain for his return or intelligence about him, she determined to go.

She then formed the extraordinary resolution of laying in a stock of sailor's
clothes, as well as female apparel, that she might, in the event of an emergency,
adapt herself to it without the hazard of delay. Arrived in America, she proceeded to the place in which she hoped to hear some tidings of the man for
whom she had made such a sacrifice, but she had passed over the ocean only
to see the turf that covered his remains. She resolved to be a sailor herself, and
succeeded in obtaining the situation of cook and steward on board a vessel
sailing for the Mediterranean. Her swarthy complexion favoured the decep-
tion, and for nearly two years she had been tossed about by sea and land, no
human being ever having suspected, during that time, she was other than what
she appeared to be, with her cropped poll and jacket and trowsers.

At length the secret was to be discovered. About six months ago she engaged at Lisbon with the captain of the *Belfast*, as cook and steward, at £2.10S a
month, and she sailed to many ports with him. One day, as she was washing in

her berth, with her jacket loose in the front, one of the crew caught an acciden-
tal view of her bosom. He immediately expressed his astonishment, and threatened to inform the captain if she refused to consent to the only terms on which
he would promise silence, and these terms being rejected in such a manner as
to show the inefficacy of any future solicitation, everybody in the vessel was
speedily acquainted with the fact that there was a 'she' amongst them.

The poor girl was, from that moment, doomed to suffer great misery. The
captain thought, as he was the master of her fortunes for the time, he ought also
to be the master of her person, and when he found that he had calculated too
much upon his power, turned her out to work amongst the men, by whom she
was upon all occasions most grossly insulted. She declared that, upon one
occasion, she saved her person from violation, by calling God to witness that
she would prosecute every man in the ship if they persevered in their attempts;
but the captain never advised any abatement of the persecution she daily and
hourly underwent. In the most desperate weather she has been ordered up the
shrouds, and her hands are now as hard as those of any man before the mast;
and the gibes, jeers, and curses of the rascally crew was the language to which
she had been constantly obliged to listen.

The gentlemen to whom these circumstances were recited, would not
permit the poor girl to return to the vessel, which sailed the next day, and the
captain succeeded, at least for a short time, in his object of pocketing her wages,
having determined to resist upon the ground that he had agreed to pay a man
and not a woman.

The gentlemen, after having provided for this extraordinary person, for the
present, in a respectable family, wrote to her father an account of the whole
transaction, and in the course of the week an answer of a very favourable
description will no doubt be received. —

This account is followed by a verbal report of Anna's interview with the
Lord Mayor in front of the now apologetic captain who pays her wages, in
return for which Anna acknowledges the captain's kindness and humanity.
The Mayor tells her: 'I trust that you will, by your future attention and care,
prove to your father that your filial affection is as strong as your courage in
such circumstances of danger and toil as you have been placed in, so immeas-
urably beyond that of the rest of your sex of modern days. Many gentlemen
to whom I have spoken on the subject looked upon the case as the coinage of
the brain, but the investigation has, if possible, added, to the interest of the
story.'

What horror such an episode evoked in those days! An unprotected woman was a threat to public morals, and only Anna's youth, her apparently determined retention of her virginity, and the influence of the Lord Mayor, saved her from public obloquy. What became of her later is not known.

~

By the 1860s tourism was well launched and increasingly large numbers of people were travelling in groups. Cook's tourists were a reflection of the social changes brought about by the wider franchise of the Reform Acts and the increasing prosperity of the middle classes. The more aristocratic tourist now moved further afield, and the antiquities of Egypt, not investigated by Thomas Cook until 1869, became popular.

HELEN SELINA BLACKWOOD
(Lady Dufferin)

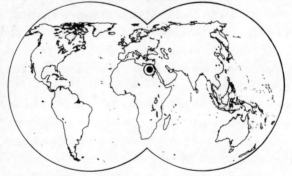

An entertaining parody of travel writing

Helen (née Sheridan) (1807-1867), granddaughter of R.B. Sheridan, was the widowed wife of the Marquis of Dufferin and Ava when, using the pseudonym of the Hon. Impulsia Gushington, she published a parody on travel called *Lispings from Low Latitudes* (1863). The title echoes her son's Icelandic travel book *Letters from High Latitude* (1856).

The Hon. Impulsia Gushington purports to be an amateur poet and is the personification of a gullible Victorian lady traveller with too much time and money. Inspired by Kinglake's *Eothen* (1844) she sets off with her lapdog for Egypt, there to fall foul of a dreadful group of British and Irish abroad, the MacFishys, the O'Whackers and the Fitzdoldrums. She is eventually rescued from this appalling crew by a coloured gentleman and attempts to travel back to Luxor on her own.

The drawings in the book are hilarious. Lady Helen wrote and illustrated it in Ireland at Clandeboye, the Dufferin family estate, to amuse a sick friend. She also wrote songs and verses, collected and published by her son after her death. Well travelled herself, Lady Helen evidently inherited her grandfather's sense of the absurd.

The following passage describes how the Hon. Impulsia hired a camel and her adventures thereafter:

— I asked for a horse – there was none to be had in the village. A donkey? *'Mafish!'* A camel? Yes, two camels! A merchant from Dongolah was even now in the town, with two camels, on his way back to Cairo.

My heart bounded with joy. I had long desired to try the paces of a camel but had not hitherto found a proper opportunity. The merchant and I were put into communication. He proved to be a ragged, pedlar-looking fellow, with a singularly dirty friend or double, who answered for him every time anyone spoke to him. As well as I could I put the question, 'How much to take me to Luxor?' The whole village, as well as the merchant and his double, answered with one huge shout of general information which, however, slept useless in my ear....

In about twenty minutes they had captured the man who spoke French and brought him to me....and I soon discovered that his whole stock of French consisted of the word 'Monsieur', by which title he occasionally saluted me, but said the rest in Arabic ... I managed to make them understand that I wished to start at daybreak, and as it was now evening I accepted the hospitality of an old woman who had been pulling my sleeve and entered her clay-built hovel with some misgivings.

It proved much cleaner than I anticipated. She spread my own cloak over a coarse mat which covered her divan (also made of dried clay), and gave me a leathery cake of bread, baked in the ashes, and a draught of sour milk, for which I was truly thankful.

I could have slept soundly, even on this hard couch, if my entertainer would only have permitted it – I was so thoroughly exhausted by the fatigues of the day and the agitation of my parting interview with the MacFishy family. But the old woman came every five minutes to see if I slept, stroked my face with her dirty hands and finally became so troublesomely inquisitive as to the fastening of my earrings, that I thought it advisable to leave the shelter of her roof, and walk up and down before the door until morning....

'Miss Gushington experiences a new sensation,' by Lady (Helen Selina) Dufferin from Lispings from Low Latitudes: Extracts from the Journal of The Hon Impulsia Gushington, *London: John Murray, 1863*

My camels appeared soon after, and my camel knelt obediently for me to mount...My boxes were fastened onto the other camel, and now, with much chattering of the attendants we prepared to set forth, when, suddenly the door of the hovel in which I had taken shelter for so short a time overnight, flew open, and the inquisitive old lady planted herself in my path with the air of an avenging fury, demanding a second payment for the leathery bannock and sour milk she had so hospitably bestowed on me...We moved forward, but as she continued to scream and skip in front of my camel, the merchant quietly took her up in his arms, wrapped her veil round her head so as to suffocate her in a slight degree, and deposited her inside her own mansion....

My camel proved to be gentle, easy and docile. I found myself often slumbering to its rocking motion, being rather worn with want of sleep and oppressed with the heat of the day....The merchant and his friend walked in advance. Two nubians trotted merrily by my side, both barefoot, though one carried a good pair of slippers in his hand. Poking my camel with a stick, or encouraging him by caresses to accelerate the dignified pace at which these animals generally progress, these interesting youths lightened the way by their native chants and songs ... The lovely scene, the balmy air, the sense of freedom and relief from hateful associations, all combined to soothe and calm my spirit....I fell into a delicious trance, half slumber, half reverie. I could have journeyed thus for ever!

I woke with a shock from the sleep which had overcome my sensibility to outward impressions. Good gracious! what spirit of evil had taken possession of my gentle camel! I found myself bounding over the sandy plain at a pace which threatened dislocation of all my members!

It was in vain that I grasped the horn of the saddle with a mad desperation that only served to fatigue my arms. These tremendous bounds lifted me out of the seat....my serviceable little hat flew like a rocket from my head, my parasol mounted like a balloon. I felt like a fly on some inexorable monster-wheel moved by the demon *steam*, that must in its next revolution inevitably crush me into annihilation. On and on we rushed, the scared cranes screamed above my head, the sand seemed all on fire beneath my camel's feet, the low hills fleeted by like dreams, the wind deafened me by its rush and roar against my ears, my breath was gone, my sight failed! When suddenly – all grew black and silent and still!

I must have fainted, and most fortunately slid down the side of the distracted animal to which I was clinging, for I found myself bruised indeed and shaken, but sound and whole in limb, upon a heap of drifted sand.....

My dress was terribly torn, but I carried in my pocket all the necessary little matters that would enable me to repair the damage.

In about half an hour my faithful Arabs came running up to me with many exclamations of surprise and alarm, fearing that I was seriously hurt. They had succeeded in catching my camel, which indeed had soon stopped of its own accord, but the other one with my baggage was missing. This was a most unaccountable circumstance, and the impossibility of comprehending the explanation which the Arabs seemed eager to afford, added greatly to my perplexity.

Time might remedy this, and I trusted that the morning would bring me news of my missing property. In the meantime the merchant and his friend invited me by signs to proceed a short distance further, as a small village lay hid behind the spur of the sandy hill.

With some difficulty I managed to drag my weary limbs so far, but the hovels to which they conducted me looked so dirty and uninviting that I refused to enter them. I had noticed some dry shallow caves in the sandstone rock we had just passed and I made my friends understand I should prefer passing the night there...

To the caves we accordingly repaired. I selected one for my 'maiden- bower' and my faithful Arabs chose another for themselves. They lit a fire there and prepared some excellent coffee, of which I gladly partook, as well as of the palatable cakes they procured from the village. I now divested myself of my upper garments and proceeded to repair the damage they had sustained. I finished my task just as the sun sank beneath the low sandhills. I can just remember replacing my gold thimble, scissors, etc. in the pocket of my dress, and with the garment still lying loose across my knees, fatigue overcame me, and I slept – a long, delicious, dreamless sleep.

I woke with a start, just as the golden dawn was tipping the extreme tops of a tuft of palm trees near me with the most brilliant orange. Perfect silence prevailed, save the distant bark of the village dogs....My dress? It was no longer on my knees, it was nowhere to be found!....I rushed into the open air, calling loudly on my faithful attendants. No voice responded to my call....nothing remained belonging to my late companions except the ashes of the fire they had kindled for our repast.

Then for the first time the awful truth burst upon my mind, and nearly overwhelmed it. —

Fleeced by the Arabs, Impulsia goes to the Sheikh of the local village, in her half-clad state, i.e. wearing only her underclothing and the 'hoop' or 'cage' of her stolen dress. After some misunderstandings she succeeds in exchanging her gold earrings for the Sheikh's 'abbah' or cloak, and he obtains a donkey and driver for her. She departs, minus her hoop, wearing the Sheikh's abbah, obliged to ride astride on the donkey's saddle.

— Towards evening we arrived at a large village on the banks of the Nile, and I at length got rid of my dreadful negro [driver], who saluted me at parting with a volley of execrations, in which the fatal word 'Bakhshish' still predominated.

With languid limbs and sinking heart I crept through the outskirts of the town and directed my steps towards the river. To my inexpressible delight I saw, moored under the bank, a small 'canja' or native boat, with the Dutch flag flying at its stern and its head lying down the river. —

The Dutchman proves to be an engineer employed on a survey for the Pasha, who speaks little French or English, but agrees to take Impulsia up to Luxor. During the journey she sleeps most of the time.

— At this distance of time, I look back with astonishment at the very little disturbance of mind I experienced in contemplating my peculiar relations with my excellent host. That exquisite sense of feminine decorum on which I prided myself, seemed for the time quite in abeyance. It is true that, from the first moment of our meeting, I felt the most unbounded confidence in the respectful nature of this gentleman's attentions. I think the Dutch character is calculated to inspire this feeling. Mynheer Van Swillanstoff was evidently a man of refined and noble qualities, and reserved disposition ... Our communications were rare but mutually satisfactory, and I think it speaks volumes for the character of this truly worthy man, as well as for his merits as a companion, that a maiden lady in my strange and unprecedented situation, unknown and unnamed, in what must be called male costume (if it could be styled any costume at all), should thus have floated calmly down the current of existence on the Nile's broad bosom, for the space of three days and three nights, in the society of a fat gentleman, with whom she had never exchanged a word in her life before, without a shadow of fear or feeling of embarrassment. —

JANE FRANCESCA, LADY WILDE

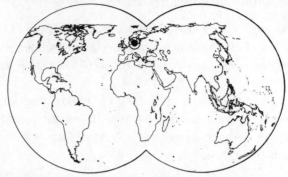

The honeymoon trip of an eminent doctor and a patriotic poet

As witty a woman as Helen Dufferin was Jane Francesca (née Elgee), born in Wexford (1824-1896), daughter of a Wexford attorney, and mother of the famous Oscar Wilde. She was in her youth passionately rhetorical and patriotic, and at the age of eighteen dropped poems signed 'John Fenshaw Ellis' into the letter box of *The Nation*, founded by Charles Gavan Duffy. Her later and better known pseudonym was 'Speranza'. She used this as her parents were dead, and she lived with a unionist uncle who detested *The Nation*.

Jane Elgee first achieved fame when her 'Jacta Alea Est' by Speranza appeared in *The Nation* of 29 July, 1848, causing the suppression of the paper by the Castle authorities. 6,000 words long, it called on Irish people to rise and fight for their liberty, to die for Ireland. Duffy, as editor, was indicted on charges of treason and felony. Jane Elgee sat in the public gallery during the trial and in a loud voice took all blame upon herself as author. Duffy, who was already in prison and had not seen the article, was dismissed.

Jane married William Wilde, surgeon and president of the Irish Academy, in 1851, and their honeymoon was spent in Scandinavia, then seldom visited. The fastest route was to Copenhagen via Liverpool, Hull, Hamburg and Kiel and they travelled second class 'for the sake of the company', paying a fare of £2 plus fifteen shillings a day for meals.

They visited Copenhagen, then went on to Christiana and Stockholm, looking at museums and art galleries and attending banquets held in their honour. In Sweden they were guests of Baron von Kroemar, Viceroy of Uppsala. William was given an *honoris causa* degree by the university there, and the Order of the Polar Star of Sweden.

The couple later had three children, William, Oscar, and Isola who died aged ten.

Portrait of Lady Wilde, or Speranza,
by Bernard Mulrenin, exhibited at the
Royal Hibernian Academy, 1864

The following extract comes from *Driftwood from Scandinavia* (1884), a belated and probably re-edited account of their honeymoon journey from Stockholm to Berlin over thirty years before, for since then William I of Prussia had become the first German Emperor:

— Again we are on the Baltic; the gentle summer sea of forest foliage and winding curves and granite crags crowned with pines, and the thirteen hundred islands, each island a verdant park lying on the calm blue water.

We see now how easily the early races in their migrations could pass from island to island and find food and sustenance in plenty, with the great shadowy pine forests for their dwelling place; and in their wild, joyous freedom, with nature, energy, independence and vigorous work, lived a healthier and therefore happier life than all our vaunted civilisation can now offer to poor, dyspeptic, nervous, depressed, worn-out, hypochondriacal humanity.

The black eagle of Prussia floats above us, the vulture, it should rather be called, as nothing escapes its talons nor the desolating swoop of its terrible wings, and German resounds on all sides. It seems quite easy to speak, after the obscurities of Danish, but we scarcely need to practise our lingual knowledge, for all the Prussian officers on board speak English perfectly.

The captain is monosyllabic and stern and quite insensible to flattery. How to reach the heart of a Prussian is as difficult a problem as to find the fourth dimension. They are a very intelligent people, but morose. They cannot help it, they are born so. Courtesy is the grace of the Gothic branch of the Teutons only.

On the third day after leaving Sweden, that land of noble hearts and noble manners, we reached Stettin. It was evening. A sea of light was around us, a roseate mist filled the atmosphere, through which soft cloud-masses rose like the snow-peaks of an Alpine world, and every peak was flushed crimson in the last rays of the setting sun. Thus transfigured, even Germany looked beautiful.

At once on arrival the douaniers came on board and there was great rending and searching of bags and boxes by rude, resolute Prussian hands. Alas, for the Scandinavian homage to womanhood! It had vanished along with the mountains and the glorious pine forests of the north.

Stettin is a handsome town, the bright, gay port of the Baltic where every traveller takes the rail to Berlin. There are fine public buildings and splendid terraces and handsome private residences, every window draped as for a festival with the gayest of painted blinds and the whitest of muslin draperies. The quays are crowded with shipping. Swedish iron is unloading in quantities to send over Europe, grapes are in cart-loads, potatoes ranged in huge sacks for export, like Ali Baba's forty thieves, fish enough to feed five thousand without a miracle, and excellent peaches at a penny a dozen.

There is much vociferation in the market place. Everyone is rapid, busy and energetic in this active population.

Rows of women were standing in tubs under the bridges at their laundry work, beating the clothes in the water with resounding vehemence; other rows of women were seated behind huge water-vats filled with live fish, which they brought up in strainers for the buyer to inspect. Altogether, after a careful study of the market prices, I came to the conclusion that in Stettin one could live comfortably, even luxuriously, for sixpence a day ...

The fishwomen all wore immense black bonnets, with a high top-knot, precisely like the old caricatures of Queen Caroline; but the nurses looked very coquettish and theatrical in short, full petticoats, showing the long red stocking to the knee, high lace cap with gold back and massive gold earrings. There was no beauty, however, amongst the women. How unlike the bright, fresh faces of Hamburg, that city of pretty maidens, are these neutral-tinted north Germans! Already we miss the oval Swedish type and dark hair, and have come suddenly upon the globular head and hay-coloured face and tresses of the original Teuton.

A wedding was going on in the fine old church of St James, and we entered unopposed. The altar was decorated with coronals of scarlet and white roses and large high pots of myrtle and orange trees in full bloom were placed at each side. Two chairs were set in front on a carpet for the happy pair, and a circle of chairs behind for the company. There was no emotion, every one looked sensible, stolid and staid. The crowd of spectators was short, square and hay-coloured, according to the national type. But a wedding is always a pretty sight. It is so interesting to contemplate the beautiful confidence of youth and love that believes the book of fate is now closed with golden clasps, and that no word of sorrow will ever be written there again.

The bridegroom was a young Prussian officer, tall, straight, handsome, with broad shoulders and slim waist, erect and manly, the regulation moustache perfect. The bride had a pale, dreamy Marguerite aspect, with her forget-me-not blue eyes and coils of fair hair, like masses of unspun silk. The upper class women have all this dreamy, mist-woven, wraith-like look, while the lower classes seem made of sandy grit, like their soil ...

From Stettin to Berlin is a four hours' journey by rail over level land, dry, sandy, flat and monotonous. No horizon, no outline, nothing to be seen except saw-mills, turf bogs, the quaint red Noah's ark, the waving skeletons of the tall, thin poplars, potato fields and hayricks precisely similar in form to the German heads. Now the dust begins from these dry plains. Dust-coloured women look up at us from the potato ridges; dust-coloured men, strong and solid, are busy at work, patient industry in their faces, a people evidently made for work, to stand in the furrows and plough and sow, and never lift their eyes from the oxen they drive.

Industry is the special virtue of the Saxon race. While the Celt is willing to die, perhaps uselessly, for an idea, the Saxon labours and lives for gain. It is the one sole ideal that stirs the sluggish current of his nature. Toil is his element, his destiny, and the greed of gain the one impulsive force of his life....In the workshop of the world the Saxon is master.

But now the empire city of Germany rises up from the circling sandy desert, stately and grand in the dim, misty, uncertain twilight. The city that proceeded out of the mouth of a king. He commanded and it was made. The capital of an empire generally expresses the life of a whole people in stone and marble, and is the product of many generations, but Berlin is the city of one man and one mind.

When the father [Frederick William I of Prussia 1713-40] of the great Frederick chose to have a capital worthy of his name and fame, he ordered the citizens to build houses, palatial residences, with magnificent frontage. Nothing at the back, nothing inside, he cared not; nor even if the unhappy builders were ruined and made bankrupt. So Berlin arose, the daughter of kings, the

Palmyra of the northern desert. The old portion of the town is narrow, poor and mean, but the grand, world-celebrated Unter den Linden is a pathway for kings.

From the great Brandenburg gate, surmounted by the Car of Victory, to the royal palace, is an avenue of architectural splendours nearly a mile in length, unrivalled in any capital of Europe. Two rows of lime trees extend the whole way. Between them is the fashionable promenade. At each side is a broad carriage drive, and beyond are the palatial houses, palaces, hotels, gardens and numerous statues, not of Greek gods and nymphs, but of national heroes who have lived and worked for the national glory. The colossal equestrian statue and monument to the Prussian hero, king and chief, the great Fritz [Frederick the Great], Rauch's greatest work, towering above all. On the palace bridge that crosses the Spree are eight fine marble groups representing Strength, Wisdom and Victory, the fitting symbols of the Prussian people. A flight of marble steps leads up to the museum. On one side is the colossal group of the Amazon and Tiger, on the other the Lion-tamer, by Rauch. The royal palace is opposite, a vast and magnificent edifice, with its grand and stately Rittersaal, the scene of the torch dance and many other grand and awful ceremonials which the Prussian court hold sacred.

These Margraves of the Marshes have been a wonderful race, and bravely fought their way by intellect, courage and hard work, from obscurity to empire, making of this poor sandy desert of Prussia, for which nature has done so little, one of the foremost nations and powers of the world — a power indeed that could crush all Europe with its immense military strength if it were so minded, and not restrained by family ties and diplomatic motives. —

Jane had her poetry collected and published in 1864, the same year her husband was knighted. A head taller than Sir William, she was by now a striking figure at her Dublin salon, clad in long gowns and oriental scarves, sometimes topped by a gilded laurel wreath.

William died in 1876, and Jane moved to London where her eldest son worked as a journalist, Oscar being an Oxford undergraduate. Here too she ran a salon, attended by an eclectic collection of people, including G.B. Shaw, Marie Corelli, Tennyson and Oliver Wendell Holmes. She also wrote for periodicals such as the *Pall Mall Gazette*. Her writing, which includes poetry, philosophy, history, legends, biography, criticism and fiction, has a tendency to put opinion first and fact second.

In old age, now short of money, Lady Wilde turned to spiritualism. Depressed by the lives of her two sons, Willie estranged and Oscar disgraced, in 1896 she caught a chill and died of bronchitis.

Nowadays Lady Wilde would probably have been a journalist. A bizarre personality in her day, but an interesting and original woman, she was frustrated by contemporary social conventions. She would have been much more at home in the late twentieth century!

MARGARET ANNA CUSACK
'The nun of Kenmare'

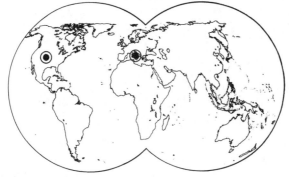

The antithesis of meekness, a nun not intimidated by authority

A woman whose travels were of a philanthropic nature was Margaret Anna Cusack (religious name Francis Clare) (1832-1899), born in Dublin to a Protestant family. Her father was a doctor to the poor in Coolock. She became an Anglican nun when her fiancé died and in 1858 a Poor Clare nun. Later she founded her own Order. Her autobiography, *The Story of My Life* (1891), is interesting on the subject of the lack of education for intellectual women. Her ideas, too radical for the nineteenth century, gave scandal and by the time the autobiography was written she had reverted to protestantism and become a sad and disillusioned person.

'The Nun of Kenmare' first became known for her writings, lives of St Francis of Assisi, St Patrick and St Clare, histories of Ireland and County Kerry, even an early detective novel. Profits from her work went to the Order. Though at first an enclosed nun she also set up a Famine Relief Fund, and then in 1880 wrote a controversial pamphlet, reprinted in the United States, on *The Present Case of Ireland plainly stated: a Plea for my People and my Race*, in which she blames landlordism for the country's woes. The pamphlet caused an uproar, she was threatened with assassination and criticised for interfering in politics by the anti-Home Rule Archbishop McCabe of Dublin. Subsequently his 1882 pastoral letter forbade women to take part in politics. Largely as a result of this Sister Clare left the Kenmare convent, about which she is very critical in her autobiography.

An outspoken person with vision far ahead of her time, many of her ideas were frustrated, and she writes bitterly as follows about leaving Ireland for Rome in 1884:

— From Nottingham I went to Rome by desire of Bishop Bagshawe, and with the best introductions. The purpose of my visit was to obtain permission from the Pope to found a new religious order, to be called the Sisters of Peace. My object in this was twofold. I hoped the very name would remind the sisters that they were called to practise peace amongst themselves before they could hope to teach it to others, and then to establish a work for the working girl, especially a work for emigrants. Besides, it was quite necessary, if I hoped to do any good, that I should be publicly cleared. This I knew would be done in Rome, for the Pope could not authorise any one to establish a new religious Order who had not lived an exemplary life according to Roman Catholic ideas.

I spent four months in Rome before a decision was made, and it could not have been more favourable than it was. I was authorised to found the Order of Sisters of Peace, and I have the Pope's authorisation. I have also a document which declares that every care was taken to investigate the charges which were made against me by the Kenmare sisters and others, and that they were made without even the least foundation. These charges indeed would appear very absurd in Protestant eyes, who could not understand that it was a deadly sin in the sight of Catholics to have left a convent, even when one was persecuted almost to death in it. But even this I did not do, and I cannot but see that the Providence of God was in this matter; for I did not leave the convent in Kenmare without the usual ecclesiastical permission. If I had done so Catholics would have believed that I had been guilty of a crime, whereas now all the facts are before them, and they know that I was not only persecuted while trying to work for them, but that I was also cruelly slandered. —

In May 1884 Mother Francis Clare was released from the Irish order of Poor Clares and authorised by Pope Leo XIII in a private audience to found the Sisters of Peace. Her first two motherhouses were in Nottingham (UK) and Jersey City (USA).

Outspoken, unorthodox women were not liked, and Cusack seems to have aroused antipathy and calumny about herself. The doctrine of Infallibility, promulgated by the Pope at the first Vatican Council in 1870, also stuck in her

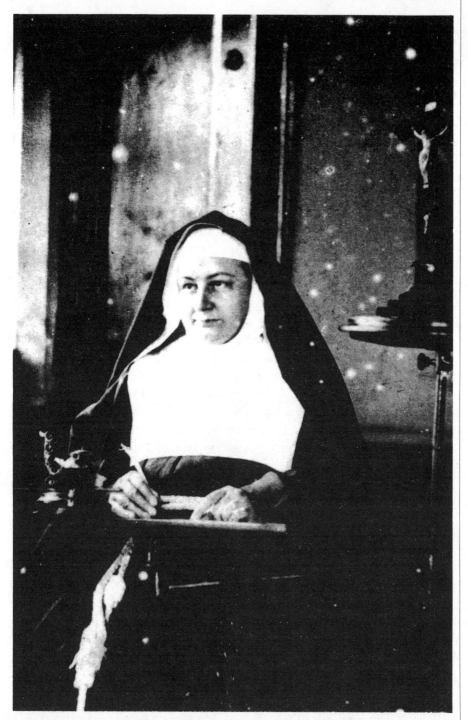

Margaret Anna Cusack, 'The Nun of Kenmare'

throat. This she discusses at length in her autobiography. Her inability to accept this doctrine may have been another source of the rumours spread about her:

— My first doubt was, as I have said before, when the doctrine of the Pope's infallibility was made an article of faith. If the Church always believed it, how was it that for so many hundred years the Church did not teach it? Why was it open to any Catholic, in, say the eighteenth century, to believe the Pope was not infallible, and even to teach that he was not, as was done in the authorised Roman Catholic catechisms, and yet be saved; and then in the nineteenth century why was it made a mortal sin, a sin the commission of which would send you to hell if you did not believe? It was surely the veriest farce to say that a Church which could make such extraordinary changes in its creed had always taught the same thing.

But my life was a busy one. The reader will have had but a faint glimpse of the extent of my work, and I have said but little of my physical sufferings. Our dear Lord has told us that what we know not now we shall know hereafter. One of the things which I must wait to know is, why our dear Lord was pleased to withhold the light or the grace from me so long, which when given led me out of Rome? I have thought perhaps that I was left in Rome for the sake of others, God only knows, but He does know. If I had left Kenmare, as I was sorely tempted to do, when I received such cruel treatment from some of the sisters, perhaps I should have known nothing of the state of the Roman Catholic Church in America, whereas now I can give information which is of the utmost importance to Christian people. —

In the US her life seems to have been no happier, for there too she clashed with bishops and found religious prejudice and intolerance which eventually affected her health. In 1888 she retired from her Order and left New Jersey, returning to England:

— I left America with a sad heart. I left behind me many Romanists whom I could have influenced for good, if only Christian people had helped me to do a work which no one but myself could have done. I was left alone, and sad, and ashamed to see the Catholics who came to me, because how could I tell them that Christian people were afraid of their Church, or to open any door for their deliverance?... They will become infidels, as the Catholics of France and Germany have become; and some one will surely have to answer for their souls.

I tried in vain to see the sisters. Protestants are persuaded by a wily cardinal or a plausible Jesuit that Rome has changed and become liberal. I think my history should be sufficient proof to the contrary. —

Cusack came to believe that Rome controlled the post office and the Press. She therefore felt persecuted and threatened at every turn, and the end of her book becomes a slightly unbalanced diatribe. Looking back at her life now, however, she appears like an early social pioneer. Her Sisters of Peace (now called Sisters of St Joseph of Peace) is a flourishing Order in Britain, Canada and the USA. She originally founded the Order to train girls for domestic service and provide lodging for factory workers far from home.

Her *Advice to Irish Girls in America*, by the Nun of Kenmare (Sister Mary Francis Clare), New York: J.A. McGee, 1872, immediately sold 10,000 copies. Written in a simple style, with simple explanations, the girls are told: 'The Angels are servants. They are God's servants,' and 'Money will not keep away death, or sickness or family troubles.' She gives advice on marriage, children, even husbands, 'Attend to any little thing you know he wishes'. Girls should avoid controversy with Protestants and put up with being called 'Papists' and 'Irish'.

Travel in Cusack's writing is always connected to her mission. She was largely misunderstood in her lifetime, and her outspoken and bitter autobiography did not help. There have recently been two biographies on her, by Irene ffrench Eagar, published in Dublin, and by Margaret Rose O'Neill, a nun in her Order from Seattle (see bibliography).

SARAH MAUD HECKFORD

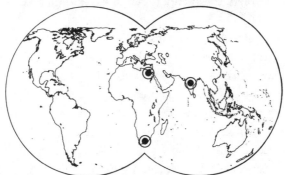

The story of a pioneer in South Africa

The first Irishborn woman to write on travel in South Africa was Sarah Maud Heckford (née Goff) (1839-1903), born in Dublin, whose obituary in *The Times* says she 'leaped the barriers of young ladydom though they were armed with painfully sharp spikes'. Vivien Allen's *Lady Trader: biography of Mrs Sarah Heckford* (1979) gives a full account of her life.

From a rich Anglo-Irish family which had been in Ireland since Cromwell's time and became Quakers in the eighteenth century, Sarah was a third child. Her mother died six months after her birth and her father, restless and unhappy, roamed the Continent, leaving his children for the most part in London, before he died in Dresden. Sarah was raised by an aunt and uncle, and from childhood tuberculosis developed a hump on her shoulder. After the death of her aunt when she was twenty she lived independently in London with her sister Annie and wrote an autobiographical novel, *Excelsior*. As an early feminist she disliked the useless life of girls of her background. She wanted to study medicine but this was then forbidden to women in both England and Scotland.

In 1866 cholera broke out, brought over via pilgrims to Mecca. This enabled Sarah to break out of her respectable upperclass life and volunteer as a nurse at Wapping District Cholera Hospital, and there she met Dr Nathaniel Heckford, born in India and part Asian. 8,000 people died in the epidemic, half from the poor East End of London.

In 1867 Sarah married Nathaniel and together they founded the East London Hospital, for both wanted to work among the poor. Sarah became hospital matron, studying medicine in her spare time. Charles Dickens was one of her admirers, and Dr Elizabeth Garrett (the first English woman to be placed on the medical register) was one of Nathaniel's students. Nathaniel, however, overworked, contracted tuberculosis and died aged twenty-nine in 1871.

Sarah was a freethinker, believing in the teachings of Christ, but not in his divinity. She wrote a short book on the life of Christ and its bearing on the doctrine of Communism. An early socialist, she was appalled at social conditions of her time. By 1874 she had given away most of her capital, so she went to India, via Egypt, travelling alone. She first worked for a medical mission in Calcutta which helped women in purdah, then travelled through central India and was for a year resident medical adviser to Shah Jahán Begum in Bhopal. Indian watercolour sketches by Sarah still survive in a Transvaal farmhouse.

Sarah was next attracted to the British Empire's newest colony when the Boer Republic was annexed to Britain in 1877. There were then some 245,000 white people living in South Africa, though this figure had doubled by the time Flora Shaw, whom we shall meet shortly, wrote her despatches to *The*

Times. Land was cheap and speculators flocked in for mining and farming.

Sarah was the only female to join a group who went out to study farming. She was by now thirty-nine and not in robust health. She travelled with Gerald Goff (23), an officer cousin and George Warner (15), whom she had known since babyhood, and who appears as 'Jimmy' in her *Lady Trader in the Transvaal* (1882), a book rare in South Africa and hardly known elsewhere, which covers the period 1878-1881. For political reasons she changed all names of the people in the book.

Sarah's biographer Vivien Allen has identified all her characters and Sarah's life history indeed makes fascinating reading. In South Africa she had all kind of troubles to put up with as a farmer, from sheep fever to malaria and labour problems. It is when these prove too much for her that she determines to set up as a smous, or itinerant trader. Later Sarah established farm schools in South Africa.

When Sarah first arrived in Durban she set out on a 450 mile journey by bullock cart and on horseback through Natal and Orange Free State to Rustenburg, north of Pretoria. Then she acclimatised herself by becoming governess to an Afrikaner family, thus learning Afrikaans.

Later on, as a smous, she would trade goods and by summer had enough money to buy more land. Her book, written in a laconic but amusing style, gives a good description of how she first set out with Jimmy and twelve men to outspan from Pieter-Maritzberg to Pretoria.

This passage comes from the beginning of her trek:

— Jimmy and I left Pieter-Maritzberg on a fine afternoon, having been there about a week, the rest of the party, together with the two wagons which had been hired by the manager, having gone on in front, the men on foot, we on horseback or rather ponyback, for neither of our steeds was fifteen hands high. I had found it very hard to get serviceable animals at Pieter-Maritzberg, for at that time all the available and many unavailable horses, were bought up by the volunteers....I cannot say much for my own two. One, which Jimmy bestrode, was a rough and ugly Basuto pony, very thin but with good qualities. My pony was larger, fat and handsome. He would have been very good except for his laziness....These two animals were the means of introducing me to the common domestic insect of this part of the world, namely the 'tick' or bush-louse, as it is called by the Boers. There were hundreds on both ponies, and the groom of the hotel being, as Kaffir grooms generally are, a useless addition to the stable, Jimmy and I had employed hours in ridding our ponies of the parasites ...

The South African tick is a wonderful creature. There are grey, brown, whitish and striped varieties, besides one exceedingly poisonous kind, yellow-green on the back with a white line with symmetrical streaks of red on it running round the edge of the podgy little body, and the belly grey. These insects vary in size from almost invisibility to the bulk of a hazel nut. They are very agile, and if you happen to be sitting on the grass you have a good chance of seeing one walk nimbly towards you, with a hungry look pervading his small person ...

With a vague idea that I was going into a wild country, and with a distinct one that Jimmy was not likely to afford much protection, I had a revolver in a case strapped round my waist and another in a holster on my saddle ... We started, and having arrived at an even stretch of road halfway up the hill immediately beyond the village, Jimmy proposed a canter. It was not a particularly fast one, but the effect was disastrous. I was a little in front when I heard, 'Hilloa! I say, look what's happening!' and looking back I beheld the road strewn with articles which had gradually fallen from Jimmy's various parcels. Jimmy looked disconsolate as he returned and began to pick them up, while I sat on my pony and laughed. This was unfair, for the loading up arrangement had been of my invention, not Jimmy's. Presently we came up to one of our party, sitting, hot and weary, on a big stone near to a handcart laden with miscellaneous articles, which had not arrived in time to be packed in the wagons. I must here observe, that the manager of our party had contracted for our being taken to Pretoria with our goods by a carrier, or what is here called a transport-rider, and the transport-rider was imperious about when he would 'in and out-span', to use a South African phrase for putting the oxen into and letting them out of the yoke....

Sometime after Jimmy and I reached the place where the wagons were outspanned. The cart was brought in, the articles in it placed in the wagons, and the cart itself sent back. When the oxen were inspanned and we started once more, we felt we were fairly en route, and being so let me describe the wagons which were to serve us as houses until we reached Pretoria.

The one was an open buck-wagon with a tarpaulin, or what is here called a buck-sail, thrown over it to protect the goods. There were eighteen oxen in this wagon, which was driven principally by the Afrikaner transport-rider, a small man with red whiskers and moustache. The other wagon was also a buck-wagon...but on the back half of it there was a tent, formed of canvas stretched on bent laths, so as to form a complete covering at the sides and top....With very few articles packed in a half-tent, its occupant may be comfortable enough, but when, in addition to cases, the entire paraphernalia which a company of twelve men, most of them unaccustomed to travelling, think necessary to keep handy, is tumbled into it, the conditions are altered. Of course each man had a rifle, and these weapons had to be kept exceptionally handy, although they did not get us more than two or three brace of birds during our whole trek, and not even one buck. The result of twelve men and one woman (myself) having these things 'handy' in a half-tent was this. The various articles underwent a rotatory movement every time one of them was wanted and became well mixed up. Later on I was able to make canvas bags and tie them up to the sides of the tent, and so save my property from the general confusion, but at the outstart my goods contributed to it.

Our evening outspan was on a bleak hilltop, along which a thick, damp mist was beginning to sweep. It soon enveloped us and rendered the cooking of the evening meal difficult. Presently supper made its appearance. The meal consisted of fried ham, bread and coffee without milk. It does not sound badly but I will describe it in the words of the man who cooked it, 'Rancid tallow candle with lots of salt in it'. He would not eat of it, but I was very hungry and did, although I confess the description was accurate. —

Later on, when Sarah became a trader, she had become much more experienced and learned to be resourceful, as the following extract shows:

— The sun had set, but there was a beautiful moon and I got into Pretoria in good time. The next morning I discharged the driver and engaged a new one. In the meantime Jimmy turned up and told me his employer had discharged him, having no further need of his services, and that he was unable to obtain any other employment as everything was very slack in Pretoria. Under these circumstances I proposed to him to come with me, to which he gladly assented. So in the evening we started, Jimmy and I riding and the new driver, a half-caste named Andreas, walking and carrying his own and Jimmy's bundles.

We were only on the outskirts of the village when we saw a great storm was imminent and turned back to the Felmans' house just in time to escape it, fortunately, for it was very severe. The next morning we started again and when we arrived at the wagon found Soldat, Clara and the dogs anxiously expecting us ...

There had been heavy rain at the Red House as well as at Pretoria and the spruit was very much swollen. The worst was that the weather looked very threatening. I inspanned after lunch and started. This time the oxen pulled much better and it was evident that, although not a good driver, Andreas was much superior to his two predecessors.

We had only got a few miles and were on a bleak hillside, when the storm I had seen approaching for some time, burst upon us. It was something terrific. There was no making head against it. I had the oxen outspanned, blanketed the horses and sheltered them as well as I could in the lee of the wagon. The flashes of lightning and the roar of thunder were almost continuous, the rain poured down in torrents and the wind howled and raved until I thought the wagon would have been blown over. I was afraid the horses would get alarmed and stood by them until the fury of the storm abated, which was not for some hours.

The rain was still falling heavily and it was quite dark, when at last, drenched through in spite of my mackintosh, I crept into the wagon along with Clara, whilst Jimmy made his bed (such as it was) under it, in the wet. When I woke next morning the rain was still falling, nor did it cease till midday, when it cleared up.

The wagon had sunk very deep in the soft ground, which was slippery for the oxen's feet, and after various efforts to pull it out, I was obliged to make up my mind to offload partially again. The evening was very fine and I trusted to being able to load up in the morning after pulling the wagon out.

The whole ground was so wet and swampy that I determined to let the horses and oxen remain loose during the night. The moon was bright and from time to time I inspected them.

The morning dawned clear beautifully, but hardly had the first rays of the sun become visible, when I saw a heavy bank of clouds which threatened hail, sweeping rapidly up from the horizon. I ordered all haste to be made to get whatever had been off-loaded up on the wagon, but before everything was ready the storm burst – such a storm, almost worse than the previous one, although the thunder and lightning was less severe....

The rain poured down all day. Clara at last managed to make a sort of little tent with a tarpaulin and some sheets of iron roofing I had with me, and got some coffee made which Jimmy and I, crouching in the wagon tent together, were very thankful for. She also managed to make some very bad griddle-cakes, but the wonder was she was able to make them at all!

Night came on, and it was still raining and blowing. It was useless to attempt to tie up the animals, the wagon was standing in a swamp, so they had to take their chance. Jimmy and I slept in the wagon, the tent of which had begun to leak, and little Roughy and Moustache begged so to come in also, that I let the poor little brutes have their desire.

When the morning dawned it was still raining, the horses were in sight, but the oxen were gone and so was the leader. I sent Andreas on foot and Soldat on Dandy to look for them and while they were away, seeing two government wagons going to Potchefstrom with strong spans of oxen, I asked the conductor to pull my wagon out, which he obligingly did.

It rained on and off the whole day, and in the evening the two boys returned, having seen nothing of the oxen. Soldat reported the spruit was in flood. I determined to look for the oxen the next day myself, as I suspected they had trekked off to the farm they had been feeding on shortly before I bought them. This is a favourite pastime of oxen. Unfortunately I did not know where this farm was, and hence it would be necessary first to go to Pretoria to see the man I had bought the animals from. —

Accordingly Sarah and Jimmy set off on horseback for Pretoria the next day taking a dog with them. They find out where the farm is and stay with her friend the Felmans, to give the horses a rest. Then they set out again to find the farm, and have to ford a dangerously swollen river twice. At the farm, however, there is no news of the missing oxen, except that the farmer, looking through field-glasses for some oxen he had also lost in the storm, had seen a number of oxen on a distant hillside, which he did not recognise as his own or his neighbours'. One wonders how the farmer identified oxen in this way at such a distance!

— The hill was in the direction of my wagon, so I thought this sounded hopeful ... We mounted once more and fording the river again in the same spot, took our way towards the hill pointed out to us, when suddenly Jimmy exclaimed he was sure he could see the oxen grazing in a valley at some distance. I could not make them out, but he was so confident that we altered our course and presently coming to a farm, we asked the Boer who owned it if he had seen any strange oxen. He told us he had seen fourteen strange beasts that morning with their heads towards the spot Jimmy had indicated. Thus encouraged we pushed on and soon came in sight of our friends, peaceably grazing. —

If times were hard, as during the Siege of Pretoria when her cattle and corn were requisitioned, Sarah traded in gold shares instead. During the Boer War she was socially active and also spied for the British.

Sarah's eyesight had almost gone by the time she died of bronchitis, aged sixty-three. She is still well remembered in South Africa.

CHARLOTTE GRACE O'BRIEN

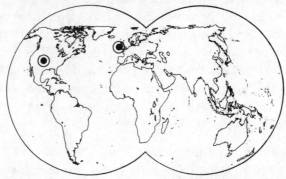

A campaigner for the improvement of conditions on emigrant ships

Another person who travelled for duty rather than pleasure was Charlotte Grace O'Brien, born Cahirmoyle (1845-1905), daughter of William Smith O'Brien (1803-64), the Young Irelander leader sentenced to be hanged, drawn and quartered for insurrection in 1848. He was reprieved, however, and transported to Tasmania for high treason. In 1854, pardoned, he lived in Brussels for two years with his young daughter. After that Charlotte returned to County Limerick.

Charlotte was descended from the O'Briens of Dromoland, the old Celtic line from the Kings of Thomond, lords of Clare, but the O'Briens had inter-married with Anglo-Normans, Cromwellian and Puritan settlers, and the only remaining R.C. O'Briens of Carrigaholt had left Ireland with the Irish Brigade. Charlotte's brothers were educated at St Columba's near Dublin. Her mother died in 1861 and she then became housekeeper in charge of a large house and her siblings, nursing her father until he died in 1864. After his death she lived with her brother Edward and his wife, who died in 1868 leaving three young children. Charlotte acted as mother to them until her brother remarried, and Charlotte remained very close to these young relatives.

Once freed from domestic duties Charlotte wrote more. Her first volume, *A Drama and lyrics*, appeared in 1880. She became active in nationalist politics, a supporter of Parnell, a founder and promoter of the Gaelic League.

In 1881 Charlotte opened a lodging house for emigrants in Queenstown. She then went to America, travelling in an emigrant ship, to supervise conditions at sea and on arrival. She was converted to Roman Catholicism in 1887. Her later life was restricted by deafness.

The following extracts come from the book published under her name as

Selections from her writings and correspondence and a memoir by her nephew Stephen Gwynne (1909). This is the account Charlotte gave to an American interviewer of her struggles to improve the lot of steerage passengers on emigrant ships:

— I tried very hard to get the Catholic clergy to establish some institution in Queenstown for the care of emigrant women, but I failed. I knew that a considerable improvement had resulted from the agitation of the matter, but I feared all would fall through if I did not take some further step. Therefore I decided to leave my own home and become a licensed lodging house keeper in Queenstown.

When this step became known, all the steamship companies saw at once that it gave me a great power over the Irish traffic, and I suppose the White Star people thought that if I settled myself there as their enemy it might prove very serious to them. Father Nugent brought about a meeting between me and Mr Ismay, the real owner of the line, who took me on his ships and gave me a chance to understand the real points on which we had been at variance.

About three thousand people passed through my lodging-house this year, but when I came to America I determined to close it altogether and to re-open it on my return. I established the house partly because there was great need of such a place and partly because I knew it would give me a direct and strong influence over all the Queenstown steamship lines.

I knew I could force almost any reform I wanted if I put myself directly in relationship with the emigrants. I did not attempt to influence their choice of lines, but to any who spoke to me I expressed myself openly. I was most anxious not to injure any line, but to work upon, write to, and visit the heads of the companies, and urge strongly what reforms I thought were needed. I went over eleven ships in May 1881, with the Board of Trade officer, and then none until January 1882, since which time I have seen them all constantly. I have paid them over one hundred visits this year. I have visited every nook and corner of them. I have had frequent letters from emigrants describing the treatment they received, and also a number of emigrants passing through my hands returning from America. Thus I have gained as thorough a knowledge of the subject as I could obtain. —

In a long article published in *The Pall Mall Gazette* 6 May, 1881, Charlotte gives an exact description of conditions on a Queenstown ship. She goes on:

— And what has been the result? When I first took the matter in hand it was a common thing for single women and married people to berth in the same rooms together, sometimes in the same tiers of beds. The companies professed to separate them, but the girls who came with parents slept with them and other married couples. Now this is all done away with on all the lines. The single women are always quite separate from every other class. Various arrangements are made. The National line puts the single women on one side and the married people on the other in what are called enclosed berths – small, separate rooms, accommodating twenty persons each. Up the centre of the compartment is run a lath partition, effectually dividing the compartment into two, with separate entrances and means of access to the decks. The Guion line has recently introduced the same system...The Inman line, as a rule, has its girls separate, but as the number of passengers varies, so do the arrangements. The Cunarders are behind all of the other lines, because, though they have enclosed berths, they are for all classes, and all open into one compartment. Theirs are the only steerages so arranged. The Allan line has a different system. For twenty-five years they have viewed with a condemnation equal to mine the systems I complain of, and have separated the men from the women altogether at night on their ships.

... There are now stewardesses on all emigrant ships. The Cunard had formerly none. The Inman had them on some ships and not on others. I have known of 400 or 500 women on a vessel with no woman in charge. Improvement in this respect is still needed. One Inman vessel on one trip carried about 1,000 steerage passengers and had only one steerage stewardess. As to lavatories and sanitary arrangements, the Board of Trade, after my letters, and what was brought out in Parliament, took action, and there has been a great improvement in this respect, and in the addition of a number of staircases and entrances, so as to give separate access to the different classes of steerage passengers. In my opinion all sanitary arrangements ought to be, as they are in the White Star vessels, so arranged that there shall be no excuse for the women to leave their steerage at night... Nobody ever thought of such a thing.. as the provision of towels and bowls, to enable steerage folks to wash.

One of my objects in coming to America was to bring the competition of improvement affecting English lines to bear upon the foreign companies, because while the foreign traffic is far behind the English, there remains a much larger margin for the English lines to fall back upon than if we could force the whole traffic up. —

She wrote the following letter to her brother's children after crossing steerage class Liverpool to Queenstown:

— Dearest Children,
I am all right after my voyage, which I enjoyed notwithstanding all the

hardships. Tell Uncle Monteagle that I have a new point for him to fight on in the need to have the law revised.

There were four horses berthed among us! It appears it is legal to berth up to ten, but these were not quite legally arranged. Captain Wilson made a great fuss about them, though they had been cleared by the officer in Liverpool. Altogether, Captain Wilson was inclined to refuse to clear the ship; the hospital accommodation was so bad, and ventilation, but it had passed the Liverpool officers without comment. I shall have a deal to tell Uncle Monteagle of my experiences.

Whenever I woke in the night there was an old woman in the next berth working away at the whiskey bottle (not an Irishwoman). I had the advantage of an empty berth on each side of me, but below and opposite were a lot of women and children. It was all awfully dirty and disgusting and the food bad enough, but on the other hand the people were so friendly, so good to one another, so cheery, I was happy enough, and in the morning we had a really beautiful scene.

The day was exquisite – bright sun, still sea – so the people were quite happy again. Some Baptists began singing hymns, and shortly all the emigrants were gathered together, and we spent the whole morning thus. I made friends especially with one young man, a Baptist, a coal miner, black and grimy, but I believe the man to be a true apostle. I have seldom come across anyone who seemed to me so transformed by Christianity, truly a beautiful and grand character under a very rough outside. I was talking a long time to him.

There were also a married man and his wife, Baptists, Bradford factory workers, very attractive, but the miner was a man of more depth I think, just the hero for George Eliot. He is to write to me and tell me of his life in the mines in America. He has a quantity of books and hymns, and is evidently the stuff to make a missionary of. It would have repaid a great deal more miserable living to have realised, even for a few hours, the life of such a man, silently working among the poor, one of themselves, but raised so far above them by principle.

I saw a share of the bad side too, and I ascertained one very important fact – that is though there were a great many children, they were hardly any trouble, but went to sleep at once, and were not at all sick, though the men and women were so, desperately. —

9th October, 1882, Charlotte writes from a convent in Minneapolis to her niece:

— Dearest Nell,

Far away you see, about my furthest point. I am very much taken with this country, it is so wonderfully more congenial than I had expected – everything more homelike looking, and much prettier too. The fact is the whole country, as far as I have seen, has a great deal of quiet loveliness, no striking or impressive scenery, but beauty of foreground almost greater than any country I know, except Switzerland. Of course the autumn is the time to see America, for the colouring is more exquisite than you can conceive in the woods. If you took your paint-box with absolutely pure new paints and gradated every shade from pale canary down to the deepest browns in madder, you would get some idea of the colouring. It is simply unbelievable.

You see on one side of you a tree of pure flame, mixing its branches with one of gold and side by side with another of rich orange above shading into scarlet. The Virginian creeper, like our ivy, twines round every tree and in grand masses over the ground, and you have acres of sumach in the swampy places, of pure blood red. It is magnificent, the country is not half as lonely looking withal as I expected.

The New England States are like a succession of beautiful English parks, the natural woods and cultivated lands alternating as in park scenery, and up and down rolling land beautifully shaped, but all in soft masses, nothing approaching to mountain scenery.

Out way West here, however, the scenery becomes more Irish. The views open and the highlands are more marked, the foregrounds, though still beautiful, are not quite so rich as in the East, and the distances are finer. St Paul's might very easily be in Co. Limerick, but the stone is nowhere visible as at home. The land out West here looks much richer than nearer New York.

I need not have worried about expenses as far as I can see. Hitherto I have been so handed on that I have spent about fifteen dollars since I left England. The railways give me passes, and people pay all for me and won't hear to the contrary.

Curiously, Father Nugent, Bishop Ireland and I had met in this far-away corner. Father Nugent introduced me to the two or three thousand people in the Hall. The next day's papers say the applause was 'terrific'. Anyhow, I have got my hold pretty tight now in this country; the Lines will know that the inevitable fact has a pretty extensive royalty. I have been speaking my candid opinion of the poor dears in a way that will hardly secure a welcome in Liverpool from some of them. I hope it will teach the backsliders to come up to mark.

I send you a sonnet you may like to see. You know Americans don't speak of 'autumn' but 'fall'. I shall make you laugh plenty when I get home, but I am now going out driving with a Mr Kelly, a very pleasing and gentlemanlike person, though a grocer. Everyone in this country is in business. I wish many of our landed gentry were as gentlemanlike as these businessmen.

Bishop Ireland is magnificent, so is his sister, mother of this convent. Such a lark! I got the sisters off singing, 'Tramp, Tramp, Tramp the Boys are Marching,' yesterday, Sunday, and as excited as any batch of pure-blooded Fenians. —

As her nephew Stephen Gwynne points out, with a reticence typical of her day, none of her letters home tell of the resentment she met with from lodginghouse keepers in Queenstown, who had been fleecing the emigrants mercilessly (as they also did in Liverpool, where emigrants flocked in from as far away as Hamburg). Stephen Gwynne writes: 'She described to me a perfect pandemonium, poor creatures from the wilds of Kerry or Connaught emerging like cattle from the crowded carriages, sick with hunger or fatigue, stupefied with grief, and then the mob of lodginghouse runners seizing them, dragging them this way and that, with noisy exhortation'. *United Ireland* 2, August 1881, tells us that there were then 64,789 Irish-born emigrants living in Boston, and another 6,749 had arrived in New York the previous week.

More light-hearted is Charlotte's description of a pony trap journey in Ireland:

— I love the country east of Mountrath, but Mountrath is impossible as regards accommodation. This time we came in there for a fair, and could get no attendance at all at either of the hotels. We had to push on to the nearest town – Rathdowney. Mountrath is not a small town, and seems to have business; it is a pity the hotels are so poor, as it would be a nice centre for cyclists. That is how it is in Ireland. You will find comfortable, cleanly inns in tiny places, and in good towns miserable, dirty hotels. —

She describes the shoeing of their pony, and then goes on:

— I own before I visited Rathdowney I did not know of its existence, but it is quite a smart little town, stirring and neat, with a large brewery, a reservoir, swans and a swan island, and, I believe, two really good hotels. Near my hotel is an old bridge with the motto, 'This bridge was erected in 1813 by the spirited and independent inhabitants of Rathdowney'. A bit of 'highfaluting' that amused me, all the more as from Davies' old dictionary of Ireland Rathdowney seems to have been rather a poor little place at that time. The go-ahead spirit was there, you see, and still at the end of near a century the words appear true. There is an appearance of energy in the place usually sadly wanting. I bought here a pair of phaeton reins, home-made, for 6s.6d., good and strong. Too seldom one can find anything homemade for sale in Ireland. Hotel bill here costs 10s.6d. Total cost from Dublin – man, horse, dog, self, carriage, and oats (but with midday dinners in basket from home) – came to £1.5s.10d to Limerick. Train fares would be about – man 10s; self (2nd) 19s; dog, 2s.6d; horse £2; carriage, about £3. People do not realise the saving of going by road when having to move horses, etc. Railway fares for horses are far too high.

Rathdowney is, I think, fifty-eight miles from Limerick, as far as I can make out on map, but pony was fresh and new shod, and I had all my Dublin weariness blown away by the splendid fresh air all day, these drives are so life-giving. So with a good courage, not knowing what was before us, we started on a rather chill morning. Wisdom was in me, but it had not fair play!

'Dan,' said I, 'the day is not too good; we'll keep the low country and go by Dundrum. At the worst there is a good room there.' Ah, yes I was wise! We drove to Templemore, then along a fine road. An evil prompting made me ask, 'Where does this fine road lead to?' 'To Borrisoleigh.' It was a word of temptation. I had been there years before and wished to return. So all my wisdom flew away, and we with it, into the heart of the wild, cold hills.

These big old roads, the old coaching roads throughout Ireland, are a real fine sight; of great width, finely kept, bordered on either side with ten feet or more of 'the long farm' [by custom commonland, used for grazing], shaded often with really fine trees. They were a great surprise and joy to me when I first began my tramps. Now I reckon on them and their park-avenue-like distances as a more ambitious soul reckons on Mont Blanc, but surely I did not expect one leading to Borrisoleigh, a little village in a gap through which the road winds that leads from South Tipperary to Nenagh.

Borrisoleigh Castle, however, must have been an outpost of civilisation long ago, for behind it lies the stretch of country between Devil's Bit and Keeper Mountains, that is even now wild and desolate to a degree. In Davies' very good Atlas, published 1837, no road is shown through this mountain district we went through, it must then have been utter wilderness. It has now a thoroughly good road, but is still one of the dreariest districts I have ever been through.

My perverse desire to see everything made us attempt a road direct to Newport through the hills. Weary on us! Hour after hour, hour after hour from Borrisoleigh, on we drove, twisting round one black-capped and rounded-headed hill after another; no trees, nor ruins, no views, no villages and yet a share of population and a creamery! See how insidious is this agent of civilisation! It has invaded even that desolate country.

It was a fearful drive. It was blowing cold, wet rain in our faces (we all know the difference between wet rain and dry!) Every hill we twisted round only opened up new and interminable vistas of black valley and black round hills. I could have sat down on a fence and cried, but it would have been no good, so instead I quoted Horatius Cocles to cheer up Dan, 'And the strong heart within him bare bravely up his chin'. As for Boss, he subsided altogether under my rug. For me, I took refuge behind my aged umbrella, but as I still wanted to see, I poked long slits in the old silk till I got a fine view of the pony's ears. This is a real practical use for an old umbrella; stick it before your nose, poke holes into it, and you have then a tent and a window, and a window frame!

... I have travelled on either side of those hills, yet surely I never realised the existence of that broad bank of wilderness in the heart of those mountains about twenty-eight miles long by ten broad. What a fastness it must have been in Elizabethan times! Then the Irish possessed immense herds, and one can fancy that even now thousands of cattle might be hidden away unknown in the folds of those hills. —

Charlotte ends the account of this journey by asking whether her readers, 'who fly all over the world in trains' understand the pleasure of getting to know their own country foot by foot. The modern reader could surely be asked the same question.

HARIOT G. BLACKWOOD
(Lady Dufferin)

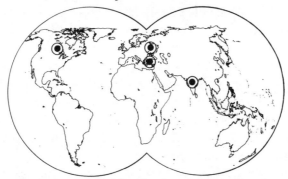

A woman who accompanied her husband from Canada to India to Turkey, involving herself with local customs

Next we meet a very charming and tolerant woman, Hariot (née Hamilton Rowan) (1843-1936), born at Killyleagh Castle, Co. Down. Her father, Archibald Hamilton Rowan, was an ally to Wolfe Tone. She married Lord

Frederick Dufferin, Marquis of Dufferin and Ava, the only son of the Lady Helen Dufferin already mentioned. Lord Dufferin had a very prestigious career, culminating in an appointment as Governor-General of Canada, and later became Viceroy of India. Hariot, to judge from her handwriting, was an energetic, open-minded and appreciative woman who travelled with her husband whenever she could, and wrote some interesting journals, constructed round her letters home, about her life in Canada, Russia, Turkey and India. While in India she established a trust for medical aid to local women and in addition to all the visits to schools, hospitals, etc. she found time, in spite of her brood of children, to go off on expeditions such as a bear hunt in Russia, or a fishing trip by canoe in Canada. She writes in a refreshingly lively way about all her experiences and seems to have been a likeable and popular person.

The following comes from *My Canadian Journal 1872-8* (1891).

— Friday 31st August, 1877. Before lunch we did about seventeen miles, and as the road was rough we were glad of the rest in the middle of the day. When we started again, we were told that we had only nine miles to go, and thought we should have such an easy afternoon. It proved a very hard one. We had five miles of swamp, and a road made with rough-hewn trunks of trees. When first made this sort of perpetual bridge is not disagreeable, but when time has worn furrows in it the jogging of the ambulance waggon upon it is not to be described!

When we had been knocked about as much as we could bear we got out and walked a couple of miles; but almost our whole journey was over corduroy road, and as we had to go at a foot's pace, it was very fatiguing.

As you may guess a 'corduroy' road is a Brobdingnagian imitation of the material worn by rough little boys, and when an occasional 'cord' has broken away altogether, when another has got loose, and turns round as the horse puts his foot on it, or when it stands up on end as the wheel touched it, the corduroy road is not pleasant to drive many miles over! In consequence of our slow progress, it was quite dark when we reached our camping-ground, and the cook did not arrive till half-past seven.

Saturday, September 1st. Ten or twelve miles of rough road brought us to the North-West Angle, where we found a beautifully decorated steamer on the Lake of the Woods....We had got up at six in order to do our steamer voyage by daylight, but our horses wandered away in the night, and it took some time to catch them, so that it was one o'clock before we had done the twelve miles, and packed our things into the boat. We had to part with Mr McKay here, and to put ourselves into the hands of twenty-six canoe men. They all came on board at the North-West Angle, which is a morsel of the United States mixed up with our land.

We had such a pleasant afternoon in the steamer. The Lake of the Woods, about which we had heard nothing, proved to be quite lovely; islands innumerable, rocky and wooded, a great variety of shapes and sizes, sometimes far away, and sometimes so close to the steamer as quite to darken it. We lunched and dined on board, and did not land till it was dark, and the setting-up of our camp was most difficult. We could only get three tents up, and I had to be one of four in mine, so we were rather crowded.

Sunday 2nd. We had such a pleasant day after once we had got into our canoes and were well started. The weather was lovely, and the River Winnipeg beautiful. We have two large and two small canoes. The first big one carries D. and Nellie and me, and eight men, and a good deal of luggage; the second, Colonel and Mrs Littleton, and eight men. The first small one had the two A.D.C's, Nowell and six men; and the other small one held three servants and six men – that is to say, there ought to be six men in the two small ones, but two left us, so our servants take it in turns at the paddles. We were most comfortable, and lay back reading and looking at the scenery, and occasionally doing a little sleeping. Sometimes the men sang the Canadian boat songs which sound so delightful on the water, and sometimes they cheered themselves up by racing the other canoes. Our tents, luggage, and provisions are distributed over all the boats.

In the middle of the day we landed to lunch, and at five stopped on a piece of ground where Sir Garnet Wolseley and his troops once camped. Nellie and I had a nice bathe, and returned to find our camp full of activity; our twenty-four men, and four gentlemen and three servants hard at work chopping wood, putting up tents, mending canoes, cooking dinners and making beds. The latter is a most important office. The bed-maker gets a quantity of dry grass and small branches of fir, which are laid one over the other so as to form a spring mattress. A buffalo robe goes over that, and then blankets *ad libitum*.

We had a dinner of hot soup, curry, stewed beef, duck and prairie chicken, and a blueberry pudding, our cook having got up early to pick the blueberries. The soup and the beef were carried here in tins, the game has been shot on the way. Monsieur Beselin, our cook, has done so well. When we were driving he used to arrive sometimes long after us, when it was quite dark, and in five minutes' time he would be hard at work, and our dinner well under way... In addition to this, he is always in a good humour, and in the daytime now he paddles away with a beaming countenance.

Strange to say, though on the banks of a splendid river, we have no good drinking water, and are obliged to suck it through a sort of baby's bottle filter! In the matter of drink we are badly off; we have brought no wine so as to lessen our luggage; we have no milk (except preserved milk), and, as I said before, good water is hard to get. Tea is our principal beverage, but without milk it is not very nice. We also have chocolate (which makes us thirsty). —

Lord Dufferin's next posting was to Petrograd and they were there during the assassination of the Czar, as Hariot recounts in *My Russian and Turkish Journals* (1916). By the time the book came out she had become the Dowager Marchioness of Dufferin and Ava. This extract is from Chapter III, 'Our Second Winter in Petrograd':

— Sunday 16th to Wednesday 19th Jan. 1881.

Real cold weather. The thermometer from ten to twelve below zero (Fahrenheit). It is not so nice as in Canada, where one could go out to walk or skate. Here one has to pay visits, and getting in and out of the carriage is very disagreeable. I kept the children in, and they amused themselves by dressing up.

Tuesday evening I went to a party. It was a really smart party in a Russian house. The rooms were large and well lighted, and every one was very well dressed, the gowns new and fresh...The entertainment began with the gipsies, who sang. The music is curious, but in a drawing room a little goes a long way, and they spoil the effect by wearing old ball dresses which fit them badly and are half-dirty. The dancing especially is spoilt by this. To see a lady in a train get up and, with wild screams, run about trembling through every fibre of her body, is, to say the least, incongruous.

Friday, March 4th. We had our third and last ball before Lent this evening, and I think it was the best of the three. There were just the right number of people, and they all looked very pretty. The invitations were for 220, and we sat down 100 to supper at 2.30. I was very pleased with this party.

Sunday, 6th. This is a great day here – a *journée folle* for most people. They dance all afternoon and stop at midnight, if the clocks have not previously done so.... There is no dancing in Lent, nor does it begin again after.

Sunday 13th. We went to church in the morning, but D. went to a *manège* where the Ambassadors have an occasional chance of seeing the Emperor [Alexander II]. D. had just come in and taken off his uniform when I went out with the two girls to visit a sick woman. She lives quite near us, and on the way we saw a wretched horse with a broken leg being dragged along by soldiers.

When we got to the house the poor woman, who was in tears, said to me, 'Is it true?' 'What?' 'Why, that there has been an attempt on the Emperor, and that, if not killed, he is wounded.' Then she told me she heard two explosions, and that he was certainly wounded. I almost ran the whole way home to tell D. and at the door I met the secretaries coming with the news, and then one of the Chancery men told us that he heard the bombs, and then saw the Emperor's carriage with the back and side blown out. D. went off to the Palace, and I have just seen Mr Kennedy, who went with him and who has left him there. He says a shell was thrown under the Emperor's carriage, which destroyed it but did not wound him. He got out and another was thrown, wounding him seriously, and they fear he will die.

I cannot tell you what a fearful impression it makes upon one, such cruel, persistent murder. I sit at the window and watch for D.'s return while I write. Soldiers are going about in every direction, and sleighs bringing all the people who have just heard it to the Palace. I believe D. had great difficulty in getting in.

The wretched horse we saw was one ridden by a Cossack close to the carriage, for you know, since these attempts, the Emperor is always surrounded by mounted soldiers.

4.30. It is all over. He is dead. D. has not returned yet, but one of the Court officials has brought word. He was insensible when D. arrived there. It is indeed terrible, and I feel much for those left. —

The following year the Dufferins had moved to Turkey where Hariot goes to a wedding:

— We were ushered into a small sitting room. All the rooms in the house were very small, and all had divans round the walls, and little other furniture. There we sat, and brilliant yellow or purple females handed us, first cigarettes, then jam, of which we ate a spoonful in the orthodox way, taking a sip of water after it, then a cup of coffee ...

We had been looking about us for some time, when it was suggested that we should go and see some of the preparations that were being made, so we passed through the central room at the top of the stairs, where guests were assembling, and saw many curious specimens of womenkind. Any one who is invited to a Turkish wedding brings her whole establishment with her, so the guests are not all ladies, and amongst the elderly it is very difficult indeed to guess which are servants and which are mistresses.

Besides these invited guests, the house is open to all who choose to enter, and even the streets are full of veiled forms, who at some time during the day will come and have a look at the bride.

When we made our move we were first shown the room where the bride would sit to be looked at, and a large throne prepared for her; and then we were taken to the 'Nuptial Chamber' ... The room was small, and in it there was a washing-stand, devoid of jugs and basins, but with two bedroom candlesticks and a few cosmetics on it, and in front of it, festooned on a horse, two gold and silver embroidered towels. Next came the bed, a squat four-poster, covered in at the top, and curtained with lovely cream-coloured satin, dotted all over with beads – really very beautiful. There were two counterpanes in rich stuffs and grand embroideries, the pillows were all embroidered in gold (comfortable!), and there were muslin embroidered covers thrown over them as well, while more cushions of various degrees of splendour were disposed along the wall side of the bed ...

Then for a change we were taken upstairs, and we saw the lady who did the honours. She is aunt of the bride, and the mother being delicate she undertook this very hard work. She was a most interesting looking women, and would anywhere have looked distinguished. Her hair was a good golden (not the fearful dyed colour they use so much). Of course her face was painted white, but it had much character and expression ... —

Later she describes the bride, and goes on to explain:

— They declare that the two have never seen each other, but I feel sure that she must have had him pointed out to her, and that he had seen her with a yashmak on, but of course they have never spoken. She is fifteen, he eighteen. When he was coming she pulled the veil over her face. He was led into the room, walked up to her, and taking her hand put it on his arm, and as man and wife walked away with her, to the room with the throne, we following. The doors were shut upon them for a second, and then out he came, the eunuchs hustling him out of sight of the other women, and bringing out whips – actually whips – to drive back the excited females. You can't imagine such a scene! A regular, common scuffle, every one pushing and pulling and screaming. I kept one child in front of me, and expected her to be frightened, but she laughed and was intensely amused, while N. took to carrying Freddie lest he should be squashed. —

MAY CROMMELIN

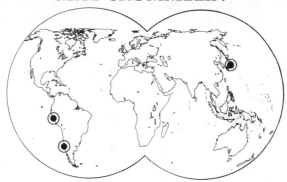

An intrepid traveller, in Peru and in Japan

One of those who could afford to travel for pleasure was May Crommelin (c.1850-1928) (Maria Henrietta de la Cherois), born Carrowdore Castle, Co. Down, descended from the Huguenot, Louis Crommelin (died 1727), a founder of the Ulster linen industry. Largely educated at home, she spent most of her early life in Ireland. As an adult she travelled widely and after 1913, when women were first admitted, she became a Fellow of the Royal Geographical Society. She listed travel as her only recreation in *Who's Who*.

May wrote thirty novels, most often set in Ireland, and many short stories. Her voyages to South America and the East also figure in her popular fiction, a complete set of which is to be found in Belfast central library.

Her travel writing includes *Half round the world for a husband* (1896), and *Over the Andes from Chile to Peru* (1896). A gifted linguist, May worked in three London hospitals during the 1914-18 war and also helped with Belgian refugees. The following passage comes from her travels in South America:

— To enjoy maté properly, the family or friends gather in a group. Boiling water is brought, probably kept hot on a *brasero*, and poured in when the maté cup has been half filled with the herb. The principal person present then begins to sip it through the silver tube, called a *bombilla*, often handsomely chased, and which is bulbous and pierced with strainer-holes at the end immersed in the fibrous mixture. There is no chance of a 'good long drink'. One only gets about as much at a time as of Turkish coffee. The gourd is again filled up with hot water, and with its *bombilla* is then passed on to the second person. Probably a fresh pinch of yerba is added for the third and fifth comers. And when the loving cup has gone all round the circle the first maté drinker begins afresh again, and so *da capo* until everyone has had perhaps half a dozen turns. A maté party therefore takes time, but then there is no lack of that.

... The Jesuit Fathers established yerba growing in that district of the Argentine still called after them by the name of 'Misiones'. The brief story of the missions is sad. Invited by the Governor of Paraquay to protect his poor Indians against the cruelties of the Spanish *conquistadores*, the *padres* arrived at the end of the sixteenth century, and spread the true Christianity of peace and industry in both Paraquay and the 'Misiones' territory adjoining it. For nearly two hundred years they protected as best they could their gentle-minded people against the slave-hunters, who carried them off at times wholesale, selling 60,000 in the market place of Rio Janeiro in two years! Cotton, yerba, manioca, and oranges were produced in abundant crops; colleges and churches erected, some being both handsome and of large dimensions....

But the Jesuits' work elsewhere in the world was presumably less blameless and excellent than this, which will always remain a crown of praise to the Order. They were expelled by orders from Spain in 1740; their missions, with arsenals and workshops, were destroyed by fire, whereupon their Indian disciples fled to the woods. Still, hundreds of acres of ruins, much of cut stonework, are to be seen overgrown with palms and wild oranges. The tracks of old roads through woods now thickly tangled, and paved fording places at streams, remain to bear witness in lonely spots that there was once a now vanished civilisation. —

May Crommelin's night-stops in the Peruvian Andes can be compared with those of Dervla Murphy, some ninety years later!

— He led me through the inner yard, littered with hen-coops, rabbits, bones, and *peones*, to a kind of cowshed door. Here, unfastening a thong hitched to a rusty nail, he displayed with pride – my room! A mud floor, four-paned window (one pane of wire sieve), three camp-beds, two morsels of matting, no chair, and a tin wash basin. And how lucky to enjoy these comforts alone, and not with strange señoras, as when crowded.

Neither bolt, key, nor door-handle was discernible. But my *capataz* was never distant in any dilemma. In a trice he ran off, then reappeared bearing a rough plank, which he planted in a deep hollow of the floor, leaning the other end against the door....

Out of doors was so uninviting, I returned to sit on my bed and lay out my travelling wear for tomorrow; the one day of probable discomfort, and certainly of a long mule ride for the best part of some eleven hours, which various friends' accounts made me anticipate like a willing martyr with somewhat 'fearful' joy. Nether riding garments, a serge skirt and warm jacket – for the cold would be bitter on the mountains before sunrise and towards evening – was the sage counsel given me, which was gratefully followed. —

May wore a wide straw hat and the ubiquitous veil of her day. Friend has also warned her not to wash her face for three days, or else cover it with vaseline or cold cream against the mountain sun. That night was a restless one for her:

— I have slept through the worst thunderstorms on land, and in a severe gale or two at sea; can dream peacefully sitting bolt upright all night in a train; yes, and even while a steamer is coaling till daybreak, with the winches working beside my cabin port. But the test of Las Vacas was too much!

Between fevered dozes and frantic starts, making vain sorties armed with candle and insect-powder against invisible attacking foes – so the horrid hours passed. Well, tomorrow would see me in Chile! —

Arrived there she later gives us this description of a rodeo:

— The fine horsemanship of the Indian has not degenerated in his half-bred descendant, the *huaso*. And the time to see the latter at his best is at a *rodeo*, which is the parting of the cattle on a big *hacienda*. This is held as a holiday by all the neighbouring *haciendados*, or farmers; by the *huasos*, or peasants, who can afford a horse; even by the poor *peones*, which, literally translated, means 'pawns', men of no account.

A great annual *rodeo* is a red-letter day for twenty miles around, and from early dawn the *huasos* may be seen jogging to the scene of pastime. Many will be riding quite poor ponies, but leading each his own animal, carefully prepared and groomed for the great occasion. Now, a *huaso* is still utterly unawakened to the sense of chivalry which stirs even the rough American cowboy, yet some feelings in his breast this morning resemble those with which a good knight used to set out to a tourney ... on his horse depend his chances of winning fame among his fellows; on it hangs often also what a true Chilian values lightly enough, the rider's life.

A *huaso's* dress is picturesque, with his enormously wide felt or straw hat, leather gaiters fastened up the back of the leg by many buckles, and a *poncho* which blows backward as he gallops. The trappings of his clever nag are no less worthy of description. Its bridle is of thin hide strips beautifully twisted into a fine rope, adorned with tassels and silver tubes, while the bit also boasts silver ornaments, ending the square flaps. To keep the neatly coiled lasso from flying loose, there also falls a trident shaped piece of leather, generally stitched or embroidered. The whip is peculiar, formed by the end of the reins plaited into a heavy thong; and the girths, often blue and red, are also of hide, the separate strips of which are joined by cross-pieces, with an iron ring for buckle. Lastly, the gigantic wooden stirrups, coal scuttle in shape, and the huge spurs, radiating like old pictures of the sun, may come from Birmingham!...

A *haciendado's* costume is not really different from this of the *huaso*, except in the finer material of his clothes, and that his spurs of shining silver are massive heirlooms. Cruel though these spurs seem, an Englishman, fond of horses and merciful to his beast, told me he used Chilian ones, their rowels being blunt, in preference to the sharp prod of the English spur ...

Once all have arrived, the scene of a *rodeo* is most animated. Within the palisades of a wide corral a multitude of cattle, bulls, cows and calves, are huddled in a surging, lowing mass. These are to be parted – a dangerous business. Outside the corral gates runs a long palisade, ending in separate yards, and by this palisade are ranged the eager volunteers for the day's sport, both gentry and *huasos*, in pairs. All take their turns in rotation, and any two men undertake to tackle any animal, however furious ...

A *rodeo* is no child's play, for there is seldom a big one at which an accident does not happen, often enough fatal. It may seem strange that the worst mischances happen in driving calves; but these are lower than the horse's shoulder, so he cannot press on them so easily: while they dodge and twist under his legs, possibly upsetting him, when his master risks a broken limb or even neck. —

May ends this chapter by mentioning a child's funeral:

— Among other sights, that of a child's wake is most interesting, but, of course, difficult for a foreigner to see ... When riding with friends one day, I was surprised to see a man trudging towards a cemetery gate, carrying a small bright blue coffin unconcernedly over his shoulder. Two women, shrouded in the usual black *mantos*, trotted behind without much semblance of grief. 'That is a very poor funeral,' said my companions. 'Generally a *huaso* gallops off after the wake with the coffin under his arm; he is half tipsy from drinking *chicha* in the house, so he and his comrades race along the roads, and maybe drop the coffin!' On enquiring further, full particulars were given me of this custom, which again reminded me of old Ireland, my native land. —

She sometimes fictionalised her travel experience. The following passage is taken from May Crommelin's first person semi-autobiographical novel '*I little Knew!*' (1908), in which the narrator, Mary Josselin, aged fifty-two (May's age at the time), from Ravarnette Castle, Ulster, travels, ending up in Japan:

– Yokohama, busy, dusty, industrious seaport often decried as commonplace, has yet its hour of loveliness. Out in the blue harbour water at six of the morning, whilst impatient travellers await the doctor's inspection, also the sun and breakfast, its April aspect is exquisite.

Afar out of a rosy dawn-mist rises a snowy-topped pink pearl.

'Fujiyama? It is! It is!' And all around, land, sea and sky are tinted in tenderest hues, clear, soft, dew-washed ...

Alone I landed therefore at Yokohama. No sign here of horses, cabs, carts. Only rikishas, and more rikishas. One bore me along the sea-front or Bund. A handcart followed with luggage. Denying myself the sour grapes of both famous Bund hotels, with their costly European Bands and luxuries, my aim was a lesser hostelry in a street of neat European houses. Vanished now my early ideas of sleeping on wooden pillows, squatting on floor mats ...

My hotel was not unlike a lesser Italian one save for the noiseless servitors who glided over the nicely polished floor of a saloon where this notice was displayed: 'Gentlemen are kindly requested not to smoke in Dining room before tiffin'. Mounting two flights to my room, neatly furnished in American style, a voice from an outer gallery greeted me through the green persienne blinds, 'Good morning missis!' Its owner, a youthful roomboy, vanished straight away. Much electric bell pressing produced a lean and slippered pantaloon with a pate so wrinkled and bald the like I had never seen before, except on Japanese ivory carvings.

'Wantee bath?' softly enquired this chief chamberman.

'Hot water, WASH,' came in clear command.

'Hot water, drinkee!' was submissively returned through an inch of door-way modestly opened.

'Washee!' I firmly reiterated.

'Yessir!' The felt-socked steps pattered away; a few minutes later followed a tap and the joyously whispered intelligence, 'Bath riddy.' Bless his heart, he had likewise brought a jug of hot water to be on the right side. Thereupon he bent his lean person in bone breaking reverence, escorting my honourable self to the bath woman to whom he delivered me with three deep salutations to her, and three to me. After which she and I began bowing....

With the siesta habit of the voyage still a tyranny, forty winks seemed desirable before issuing on my first walk in Nippon. Hardly were my eyes closed, however, before a discreet tap at my bedroom door evoked a sleepy, 'Who is there?' Immediately a tall Chinaman entered and with a look of blessing almost tempting me to imagine him a ministering angel, stood straight in the centre of the room, announcing benevolently. 'Me Shing Shang, come from Ah Long. Me topside tailor. Me makee you one piecee skirty, first chop. One piecee blousy, number one fash'. Leaving his printed card Shing Shang lingeringly departed.

Hardly was I lain down again, the door bolted this time, when there came another knock. A young Japanese in European clothes stood in the passage bowing. 'I am best silversmith in Yokohama'. I was nearly asleep when for the third time came a succession of deprecating taps. These heralded a 'washman', a photographer, and a picture card dealer, all in their native kimonos, reminding me of low-necked dressing gowns.

Wide awake now, it was clearly best to sally forth and do my own shopping in the famous Benten-dori, i.e. street named after the goddess Benten (Luck). It was so pleasant to tread solid earth again that till late I wandered past the fascinating shop fronts, some glazed, some booths, admiring bronzes, ivories, lacquer, silk and crepe embroideries, Satsuma china and how much more. —

MARY CHAVELITA BRIGHT
(George Egerton)

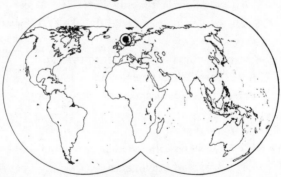

A writer on Norway

Some Irishwomen used their travelling experiences to write fiction, such as Mary Chavelita Bright (1859-1945), née Dunne, whose pen name was George Egerton. Born in Melbourne, Australia, she was one of six children of an Irish army officer who fought in the Maori war. Back in Dublin her father was evicted as a bankrupt. A relative paid for Chavelita to go to school in Germany. She acted as stepmother to her siblings when her Welsh mother died, nursed in a London hospital, and worked in New York, then she became companion to the second wife of Henry Higginson. He – unbeknown to her –

had another wife living and an impending summons for bigamy. Chavelita's father tried to prevent her affair with Higginson by threatening him with an unlicensed gun. Higginson charged Captain Dunne with assault and the Captain was put in jail.

Meanwhile the pair eloped to Norway and bought a small estate. Here Chavelita became imbued with Ibsenism and translated Knut Hamsun. When, after two years, Higginson died, she returned to England and Ireland, and in 1891 married Egerton Clairmonte, a minor novelist whom she called 'an idle, destitute Canadian', for he drank. She left him after a year then divorced him in 1901, telling her friends she was a widow.

Chavelita (George Egerton) achieved a great success with her first novel, *Keynotes* (1893) dedicated to Hamsun and militantly feminist. The Norwegians liked it and Aubrey Beardsley designed the cover. She became known as a 'new woman' novelist with a heroine who admitted to sexual feelings. She is said to have become the mistress of John Lane, the book's publisher. In 1893 her autobiographical novel *The Wheel of God* followed, about a young Irish girl who travels to New York and supports herself as a journalist.

Having got rid of the Egerton husband, whose name she had borrowed, Chavelita made a third marriage in 1901 to her agent Reginald Golding Bright, and herself became a leading dramatic agent for writers such as G.B. Shaw and Somerset Maugham. Her only son (officially Egerton Clairmonte's), born in 1895, was killed in 1915. Her third husband died in 1941. Her cousin, Terence de Vere White, in *A Leaf from the Yellow Book* (London: Richards Press, 1958) sorts out some of the details of her life as it was, rather than as she reported it to be.

Two other Irish fiction writers whose travel was embodied in novels of this period are Bithia Mary Croker (born Roscommon, 1860-1921), who spent fourteen years in India and Burma, and Frances Sarah Hoey (born Dublin, 1830-1908), a prolific novelist and translator who knew France and Italy well.

FLORA LOUISE SHAW
(Lady Lugard)

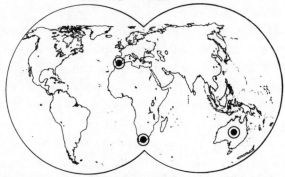

**A crusading journalist, investigating the Queensland sugar industry,
among other activities**

Flora (1851-1929) was born in Ireland, the daughter of an army officer who
became a general, and the third of fourteen children. Her French mother died
when she was nineteen and she was left in charge of her younger siblings.
Then, as they matured, and her father remarried, she was free to live her own
life. She had by this time already written a children's novel, *Castle Blair* (1878).
In 1876 she became companion for two years to an elderly couple named
Younghusband and travelled with them to Gibraltar, from where she rode on
horseback far into Spain, then on to Tenerife, Morocco and Egypt. She wrote
articles upon her travel experiences for *The Manchester Guardian* and *The Pall
Mall Gazette*, to such good effect that the *Guardian* sent her as correspondent
to a Brussels congress on the suppression of the African slave trade.

By now a friend of W.T. Stead, who moved from *The Pall Mall Gazette* to *The
Times*, Flora also knew Moberley Bell, that paper's assistant manager, and she
was sent by him to South Africa, a year later becoming *The Times'* colonial
editor. The paper next sent her to Australia. She returned home via New
Zealand, travelling from Auckland to Samoa with R.L. Stevenson (who died
in 1894) and his wife, then on to Hawaii, the U.S. and Canada.

As a senior journalist to *The Times* her sex was not known until after her
dispatches had been collected and published anonymously as *Letters from
South Africa* and *Letters from Queensland* (both 1893). The following extract
shows the care with which she went into investigations, in this case labour
conditions in the North Queensland sugar industry:

— The question of the employment of alien labour in Australia is nowhere

more vividly presented than at this northern end of the belt of sugar cultiva-
tion. Besides Chinamen there are in the district considerable numbers of Malays and Cingalese, Japanese and Javanese, but the principal open-air labour of
the sugar plantations is furnished by Kanakas, who are the native inhabitants
of certain groups of South Sea Islands not at present under the protection of
any European flag. They are a very intelligent, active and docile people, and
their labour was looked upon as the mainstay of the Queensland sugar industry, until in 1890 their further importation from the islands was forbidden.
Already the fall in the prices of sugar and the over-capitalisation of many of the
plantations which had been bought at excessive valuations at a time when the
price of sugar was high had caused a depression in the sugar industry.

The prohibition to import Kanaka labour was received as its death sentence.
The owners of some of the principal mills and plantations prepared to wind up
their affairs; others determined to move their whole plant and establishment to
Fiji. The small farmers, who were dependent upon the central mills for their
market, saw themselves about to be ruined and obliged once more to begin the
world. Fortunately for the fate of tropical Queensland, the majority of the
Kanakas then in the country had three-year contracts still to run. The prohibition would not have come into the full force of its disastrous operation until the
next year, and in the meantime, seeing what the result must necessarily be
upon an industry which promises to do more than any other single industry in
the colony to settle an agricultural population upon the soil, the Queensland
Parliament has rescinded its decision. A Bill brought in by the Government this
year permits the continued importation of Kanakas under certain very strin-
gent regulations. —

She goes on to explain why a tropical country must be developed by
tropical labour, what a crop of cane may produce per acre, and how white
labourers cannot support the heat while cane-cutting, which can only be done
by hand.

— While one row of blue-shirted Kanakas is busy under the waving plumes of
green, which gradually fall before the advancing knives, another row is
engaged in picking the cut cane from the thick litter of leaves amongst which it
lies and passing it on to be piled in sheaves upon the trains of waiting trucks.
The work is heavy, for a sheaf of cane is a bigger burden than a sheaf of corn,
and the bearers sink sometimes knee deep in the trash that lies upon the
ground. —

One Kanaka is employed to each five acres, but 'Whatever may be the
possibilities of white men learning eventually to work under the tropical sun,

it is evident that a plantation which had to pay for this labour at the prevailing rates of Australian white wages could not, all other things being equal, hope to compete in price with, say, a Cuban plantation obtaining black labour at a rate of 4d or 6d a day. Putting the average of Australian white labour at 26 shillings a week, without rations, the difference between the Queensland and the Cuban labour bill at the end of the year would be nearly as possible £12,000.'

Flora gives the estimated cost of a Kanaka labourer as fifteen shillings a week, 'or about the price of agricultural labour at home'. She is writing this letter to counteract what she calls 'so much general misapprehension' about the employment of Kanakas, so she gives exact details of this.

They are recruited from the islands in which they live by ships sailing under the strictest regulations as to tonnage, crews, cargo and sanitary conditions. Each ship is accompanied by a government agent, whose duty it is to see that before any Kanaka comes on board the nature of the contract into which he is entering is fully explained to him, and that he does not come otherwise than of his own free will. The captain of the ship is bound under a penalty of £500 to countenance no irregularity. Their contract is to work for three years, be provided with food, clothes, quarters and other necessities, to receive not less than £6 a year in wages and be given free passage home to the island they have come from. Married woman only are also engaged under the same terms.

Flora interviewed ships' captains, government agents, Polynesian inspectors and the Kanakas themselves and admits there have been 'grave abuses in the past. Men are, I believe, still undergoing punishment for the part they took in them'. She continues with more details. After expiry of their three-year contract the Kanaka is entitled to free food and shelter until the ship for his particular island arrives. 'I had read accounts so harrowing of the sufferings of these unfortunate aliens, of the disregard for life which was shown by their temporary masters, of the want of food, the bad accommodation, the overwork and the ill-treatment by overseers to which they were subjected, that I was prepared to give the most careful attention to the subject. Having now visited plantations throughout the whole length of the sugar belt, including some of the principal plantations of Bundaberg and Mackay, having been allowed everywhere to inspect the Kanaka quarters and rations, and to have perfectly fair talks with the Kanakas, I am in a position to say that not only are they not ill-treated, but that I have never in any country seen the lot of the average manual labourer so well cared for.'

Some Kanakas elected to stay on after their contract has expired. 'The time-expired boy, as a rule, has adopted the household customs of civilisation. He has a bedroom and a living room, his beds rise to the dignity of mosquito curtains, his kitchen boasts of table, chair, pots and plates. His wife becomes a fairly good cook and I have seen suppers prepared in Kanaka huts which an epicure need not disdain.'

Flora's standards are, of course, based upon the social conditions of the era, and her readers are assured that 'there is no detail of their material condition which is not more fortunate than that of our agricultural and factory hands' none of whom, one might suppose, received government rations of 1½ pounds of meat per day, plus all the plentiful fresh fruit they can eat. 'The manager of one plantation told me that bananas were consumed in his Kanaka quarters at the rate of twelve dozen per man per week ... Married men who prefer it can have their rations served to them raw for their wives to cook. For the others, the rations are cooked and three meat meals a day are served to them either in the quarters or in the fields, as may be most convenient.'

Flora concludes, 'The more I have seen of them the more I have been at a loss to comprehend how the absurd stories which have gained currency regarding them can have originated. One fact in itself speaks volumes. Two-thirds of the Kanakas now in Queensland are time-expired. Most of them have been home and have re-engaged for a second term of service. Some have preferred never to leave the colony'.

After her identity as the author of these letters to *The Times* had been revealed, Flora was invited to read a paper, well reasoned and wide in its scope, on 'The Australian Outlook' to the Royal Colonial Institute, marking the first time a woman had ever addressed this illustrious body.

Among the compliments paid her after the lecture was one from Sir Saul Samuel, who said: 'Those who know those Colonies must have marvelled at the extraordinary way in which that lady travelled over the country, in a manner very few men would have done, encountering and defying difficulties which would have been faced with reluctance by experienced bushmen. She has acquitted information with which very few people, even those long resident in the Colonies, are acquainted, and she has imparted this to us this evening in a manner which must be agreeably surprising to all present'.

A woman of that time would have found this flattering rather than patronising!

The population of Australia was then less than four million. As a loyalist and great believer in the positive aspects of the British Empire, Flora Shaw saw the Colonies as places of opportunity which needed more publicity. Her paper is enthusiastically glowing in its praise of the immense potential of Eastern Australia, its fertility and its opportunity. Of the Victoria area she says:

— The houses at present are mostly log huts, but they have their flower garden and orchard, their fence and their gate, their pine tree or other distinctive feature. There is no labouring population in the ordinary sense. Everyone is young, and everyone, whether he be a ploughman or an undergraduate, is working for himself. The general tone is of a prosperous, intelligent, self-respecting independence, and of a consequently enlarged plane of interest which enables the man who appears to be wholly absorbed by the varieties of American ploughs at one moment to be equally keen upon the diversities of American poets in the next. —

Flora Shaw also possessed considerable prescience. Of the future she wrote:

— Some of the best aspirations of the rising generation are centred upon the ideal, which they believe to be a patriotic and disinterested one, of an entirely independent national life. The radical democratic ideal may, I think, generally be said to favour separation. A good deal of the mature liberal thought of Australia, preserving the remembrance of what used to be resented as undue interference from home in local affairs, and not fully recognising perhaps how entirely any desire to interfere has passed from the traditions of the Colonial Office, is disposed also to nourish the belief that the best possibilities of the Australian future can only be attained under conditions of complete freedom from Imperial restrictions. —

Flora lived in London with her sisters Allie (an R.C.), Marie (a Protestant) and Lulu, who wrote articles. She became one of the most influential newspaper correspondents of her day. In 1898 she wrote another series of articles on the Klondike gold rush, and two chapters of Amery's *The Times* history of the South African war.

In 1900 Flora, aged forty-nine, considered elderly in those days, resigned from *The Times*. Directly the Boer War ended she set off for South Africa with a maid to visit the refugee camps. She subsequently met Sir Frederick Lugard, whom she had known for seven years, when he was on home leave from Nigeria. Before her marriage to him the following year she wrote another book, and articles on the Sudan for *The Manchester Guardian* and *The Times*.

After marriage Flora went to Hong Kong with her diplomat husband and visited Peking.

Back in England by 1912 she became interested in the Irish question. In 1916 she was awarded a DBE for her work with war refugees in Belgium. Her husband died in 1919, ten years before she did.

Flora Shaw deserves another autobiography to supplement that written by E. Moberley Bell in 1947. She was a remarkably able woman and according to her obituary in *The Times* also a traveller 'of unusual pluck and nerve,' and 'so much more interested in the thing she was discussing than in herself, that men forgot she was a woman and talked to her as freely as to another man.' That in 1929 was praise indeed.

EMILY LUCY DE BURGH DALY

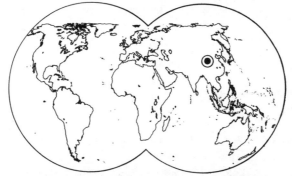

A picture of China at the turn of the century

The first account of travels from an Irish missionary doctor's wife was published by Emily (née French), sister to Percy French the songwriter and artist, born 1859 at Cloonyquin, Co. Roscommon. Emily left home in 1888 and lived in China and Manchuria for over twenty-five years, through the Opium War, the Boxer Rebellion, and the Japanese occupation. Her interesting book *An Irishwoman in China* (1915) was written after she returned to Dublin. As she says on her opening page:

— It's a far cry from the beech-groves and grasslands of Roscommon to the tea-plantations and ricefields of Mid-China, farther still to the frozen plains of Manchuria; but people do not think much of long journeys in Ireland, where practically every family has some members Empire-building overseas, or spreading the knowledge of Christianity and civilisation among alien races, and where a simple country girl, who has hardly ever left her own townland, will start for U.S.A., Australia, or New Zealand, without any fuss, on receipt of a letter from her 'mother's sister's son', sending her passage money, and assuring her that 'great wages she'll be gittin' in that land beyond the say.' —

After training in London, Emily travelled out to Ningpo as a nurse and was shortly put in charge of a hospital for Chinese women, but soon after this she stopped nursing to marry Dr C.C. De Burgh Daly, the Port Doctor in Ningpo and director of the CMS Hospital (married ladies did not 'work' then). Later they were moved to Newchwang, in S. Manchuria. She writes wisely about the difficulties of the young wife overseas:

— The first summer in the East is very trying to a young wife. Her husband is probably occupied during a great part of the day; she misses her own people, her young companions, feels the heat and discomfort, and unless she has a strong character, is adaptable and unselfish, and takes some intelligent interest in her new surroundings, is apt to degenerate into the bored, vapid person, who spends all her time paying calls, dressing, supervising her tailor, or flirting (harmlessly enough at first) with that 'Tertian Quid' at whose door lies the blame of many a domestic catastrophe. —

The couple travel a good deal in China and every few years take home leave.

— In the autumn we took a house in Dublin, not intending to return to China for nearly another year. Dr Phillips, who had become my husband's partner, was in charge, and all seemed going on smoothly. But shortly after Christmas came a bolt from the blue ... ' Plague bad, community want you. Phillips'....We packed up and went out again via Siberia as quickly as possible... We did not 'stop off' anywhere, and until our arrival at Irkutsk we heard no news about Manchuria. —

They went on to Manchouli where they found that plague had broken out. The Russians had segregated four thousand Chinese in railway carriages, and kept suspects separate, thus saving the town. Emily goes on:

— As we travelled through Manchuria it looked like a dead country; no business seemed to be going on, no long strings of carts laden with produce were to be seen, no mellow mule bells to be heard. The dread of the pestilence was over the land; already many thousands had died, and there was not one authenticated case of recovery. —

Photographs from Emily de Burgh Daly's An Irishwoman in China *(1915).*
Top: Great mneumonic plague, Manchuria 1910, examining rats.
Bottom: old Chinese doctor, who took no precautions and proved immune to infection.

When they arrived back at Newchwang Dr Daly immediately took over quarantine work, for as yet there were no cases there:

— We have all been working with frantic energy, and if we *are* scared, no one says so. This plague is said to come from the marmots; the infection is chiefly from inhalation, so we all go about wearing respirators. —

They were both inoculated. Amid the snow and ice of winter, quarantine buildings were erected. The plague chiefly attacked those in the prime of life and in one family of fourteen an old woman of seventy-one and a baby of two were the sole survivors. In the end, though Newchwang escaped, the epidemic killed at least forty-five thousand.

Emily writes well about Chinese women. Apart from footbinding to give what was called the golden lily gait, of which she disapproves, she writes:

— Chinese women are no dolls, but possess strong characters, are intelligent and capable. They sew and embroider extremely well, and often have good business capacity. Amongst shopkeepers the wife has charge of the cashbox, while the mandarin commits that most precious possession – his seal of office – to the care of his T'ai-T'ai.

Old residents in China all agree that women possess much influence in domestic, commercial, and even political life. The immense power wielded by the late Empress Dowager is a case in point, and amongst humble folk very shrewd old ladies are to be found ...

In Ningpo there are certain square brick towers outside the city wall known as Baby Towers, about which very erroneous ideas are held by many foreign visitors, who are persuaded that live girl babies are thrown into these towers by their unnatural parents! As a matter of fact, they are built by charitable people, so that the bodies of the children of the very poor (who cannot afford coffins) may be placed in them, and thus saved from prowling dogs, pigs, and carrion birds. Once or twice a year, at a time considered propitious by the necromancers, these towers are cleared out and the remains cremated. —

A philosophic and even-tempered woman, Mrs Daly becomes a seasoned traveller. Her last trip home is via Japan and Canada, travelling slowly with stops. While in 'The Empress of Britain' they collided with a collier and cut her in two. The crew were all saved, but their ship had to return to Quebec, pumping out water as she went.

EDITH SOMERVILLE

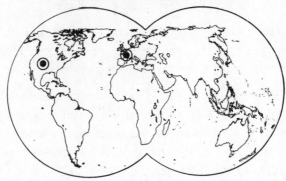

Amusing glimpses of the United States and of the Eiffel Tower by one of Ireland's most entertaining writers

Edith Somerville (1858-1949) is well known for the fiction she wrote with her cousin Violet Martin (1862-1915), as 'Somerville & Ross'. Edith was also a competent artist. Apart from light, amusing travel books about Ireland, Wales and the Medoc vineyards, written earlier with her partner, Edith also wrote *The States through Irish Eyes* (1930), after being invited to go on a lecture tour. She needed the money, so aged seventy-one she set out with her sister Hildegarde, and visited New York, South Carolina, Boston, New Haven and Philadelphia, being lavishly entertained everywhere. Warned by a friend that arrival at the New York docks was 'hell and bedlam', she went ashore:

— Neither Hell nor Bedlam was suggested by this vast, dim place, almost desolately empty – we had indeed been the last to leave the ship – where the courtesy of the Port was matched by the courtesy of the porters. —

In this, her first visit, 'Save to cross a sidewalk, foot of ours was never set to ground. Seated serenely in our hostess's car, we learnt what it was to race the red light from block to block, staring at the streets whose names were so familiar'. She went to the Morgan library, a Philharmonic Concert conducted by Toscanini, to a 'blurred dazzle' of dinners, lunches, picture galleries, theatre parties, and to Long Island.

Travelling overnight to Carolina was also a novel experience:

— No *wagon-lit* accommodation in European trains could compare with the comfort of the 'drawing-room' apportioned to us. Large, airy, with immense windows, and generously endowed with gadgets, electric and otherwise, to meet every conceivable need of light or heat. Even had the berths been less

Somerville and Ross (Violet Martin, 'Ross', on right) about 1895

comfortable than they were, there would have been compensation in the sight of the species of earthquake from which throes they arose, and having expired as armchairs, were reincarnated as beds. —

Edith's younger travel accounts were written in the 1890's for *The Lady's Pictorial*, with Violet Martin (pen name Martin Ross), tailored to the requirements of the magazine, though later published as a travel book, illustrated by Edith's sketches. In 1893 the pair also travelled to Denmark for the same magazine and the subsequent articles on 'The State of Denmark' were included by Edith much later in her 1920 volume *Strayaways*, in which she explains that most of the articles were written by Violet. In these articles Violet Martin comments about 'being Irish'. Irish Ascendancy women, until the mid twentieth century, enjoyed dual identity. They could be either 'Irish' or 'English' (the term 'British' being seldom used then) at their convenience. 'British' came into use only after the British Empire had broken up, and numbers of people, including many non-Europeans, claimed their right to British nationality. As Edith writes in chapter 14 of *Strayaways*:

— There is nothing aggressively superior about being Irish – at least, other people do not think so, and however that may be, there is a sense of kinship between the Irish and those who are not English that is curious, yet unmistakeable. Taking this into consideration, we ventured to hope that it was intended as a compliment when we were assured that we were quite unlike the English, but it was not altogether so gratifying to discover subsequently that Englishwomen were specially remarkable for their rich and handsome clothes. —

Here is a passage from Somerville & Ross's *In the Vine Country* (1893), in Paris on the way home. The Eiffel Tower had been built in 1889 for the Paris Exhibition:

— People who would go to sleep if we talked to them about the vineyards, would wake to active contempt if they heard we had not been to the Eiffel Tower.

We were deluded into getting off our tram too soon, and consequently had a long crawl through the empty Exhibition buildings and grounds before we reached our destination ...

We found ourselves at last under the four arching dachshund legs from which the Tower tapers improbably into space, and strayed round on the gravel underneath it, lavishing upon each other truisms appropriate to the occasion and expressing artificial regrets that we had apparently come too late in the afternoon for the lift. While we spoke, a clicking sound dropped to us from the sky. We looked up and saw, amidst the cobwebs of iron, a large square fly descending. I hardly know how we came to find ourselves at the entrance of the *ascenseur*. We both dislike lifts, and my cousin can repeat many rousing tales of lift-accidents...We held our breaths as we slid upwards through the girders that looked like all the propositions in Euclid run mad ...

We walked round the long galleries, my cousin making herself both conspicuous and absurd by her determination to find out how many dragoon- like strides went to each side. It will doubtless be a blow to the designer to hear that the four faces of the Tower vary in length, two of them measuring ninety-seven yards, another a hundred, and the fourth ninety-nine and a hop. We had thought of going to the top – thought of it vaguely and valiantly for some little time after the lift had shaken us out on the first *étage*, and before we had looked over the edge. One glance, however, down at the black specks crawling on the strips of tape that represented the gravel paths of the Exhibition grounds, satisfied us that we were as high as we wished to go. Even here the height was making my fingers tingle and my cousin had retired unsteadily from the verge under the pretext of buying a photograph at a neighbouring stall; while as to the view, all Paris was already far below us, a marvellous grey and green toy, with the afternoon sun striking flame out of the tiny gilded domes and spires and the pale thread of a river winding from one microscopic bridge to another, all showing clear in the smokeless air with a magical precision of detail.

There is a staircase that circles dizzily down the Tower, a Jacob's ladder that would make an angel giddy, and rather than enter again the lift that was even now sliding down to us on its steel cable through the iron network, my cousin said she would walk down. It was the final dispute of the expedition and, after affording much amusement to the bystanders, it ended by my leading my cousin, with her eyes tightly shut, and the expression of Lady Jane Grey on her way to execution, into the box with the sloping floor, in whose safety it was so impossible to believe.

We sit safely now in the ground floor of a two-storeyed house, and as we look back to that experience, it seems to us that no dentist's chair can have cradled more suffering than the lift of the Eiffel Tower. —

Edith was, of course, familiar with other countries from an early age. Born in Corfu, she later studied art at Düsseldorf and Paris. Because of their ironic and sometimes patronising tone it has taken time for the work of Somerville and Ross to be regarded dispassionately in Ireland, and thus fully appreciated.

HANNAH LYNCH

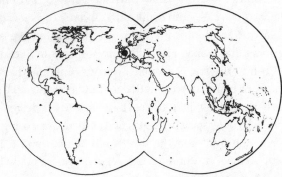

How to live in Paris on a tiny income

Hannah Lynch (1862-1904) was born in Dublin and joined the Ladies' Land League, which supported evicted tenants and encouraged the withholding of rents from rapacious landlords. Irish nationalist and friend of Anna Parnell, when *United Ireland* (the organ of the National Land League) was suppressed, Hannah took the type to Paris and printed it there, living as a political exile. She also became Paris correspondent to *Academy* (forerunner to the *Times Literary Supplement*).

Hannah's writings include fiction, often as an outlet for political feelings, a study of George Meredith and several travel books. Her *Toledo, the story of an old Spanish capital* (1898) shows a knowledge of Spain and the Spanish language, but it was France which became her second home. This is her impression of *fin de siècle* Paris from *French Life in Town and Country* (1901):

— It is a settled thing that Paris is the home of vice. French novels of the day attest to this fact ... so, above all do the songs of the unpublished poets of Montmartre, who fondly and seriously take themselves for misprized genius in the lump, and pose as so many Verlaines. Yet nothing in Paris offends the eye of the casual lounger through its streets as the eye is offended constantly in London. In Paris you have to look for manifestations of wickedness, and then it is known that you will find them in abundance, but they are not thrust under your nose at every street corner. You may walk the streets and boulevards at the small hours of the morning, or in the full glare of evening gas, or in the gathering gloom of midnight, when the lights are being put out, and if nobody assassinates you, you risk no evil sight or sound. There are quarters, we know from the daily papers, where vile creatures of both sexes group themselves for the peril of the passer-by, where blood is shed, and hideous language befouls the air, but these lie off the travelled highways of the city; and if you never read a newspaper, you might live for fifty years in Paris and never suspect that such a thing as crime took place within its fortifications.

Rents in Paris are comparatively high and space is precious; hence the exiguity of the average home of the middle and lower classes. Spare rooms are unknown and closets and presses must be packed with the nicest precision. But it is surprising how soon one becomes reconciled to want of room in a French flat, and in how short a time one learns to pity the London householder, above all his wife and servants, for his superfluity of chambers. Once you have climbed up the stairs of your flat, there is no more climbing, no futile running up and down stairs. Everything is to hand. You walk from your dining room into your salon and across a level floor into your bedroom; and it needs no excessive labour to keep all things straight, and polished and spotless. If you are fond of experimental cooking and light housework, you can dispense with the trouble and cost of a servant; avail yourself of the services of a *femme de ménage*, in a land where women of the people are admirably competent and honest, and potter about your dolls' kitchen to your liking. Fuel you will find much cheaper than in London, thanks to the little charcoal furnaces in enamel fireplaces, which can be lit and extinguished at will, at a nominal expense. And so a poor lady, a teacher, or a student, can live respectably and agreeably in Paris, on an income that would mean squalor and misery in London. A flat consisting of three bright rooms, a kitchen, several presses, a closet large enough to stow away endless boxes in, and serve as well as a hanging clothes closet, plenty of water, and excellent sanitary arrangements, may be had in an enviable spot, with pleasant outlook and good entrance, for six hundred francs a year (£24). A *femme de ménage* will cook, market, mend, clean up as a French woman knows how, for six sous (threepence) an hour; and if you treat her fairly well and secure her loyalty, she will give you devotion and friendship, as well as excellent service, and amazingly intelligent speech. For here you need never be at the expense or trouble of cooking complicated dishes. These are sold at the pastry cook's or the baker's, for considerably less than they will cost you at home; so that you can live well and keep your household bills within your means, even if meat in Paris be dear.

And then, when you want amusement, should your income not permit of frequent theatre going, what need to open up your purse? You have but to open your house door, and emerge upon the public place. On a summer afternoon or evening a ride on the top of an omnibus or tram is better entertainment than that offered by many a theatre of London. A walk through old Paris, or along the ever lovely quays, is refreshment enough for eye and fancy. Three sous will take you from the Madeleine to the Bastille; and where is it you may not reach from the Bastille for another three sous? If the chestnuts are in bloom, on foot, or on the *impériale* of a public vehicle, in imagination you are wandering through your own avenues, and you really have little to envy the rich in their cushioned victorias.

This is why I contend that the philosopher of either sex, whose purse is light, and whose tastes are frugal, can make shift with less in Paris than elsewhere; can live and be infinitely happier there on small means than in London. So much beauty is provided for him gratis, that he must be a churl who can spend his time in moaning and whining because his private walls are undecorated, or costly carpets do not cover his floors. Let him go to the Louvre or Cluny Museum when the fit takes him, and count himself a king without the cost and care of sovereignty. Let him sit in the Tuileries, and call them his private gardens while he feeds the sparrows; let him loaf among the bookstalls of the Seine, and leisurely turn the pages of books he means not to buy. Where will he better such luxuries, even at his own price, if fortune stepped his way?

In London poverty is galling, because there is no escape from its meannesses and its miseries. That is why the poor in London may be pardoned for taking to drink. That seems the only door, for it would need that a poor man living in a London slum should be very drunk indeed to find beauty of any kind in his environment. But poverty in Paris may be found both amusing and instructive.

I am not sure that it is not the poor, the needy, the small clerk, the overworked teacher, the shopgirl, the underfed student, who do not get the best of Paris; feel to the fullest measure its common joys, which lie not in wait for the rich and worldly. —

Later in the book Hannah Lynch makes some interesting comparisons:

— I have said the lack of material comfort and plenty in middle-class French homes is striking ... I have had a glimpse of all these classes of homes, and in winter found them unseasonably chill and frugal.

Thirty years ago, I am assured, it was far worse, for then carpets were unknown, and fire was far more scant than today. Such economies are practised here as in England would only accompany harsh poverty, but they must not be taken as the symbol of such. Your grocer and his wife, who eat behind the shop in a sanded and comfortless space walled off, and on Sunday afternoon go out, neatly arrayed in well fitting but utterly dowdy and serviceable garments, have tidy fortunes stowed away, while their flashy, splash-loving brethren of the British Isles, with their dogcarts, bicycles and up-to-date attire turned out by fashionable tailors, dressmakers and milliners, are pulling the devil by the tail and stupidly patronizing their betters, contented with less display.

I retired lately to Ireland to write this little book, and there found such a violent contrast between French and Irish character in these respects after long residence in France. I was used to the simple, courteous, willing, active tradespeople of Paris, who give themselves no airs, dress dowdily, live modestly. I found the same class in Ireland, even in a small village, dressed daily as Solomon never was in all his glory, with tailormade gowns of ten and twelve guineas, with high and haughty manners to bewilder a princess of the blood, the one cutting the other, Heaven only knows on what assumption of superiority, and all hastening from their counters in smart turnouts, duly to subscribe their loyal names to the list of the Queen's visitors. I felt like Rip Van Winkle, as if I had waked in my native land, and found every one gone mad with pride and pretension. When I ventured into a shop to make an insignificant purchase, a gorgeous dandy with a lisp condescended to attend to me, or a lady looking like a duchess, and most desirous that you should take her for such, dropped from the height of her grandeur to my humble person, and was good enough in her superior way to look after me. Everybody was so seemingly above trade or business or breadwinning of any kind, that I was glad enough to pack up my papers and things, and come back to a race more simple and less pretentious, where the people work with good will, and sell you a yard of tape or a hat without insufferable condescension, and where tradesmen and their wives do not think it necessary to confer on crowned heads the honour of their call. In pursuit of my investigations on this subject I was taken to the house of a very small trades person, who lived over her shop. The owner wore a twelve-guinea silken lined gown trimmed with Irish point. I can well imagine what sort of residence hers would be in France.... Majesty indeed might have sat in that sitting room ...

Another time I obtained a glimpse of the interior of a bankrupt widow of a 'little burgess' who had to vacate a house with grounds to take up her residence in a more modest dwelling. Such a woman in France would be content to live and die a very plain and simple person, and having had to compound with her creditors would have considered herself bound to lay her new existence out upon the lines of the most rigid economy, above all, having a large family of sons and daughters not yet of an age nor having education to provide for themselves. The house I visited was one of a row, a poor, mean quarter, where no sane person would look for any appearance of affluence. Over the fanlight the house rejoiced in an imposing Celtic name in three words in raised white letters, not the cheapest form of house nomenclature. A gardener was engaged trimming the infinitesimal garden front; the youngest girl of twelve, was mounting her bicycle to career off with a companion; in the hall were three other bicycles belonging to different members of the family. The furniture in the drawing room was new and expensive, and a young lady was playing up-to-date waltzes on the piano without a trace of concern or anxiety; no sign anywhere of economy, of sacrifice, of worry. Yet I knew I was entering a house where there was practically nothing to live upon, and where the proceeds of a sale that should have gone to the woman's creditors had been squandered on unnecessary things.

One may criticize the meannesses to which thrift drives the frugal French, but I never felt more near to falling in love with what is to me an uncongenial vice than I did on leaving my native land after this visit, to have commercial dealings once more with people not above their business, instead of trading with the spurious descendants of kings, whose sole anxiety is to make you feel their social superiority and extraordinary condescension, to find these excellent French 'little people' all that Lever told us the Irish were and have ceased to be: cordial, delightful, intelligent and simple. For that is the great, the abiding charm of the French middle class – the absence of vulgar pretension. Every man to his trade, and an artist at that – such is the wise French motto. —

MAUREEN HAMISH

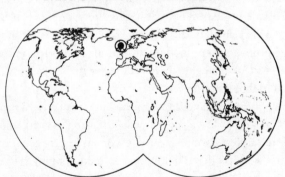

Life as a working girl, living away from home

Maureen Hamish (real name Mary Loughran) was born in Cookstown, Co. Tyrone, around 1870, and she is included here because her only book, *Adventures of an Irish Girl at home and abroad* (1906), gives us a glimpse into another way of life, one experienced by many Irish women yet seldom recorded.

Maureen tells us she had a national school education, and did her writing at dawn or very late at night. She wrote to earn money to take her sick father to Lourdes.

Aged about sixteen Maureen went to Scotland as a maid, then to Yorkshire and on to London. She began as a kitchen and scullery maid, and later tried to rise to cook. She evidently has literary ambitions for her book ends with nineteen pages of verse. Here she is in Yorkshire:

— When engaging me the lady told me there was a Catholic church two miles from her residence. As soon as I found out the name of the place where the church was, I wrote to the parish priest, although I did not know his name. In due course I received a reply from a minister of the Church of England, referring me to the Prior, Ampleforth College, and telling me there was no Catholic church in the district. The good lady had made a mistake. I wrote at once to the Prior and received a reply saying the nearest church was in Kirbymoorside, six miles distant. There was no train on Sundays, and I would have to walk both to and from, making twelve miles. There was no help for it, but it was a sad disappointment to me, and I had been so anxious about it before I engaged, and so sure all was right. However, I must just make the best of it.

The good sub-Prior introduced me by letter to some very kind people in town, who received me in their house, and made me feel quite at home. The church was very small and humble – it had once been a mason's shed. The congregation was mostly converts; the mission was served from Ampleforth College. In time I learned to love the long walk; I went to Mass once a fortnight. After Mass I had dinner with my friends, rested a little while and then walked back.

The people I was with had a residence two miles from Pickering, I will call it Wilton Hall. When we had been there for a few days there was a meet in the neighbourhood; the master was hunting, had an accident, and was laid up for three weeks at another gentleman's residence. There was only my friend and I, the other servants and the children (who always spent the winter in Edinburgh), had not arrived. We were left alone in a large house in a district we knew nothing about, with very little provisions. Only we happened to have a little money of our own I don't know what would have become of us, for we had the greatest difficulty at first in making out the dialect.

The mistress was with Mr – when he was hurt, and remained in close attendance on him. She was a good kind young lady, but I cannot say I ever liked the master, he seemed to always treat his servants with distrust and suspicion, and I thought he was not as kind to the mistress as she deserved. I often heard him speak harshly, and then would find her in tears. My heart was sore for her, though she never complained; but she was so sensitive and so gentle.

The avenue opened into a village street. When my friend and I were left alone, the young men made a practice of standing outside the gate, and trying all in their power to attract our attention as we passed in or out. We took no notice, but one morning when we came downstairs, we found letters waiting for us under the kitchen door, enclosed in one of the letters was a cartoon, a young couple going on their honeymoon. On the back of the cartoon was drawn rabbits, hens, a local preacher, and at first the couple on the cartoon seemed to get on well, then he was using a stick. The sender hoped that when we went honeymooning we wouldn't do like this. At first I decided to follow my usual custom and take no notice; but my friend pleaded so hard and I was sorry for her, and hoped to distract her mind from her trouble; so we asked a man who worked in the garden attached to the hall for the names of some of the young men who loitered about the gate. —

Maureen then sent the young hopefuls a reply in excruciating verse! As a result their letters back became a 'regular nuisance', so that she was glad when her family arrived. Soon after this, smallpox broke out in Kirbymoorside and she started going to Mass in Malton, thirteen miles away. She walked two miles to the station, took the train to Malton, then had to walk all the way back. Again someone invited her into their house to eat and rest. Only perhaps in parts of Africa nowadays would a young woman take such pains to get to Mass.

In Scotland Maureen works for a widow with four daughters and one son. Here again she walks miles to Mass every other Sunday. She then by accident discovers that there is a private chapel for Mass near where she lives. It is astonishing that the family she worked for did not take the trouble to find this out.

Finally, after the following incident, she decides to seek another family:

— One morning I awoke with a feeling of suffocation. I tried to leave my bed, but found that almost impossible. By a strong effort I dragged myself to my bedroom door, which I had fortunately left slightly ajar the previous night. There was a fine fresh breeze coming upstairs from a garden door left open in the morning to air the house. It revived me almost directly, and I turned into my room again to find out if possible what was wrong.

During the night a mouse had gnawed the gaspipe in my room. It only left two very tiny toothmarks, but the gas was escaping and had very nearly suffocated me. The pipe was repaired at once, but I felt more unsettled than ever. The mistress was anxious to keep me, but I could not make up my mind; however, the next accident decided me. I was told to keep a tiny peep of gas alight during the night, and to keep my door ajar as well. I had fallen into my first sleep when I felt a choking sensation. I jumped up in bed, and a big rat rolled off my neck. It ran across the floor and I was after it in a moment. I discovered next morning that it had eaten a square meal out of my pincushion which was stuffed with bran, then somehow it got into my bed between the sheets at the foot of the bed and had made its way right up to my face. I can feel the awful sensation yet, as I realised how near I had been to having my throat cut. —

After that Maureen gets another situation with an Edinburgh family. During her first ten years 'out' she only managed to go home once, but by the end of this time her family are better off. Her brothers can now help her father, and they have started a stone factory on the farm. She goes back to Ireland for a two week holiday. Quite unable to consider a mixed marriage, Maureen seems to have remained single.

DAISY MAY BATES

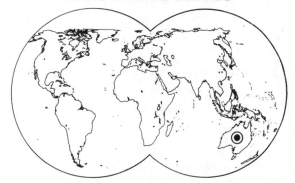

Struggles on behalf of the Aborigines of Australia, for over thirty years

Daisy May Bates (née O'Dwyer) (1861 or 1863-1951) was born in Co. Tipperary, and claimed that her father's branch harked back to William O'Dwyer, Baron of Kilnamanagh, but her branch had turned Protestant.

Julia Blackburn, in her recent *Daisy Bates in the Desert*, a highly personal and semi-fictionalised account of Bates' life, has outlined the latest version of Daisy's origins, and states that Daisy came from a poor Catholic family. Her mother died, her drunken father ran off to America but died en route. Daisy was then raised in an orphanage near Dublin and trained as a governess in a charity school. This account differs completely from Daisy's own. Daisy states that she was raised by maternal grandparents in Roscrea and that she and her siblings were 'a dreadfully happy-go-lucky, careless, misruley lot'.

Daisy evidently wished to acquire a higher social status than that endowed by her birth. She was clever, pretty, well-educated, possessed of a vivid imagination to the point of being psychic, and had a gift with words. She could dance and ride well. If the miserable circumstances of her childhood are true, her desire to rise above them in Australia, her new country, is understandable. Her inaccuracy about dates in her book, *The Passing of the Aborigines*, is also excusable. The book was written in her mid seventies, after years of living an isolated, totally withdrawn life.

Was her own account of her childhood merely a traveller's 'tall tale'? It seems too circumstantial to be entirely untrue. Whatever the facts, it is amusing to read two contrasting accounts of Daisy's youth provided by Elizabeth Salter's *Daisy Bates* and Julia Blackburn. Such is the confusion that Daisy Bates has now become a legend, fact and fancy being inextricably entwined. Daisy's equivocacy with truth has unfortunately also tainted her undoubted expertise in aborigine culture.

When Daisy arrived in Townsville in 1883 Irish emigrants provided nearly a quarter of Australia's population. She first worked as a governess on a North Queensland cattle station, and in March 1884 married a stockman named Edwin Henry Morant. This was the famous 'Breaker Morant' later executed by a British firing squad during the Boer War. Morant, like Daisy, had social pretensions, and claimed to be an admiral's son, not the offspring of a Devon workhouse keeper. He and Daisy were perhaps too alike. They separated after less than a year, and in January 1885 Daisy bigamously married Jack Bates of Nowra, New South Wales, a tough cattle drover and hero of the outback, who also played polo. Daisy became a Protestant on this marriage certificate, and remained the same age, hence the doubt about her date of birth. In August 1886 their son Arnold was born. The marriage was a disaster, as Daisy rapidly discovered, but at least she learned bush lore from Jack and how to pitch a tent. After Arnold's birth she seems to have refused sex with Jack, and that did not help either!

According to her own account, during this early period of her life Daisy roamed about Australia, staying with friends, or others to whom she had been introduced, one of whom was the Bishop of Hobart. While living in Tasmania Daisy heard all about the hardships of the early settlers, and what

had happened to the aborigines, by this time extinct on the island. Then in the economic crash of the 1890's Daisy lost what remained of her capital. In 1894 she left her son in the care of his father, and sailed to England in a wool clipper.

Daisy lived first with a cousin in Ireland, but she had to earn her own living. She obtained an introduction to W.T. Stead, then editor of *Review of Reviews* and the *Pall Mall Gazette*, known to be sympathetic and helpful to women, particularly since 1885 when he had revealed London's sexual iniquities and slave traffic in young girls.

Daisy lived in the Countess of Meath's hostel in Cavendish Square, London, working as a general dogsbody for W.T. Stead at £1 a week. Later she recalled this period as the two happiest years of her life. She moved to another hostel for 'gentlewomen' where she paid 7s 6d a week for board and lodging. She soon advanced from dogsbody to associate, and became a journalist.

Daily worked on W.T. Stead's new quarterly *Borderland* but often disagreed with his editorial policy, and said so. Daisy called New Women of her day 'public nuisances' after Stead's secretary completed a woman's first bicycle tour of the British Isles wearing knickerbockers! Daisy was conservative about dress all her life, unbending in her own social and moral ideas, however lenient she later became to those from other cultures. As W.T. Stead became interested in spiritualism, of which Daisy disapproved, she drew apart and in the end resigned her job on *Borderland*, which she regarded as anti-Christian.

When the National Bank of Australia refunded her deposits at the rate of a shilling in the pound Daisy used the money to pay her fare back to Australia, a decision perhaps hastened by her growing love for a married man. After an absence of five years from her son and estranged husband she returned to Perth. En route she met an elderly Catholic priest, Dean Martelli, who worked with Matthew Gibney, Bishop of Perth, on behalf of the aborigines. On board ship Daisy learned about the history and beliefs of Australia's native people. Martelli believed they were doomed. This gave Daisy the idea of recording the languages and customs of those tribes which were left, an idea she subsequently discussed with the Irishman, Bishop Gibney, in Perth.

A year later, having left her son now at a Christian Brothers school in Perth, and with the encouragement of Sir John Forrest, Premier, who was then planning an Aboriginal Protection Act, Daisy set off in a coastal steamer for Cossack on the North West coast, where she met her husband Jack. This was her first taste of this still wild area. They negotiated for an outback estate, to be named Glen Carrick. Jack may have hoped that Daisy would now settle down.

Later that year she accompanied the Bishop and Dean Martelli on a visit to the Trappist Mission in remote N.W. Australia for the purpose of writing articles about the work of the Trappists. Daisy has given an account of this expedition in her book *The Passing of the Aborigines* (1938), in which she says 'the four months that I spent there were nothing but the sheerest hard work under the most trying conditions,' as they confronted willie-willies, fires and tropical weather in the North West near Broome. She discovered that the aboriginal men traded their women to the Asiatics in the pearling ships. The women returned dying and diseased. The women were normally betrothed in infancy to rightful tribal husbands. They were the property of all their husband's brothers, and then 'on hire' to all the Asiatic husband's brothers, who paid for sex with her. Daisy Bates had trouble convincing the Bishop and Dean of this custom. The Bishop then stopped the practice.

Daisy describes the end of her four months' trip thus:

— I camped in the hut that the previous missioners had erected at Disaster Bay, and the others camped outside it in the moonlight. I had scarcely snatched an hour of sleep in one of the four dust-bag bunks that hung to the walls when I was rudely awakened by the presence of thirty naked women, of all sizes, giggling at me. From the neighbouring camps the natives had been rounded up by one of the Beagle Bay boys for the Bishop's visit.

Being quite unsophisticated they were as much amused by my appearance as I at theirs. I have always preserved a scrupulous neatness, and all the little trappings and accoutrements of my own very particular mode of dress, sometimes under difficulties, but I think I never made a more laughable toilet than that one. Every motion of mine, as I laced my corsets and eased my shoes on with a shoe-horn, brushed my hair and adjusted my high collar and waist-belt, was greeted with long drawn squeals of laughter and mirrored in action, though the slim black daughters of Eve about me had not even a strand of hair strung between the whole thirty.

We could not spend more than a few days at this outpost, and next morning my Lord the Bishop baptized and confirmed every man, woman and child that could be gathered in, including babies in arms. Father Nicholas dutifully had brought along the wreath and veil, and there it was, the only article of wearing apparel in evidence. Vividly I can see again the spectacle of a hairy savage with a bone through his nose, a wreath and veil, and nothing else whatever. —

They give food and clothing to the natives, brought from Perth, then Daisy goes off with a few natives for her first sight of a crocodile, wading in the mangrove flats. Treading on poisonous shellfish her feet swell so much that she can only fit them into sugar bags, and in much pain as a result, she returns with the others to the Mission at Beagle Bay.

They get as far as Broome and walk the last nine miles, the Bishop and Daisy with four natives carrying their luggage, so presumably her feet had recovered. En route the Bishop, an elderly man, shows sign of collapse in the excessive heat, and leans on Daisy's shoulder.

— The journey would ordinarily have taken three hours, but we had only reached the five mile well when darkness came. The Bishop showed signs of slight delirium, calling me 'Margaret', the name of a beloved sister in Ireland. It must have been ten o'clock when the natives whispered to me that we were at the beach, where he sank down unconscious. We straightened his weary body, the natives and I, with part of my rug-strap under his head. There we camped, unable to see the ship offshore, and I quite ignorant of our surroundings. The only sound I heard was the tide sucking at the mangroves. To make matters worse, the natives came, in frightened whispers, to tell me that 'big pindana (inland) mob blackfellows come up' close by, strangers from the inland bush. I said: 'Don't be afraid. Eebala (father) and I will take care of you'. Then I placed two of them lying one at each side of the Bishop, and I lay down with my head on the rug-strap and my feet in the opposite direction, the other two natives on either side of me.

The Bishop slept in utter exhaustion, and I not a wink. Stamping of feet and wild cries came to us clearly. Now and again a black form between me and the stars told me that our natives were listening, and in terror they would whisper to me of these bad *pindana-womba* who sometimes hung about the outskirts of the Mission to steal their women and to fight. I changed the subject to the stars and the sky, and they told me of a dark place in the Milky Way which was once a native road to the star country, until one day some women on the way lighted a fire and burned the road, which was really a sacred wooden emblem. Our heads were together as we whispered, the Bishop's white unconscious face beside us. Then a fiercer chant and the mound-beating of the pindana men would send us all noiselessly on our backs again. Through the false dawn we were particularly watchful, but nothing happened. —

Daylight brought the boat, owned and run by Filipinos, and the Bishop was laid on deck. Throughout the hundred mile voyage Daisy remained by his side, listening to the same haunting tune being sung by a crew member which 'always brings the scene vividly to my mind — the filthy boat that was once a miniature floating palace, the sleeping Bishop lying on a sail-cloth, and the Manila helmsman looking up at a sort of calico cornucopia which, when filled with the winds, was his steering compass.'

— Just before we entered Broome waters the Bishop opened his eyes and looking round wearily, saw the old Manilaman lying naked and unashamed nearby.

'Go and put your clothes on!' he called to the poor old fellow, who had neither clothes nor need of them in his rough life on the sea.

A typically Irish ending to a difficult work accomplished. —

Daisy Bates first lived on a cattle station near Broome for eight months to study the Koolarrabulloo tribes. Broome was a prosperous pearling port with a polyglot population of Chinese, Japanese, Malays, Filipinos and dealers of many European races.

She writes: 'Within his own tribal laws, the aborigine is bound hand and foot by tradition; beyond them he knows no ethics,' and she realised that 'to glean anything of value I must think with his mentality, and talk in his language.' She began compiling a dictionary of several dialects, two thousand words and sentences and notes on myths and legends. She pretended to be a magic woman, one of the twenty-two wives of a patriarchal 'dreamtime' father, and they accepted her. Daisy was admitted to the sacred ceremonies of the initiation of men, normally forbidden to women under pain of death. In the end during thirty-five years of journeying, Daisy Bates was accepted as the age old spirit of Yamminga, keeper of all the totems. She learned many aborigine dialects, more than any other outsider, before or since.

The aborigine tribes were both circumcised and uncircumcised, for the latter had been chased south, east and west by the former who had come in from the north. The Broome tribes were circumcised. The men made all the decisions, women being subjugated and despised. Boys were separated from girls at the age of eight to start small game hunting and boomerang throwing. Aged about twelve, a boy had his nose pierced preparatory to his circumcision, a long and complicated ritual of which Daisy gives an exact description. Some tribes also knocked out the two front teeth.

After circumcision the young men were kept apart from women. Any woman who approaches them is killed. They then passed through another initiation lasting a year, which terminated with the drinking of relatives' blood. For several weeks the boys only drink blood, or eat dried blood, even while the men eat meat. After this, still nourished only by human blood, the boys go on a long journey, and undergo more trials until they emerge at the end of this lengthy process, which may take years, freed of restriction and allowed to marry their brides, betrothed to them in childhood.

Still trying, at intervals, to make a go of her marriage, Daisy next decided to drive 770 Herefords from near Broome to Glen Carrick, the estate Jack had bought, a thousand miles south. She rode with eight drovers and a half-caste cook for six months, 'Three thousand miles, as I rode it, zigzagging behind the mob at six, eight or ten miles a day, and every one of the 770 surpassing the Irish pig in contrariness. My equipment was a good English pigskin side-saddle with ordinary stirrups; three pairs of laced wallaby-skin shoes; three habits; a felt hat; three pairs of riding gloves and plenty of fly veiling'. Besides four draught horses they took thirty-six riding horses for the use of Daisy, the drovers and her son Arnold, aged twelve. They forgot, however, to take a cattle dog.

After that Daisy does not mention Jack, whom she still met at intervals until they finally separated in 1912. Her article on 'Three thousand miles in a side saddle' was later published in *Australasian* more than twenty years later. Part of the journey she called 'gruesome' and the memory of it certainly never left her. 'I saw myself after a long's day ride through the dusty, curly, wattle scrub, covered with dust and mud, coat and habit hanging in ribbons, face begrimed with dirt, added to by vexatious tears caused by the vagaries of a mob of the most malignant beings in creation, the so-called mild-eyed cow that artists so love to paint.' Sometimes the day lasted for eighteen hours, '... from dawn till the sharing of the night watches we plodded on'. Cattle died, and at one point six hundred of them stampeded looking for water. Daisy made £1,000 profit in the end for all her pains, though she was left with no stock for Glen Carrick. She said this experience aged her fifteen years, and after it, fourteen pounds lighter, she was completely exhausted.

Now regarded as an authority on the aborigines, Daisy next worked with the uncircumcised Bibbulmun tribe, once the largest in Australia, in the Perth area. Women of this tribe, though still a man's property, had more liberty. Infanticide was rarely practised except on twins, they used palaeolithic tools and wore kangaroo skins, spears and clubs being their only weapons. Only about forty stragglers of the original tribe remained. They had believed that the first white men were the returned spirits of their dead relatives. Daisy does not blame the early settlers' treatment of the natives, five were even sent to a Benedictine seminary in Rome, but she remarks, 'The Australian native can withstand all the reverses of nature, fiendish droughts and sweeping floods, horrors of thirst and enforced starvation, but he cannot withstand civilization'.

For two years Daisy lived in a fourteen foot diameter tent overlooking the Guildford River, 'trying to conjure a nation of the past from these few and homeless derelicts' as they died about her one by one. She then began travelling round the area to visit dispersed groups of aborigines who said 'the smell of the white man is killing us'. She went to a native reserve and nursed the sick in a measles epidemic. About this she writes: 'I believe that in heaven, in 40,000 years time, if somebody uncorks a bottle of native odour I shall be able to tell them the tribe it comes from'.

Although Daisy had read papers to the Royal Geographical Society, was requested to write papers for the Royal Society, and was known as an expert on aborigine culture, she was self-taught and still regarded by those in authority, and by anthropologists, as an amateur, so she often had difficulty in obtaining backing for her work.

In 1910 she was, rather grudgingly, appointed as a travelling protector to the aborigines, to be attached to an expedition from Cambridge led by a man named Radcliffe Brown, who would become Australia's first professor of anthropology. Daisy travelled with Brown, Grant Watson, a biologist and photographer, a government attaché and a Swedish male cook. Daisy had to convince the natives that these men were not police, so she called Brown and Watson her sons! She clashed with the patronising Brown, and later accused him of plagiarising her notes.

Daisy had by now gathered an enormous amount of anthropological information, much of it by talking patiently to old and sick natives. She discovered the importance of place to them. Diseased natives, isolated on an island in Shark Bay, were uprooted and believed that upon death their souls would be orphaned in this strange place. Adopted as one of themselves she became Kabbarli, the Grandmother. She describes her research method thus:

— The first lessons I learned were never to intrude my own intelligence upon him, and to have patience, the patience that waits for hours and years for the links in the long chain to be pieced together. A casual soul, he knows no urgency. Yesterday and today and tomorrow are all the same to him. —

So most of her data were a gradual compilation over many years. She claimed, for example, that baby cannibalism was rife among the central-western tribes. In one group she found every woman had eaten her babies immediately after birth, dividing them with her sisters who in their turn reciprocated, so that the group had not produced a single living child for some years. It was a form of deliberate genocide. Because Daisy was given to exaggeration and inaccurate recording of some of the facts, much of her aborigine research remains unacceptable to academics.

Daisy also learned about the complicated system of totems:

— In this comparatively desolate country, the totems were entirely different from the brotherhood with nature and the food totems of the Bibbulmun. Kangaroo, emu and dingo totems are common throughout Australia, and here, among them, I met men of the *moolaiongoo* or wombat snake, and the *googara*, or prickly acacia. The *googara* provided the best *bomburu* sticks and also the wood for the best come-back boomerangs. —

Daisy learned about feuds between totem groups and their blood magic:

— One evening, as we sat round the camp-fire, this native, Jaal, by a weird aboriginal sleight of hand, apparently from his stomach, produced an initiation knife, with it a piece of dark stone shot through with veins of galena – or was it gold? I did not know. He gave them to me. 'This,' he said in his own language, 'is what the white man likes, but we don't let him come for it. The knife is from Maiamba, and it is my totem, jeemarri'.

I questioned him further, and found that the *jeemarri* group was the most important in the widest area that I could compass there. Jeemarri knives were peculiar to the region, of a hard, dark flint. The shrine Maiamba was a secret and sacred place visited only by the older men, who are possessed of the magic of extracting these initiation knives from their stomachs. The surroundings of the shrine possessed a peculiarly Scottish name, Munro, and the area was called Yarnder. The jeemarri knives found there were bartered south, west and north to the confines of the continent. They were so hard and strong, and having come from the stomachs of the old men, their magic was so potent that they could be sold for 'spears and spears and spears,' making the group a rich one and of outstanding importance.

Jaal told me that he was the last man of his group, and to me he left this shrine Maiamba, from which he and his people had headed off the white man who had come many times looking for gold. I was not to take anyone there until all of the natives who belonged to it were dead and gone, and Maiamba an orphan water. Jaal said he would go with me to Maiamba, but soon after this episode he was taken to Bernier Island [the island where diseased natives were isolated and usually died. Abandoned in 1911]. I showed the stone with its rich content to an assayer. He was deeply interested.

'An excellent specimen, Mrs Bates. Seventeen ounces to the ton. Where did it come from?'

'I am not sure of the name of the place,' I evaded. 'A native brought it in.' Jaal's country and its Maiamba shrine lay east of Meekatharra at Lake Way, now the extensive gold mines of Wiluna, to which by right of bequest, I am the hereditary heiress, for the *jeemari* area is mine, by deed of gift of my last grandson there. —

In 1912 Daisy returned to Perth now 'a confirmed wanderer, a nomad even as the aborigines. So close had I been in contact with them that it was now impossible for me to relinquish the work. I realised that they were passing from us. I must make their passing easier,' and she decided to dedicate the rest of her life to studying and helping their race.

— A glorious thing it is to live in a tent in the infinite – to waken in the grey of dawn, a good hour before the sun outlines the low ridges of the horizon, and to come out into the bright cool air, and scent the wind blowing across the *mulga* plains. —

Each night she covered the fire with soft ash, as she had watched her compatriots cover turf fires in Ireland.

— As the sun came up it changed that plain white room into the most exquisitely frescoed pergola, with a patterning far surpassing the best of Grinling Gibbons' handiwork. In a constant play of leafy light and shadow I would eat my tea and toast in absolute content, while outside the blue smoke of the fire changed to grey in the bright sunlight. —

Daisy visited an aboriginal prison at Rottnest, an island fourteen miles out. Offences ranged from murder to sheep or cattle stealing, 'and other breaches of the white man's law of the enormity of which they were, for the most part, ignorant'.

Chained in gangs the convicts worked in the salt lakes or making roads, and on farm work. They slept in stone cells and died in appalling numbers. Daisy calls Rottnest another tragic mistake of the early colonists and soon after she went there it was abandoned.

In 1914 Daisy Bates was invited to a Science Congress in Adelaide. To get there she hired a camel buggy and a pair of camels for the 240 mile journey from Eucla, her present camp. She went with Gauera and Balgundra, Gauera's fourteenth husband, who had bought her a few weeks before from his brother in exchange for two shillings and a well seasoned pipe.

They had to cross the then still unsurveyed Great Nullarbor Plain and before leaving they sent a smoke signal of farewell. On the way they met, and were joined by, one of Gauera's previous husbands, who had sold, not lent, her, and though she built his breakwind, he lit his own fire and cooked his own food. En route they ate edible ants, lizards, land-snails, kangaroo, emu, dingo, wombat and wallaby, also a long fat goonia snake 'rolled into lengths and roasted'.

Daisy stopped for several weeks at a sheep station and completed her journey to Adelaide alone by boat just as the 1914 war broke out. She gave many lectures at and outside the conference, and obtained a good deal of press coverage, but she failed to get financial aid from the government to help her work.

Daisy next moved camp to South Australia near Fowler's Bay. 'The animism and totemism of the aborigine are his religion, the initiation ceremonies his baptism of blood, and are there not sacred pagan places in our own Catholic Ireland?' she asks, adding that the rock drawings of Australia have their counterparts in England, Scotland, Ireland, Brittany and elsewhere and hold similar meanings. 'They cannot catch up with us in one generation.' The government aboriginal department continued to regard her as a self-willed eccentric, and the anthropologists did not accept all her conclusions, especially her evidence for the existence of cannibalism, published in various articles.

In 1920 Daisy Bates was appointed the first female J.P. for S. Australia and asked to arrange a display of aborigine life at Ooldea in honour of the Prince of Wales travelling down the new transcontinental railway. She collected 150 natives and went down the line with them in the goat-van of a goods train, 'the two distinct odours definitely conflicting'. Daisy arranged a demonstration of native arts, crafts and skills, a corroboree welcome for the Prince with singing and dancing. In exchange the men received sheep to roast, flour and tobacco.

Living among the natives at Ooldea Daisy had to treat VD, debility, senility, ophthalmia, broken bones, burns, spear wounds, ringworm, measles, sandy blight and pneumonia. She stayed in that area until 1934, and no more half-caste children were born to women 'hired' to the railway workers, due to her quiet persuasion. She became an expert bird watcher and nature lover, living through drought and bush fires, eating very sparsely and always short of money. She claimed she could live on ten shillings a week.

— A little while later the drought broke, after nearly eight years. On a day of scorching wind, 106 degrees in my tent, I looked out upon the amazing phenomenon of a great grey mountain range moving slowly towards me across the plain, a cloud range hundreds of feet high with many clefts and crevices, blue and glacial or dark and cavernous, with outjutting ridges exactly like weather worn granite. The contours never changed, although within it a ground wind whirled and spiralled horizontally. The natives were terrified at this moving mountain.

Suddenly it was upon us. The mountain became a whirling mass of sand and wind and rain. I clung to the ridge-pole and shut my eyes in a tornado of blowing canvas and lashing branches and corrugated iron, while the thousand and one water-vessels beat about me in pandemonium.

There followed many gusty showers, and after the parched years, a vision beautiful. Green returned to earth, and the world was filled with the sweet fresh scent of herbage. On my way from the siding I now gathered armfuls of flowers, the slight rare glories of that barren bush. —

During these latter years Daisy wrote forty-seven articles for Arthur Mee's *Children's Newspaper*, and regularly for the *Australasian*. The Australian writer Ernestine Hall stayed with Daisy in her tent, and afterwards wrote about this woman who lived as a tribal matriarch among the aborigines. Daisy became better known, though many were still sceptical about her, and in 1933 she was invited to Canberra to give advice about the aborigines. Daisy recommended that the natives should live in 'a large central contiguous reserve' to work out a community as they wished it to be, where they could live in the way they preferred, using their own medicaments, but they should be given some farming and road-building assistance. Her plan was dismissed as impractical. She was still regarded as an amateur, and now out of touch as well.

Daisy might be poor, but she was also obstinate and intransigent. She wanted to prepare her lifelong material for publication and refused any offers of collaboration. At least some recognition for her humane work with the aborigines came when she was awarded the OBE (1934), and when *The Passing of the Aborigines* came out four years later it was a bestseller in Britain.

In Canberra on that 1933 visit Daisy, now in her seventies, had her first bath for twelve years. She found Australia had changed, 'quite alone and in my old-world garb I felt a stranger and an anachronism'. New South Wales had a brand new 'synthetic' city. She met the Prime Minister who feared for her health. Yet the government did the minimum to help her. Her unpublished research remains in the National Library of Australia at Canberra.

Daisy wrote: 'There was not an hour of my time wasted in all those years. I did what I set out to do, to make their passing easier and to keep the dreaded half-caste menace from our great continent'. She believed that the aborigines, 'the last remnants of paleolithic man,' were doomed. When Daisy's book was published there were a mere 60,000 aborigines left, but, although co-inhabitation between races remained illegal until 1967, many did intermarry. An Australian writer, Bill Harney, married an aboriginal girl he had first seen harnessed to a plough with twenty other women in 1938. Daisy's abhorrence of mixed race was typical of her time. The aborigines have today increased to some 200,000 and prospered far beyond anything she could have imagined.

Daisy's 1938 book did not appear in Australia until 1946. By this time she was still wearing clothes bought in 1900. She had obtained a Commonwealth Literary Fellowship in 1944, but it was only when she was hospitalised for malnutrition that the public sympathy was awakened. Daisy had by now become eccentric, according to the ways of the white man, and snide remarks were made about her being 'slightly mental'. In fact she was far from that, but she still needed to be in the bush. She discharged herself from hospital, and took a bus 400 miles to Streaky Bay. Here she planned to compile a book of aborigine legends from a hotel bedroom. What she really wanted was a horse-drawn caravan in which to search for 'my natives'.

Helped by Ernestine Hill, in the end Daisy obtained a pension of five guineas a week and she moved to share a bungalow in the hills behind Adelaide. Daisy died, over the age of ninety, in an Adelaide rest home.

MRS AUBREY LE BLOND

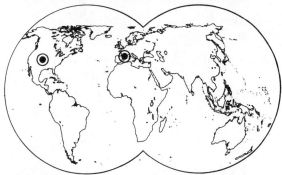

An expert in climbing and photography, giving a vivid description of the Alps, and of driving to Santiago, as well as cheap travel in the United States

Known as a writer by the name of her third husband, Elizabeth (née Hawkins-Whitshed) (1861-1934), had two other married names, Burnaby and Main. She figures as an intrepid woman climber in both Mary Russell's *The Blessings of a Good Thick Skirt* (1988) and Maria Aitken's *'A Girdle round the Earth'* (1987). Elizabeth's autobiography *Day In, Day Out* (1928), tells us that she spent her childhood in Killincarrick House, Greystones, Co. Wicklow. Her paternal great-grandfather was Irish and also her mother. When her mother was widowed Elizabeth became a Ward in Chancery. She used to spent a few months annually in England with her father's relatives. Aged seventeen she married Fred Burnaby, twenty years her senior, who died five years later. She then married an English doctor, J.F. Main, and settled in San Moritz, becoming expert at snow photography upon which she produced a textbook. She took up mountaineering and skating and wrote guide books on Spain and Italy.

Mary Russell writes of this period: 'By the time Elizabeth Burnaby arrived in the Alps in 1880 women were finding themselves faced with Hobson's Choice. If they conformed to the conventions of the time, they were likely never to travel at all; if on the other hand they appeared too spirited in their approach to climbing they risked the danger of being labelled a New Woman – a terrible thing to happen to a well brought up young lady...' So Elizabeth had to fight the disapproval of her family, and scandal in her social circle. Unable to wear breeches in public, she wore them beneath her skirt. Once she hid her skirt beneath a boulder and it was carried away by an avalanche. It is difficult to imagine nowadays how shocking it was for a woman to walk

Elizabeth Le Blond. left, with her mask and goggles in place, and above, climbing on Mont Blanc, where she wore breeches beneath her skirt and removed the latter on the higher stretches.

about in knickerbockers!

Elizabeth's second husband was killed on the expedition for the relief of General Gordon in Khartoum, after which she settled in France, still climbing, and then married Aubrey Le Blond, travelling with him to Russia, China and Korea. During the 1914 war she worked as a nurse in Dieppe, and lectured to troops on her climbing career, for in 1907 she had become the first President of the Ladies' Alpine Club in London, a post she held all her life. During summers Elizabeth used to climb in Norway, where she went up over twenty unclimbed peaks.

Elizabeth Le Blond wrote seven books about her climbing experiences, apart from her early guide books. The following excerpt from *Cities and Sights of Spain: A handbook for tourists* (1904), tells us about Santiago:

— I have a great dislike to travelling by diligence, so with two friends I decided to take a private carriage to Santiago, and keep it there till our return. The owner asked us 280 pesetas for the three days, but eventually agreed to do it for 150, everything included. I am bound to say that he stuck to his bargain, and did not suggest a *pourboire* when we paid him off on our return to Coruña. He gave us a comfortable carriage and four horses.

When the carriage drove up it was closed. We asked the driver and another man, whom for some inscrutable reason he took with him to Santiago, to open it. They demurred. 'The ladies will be cold'. It was a cloudless day, the hottest for weeks. We still insisted. 'It is impossible, it does not open'. 'Then get us a carriage which does'. By this time we had one of those orderly and deeply interested crowds round us which any prolonged episode causes to assemble in Spain. To shorten the story (which is a very long one), a blacksmith was fetched, half the carriage was demolished, the horses relieved of a great and superfluous weight, the crowd satisfied, and the driver obliged to confess that we were in the right.

Half an hour late, at 10.30, we started. I may say here, for the convenience of readers, that we took 8½ hours to reach Santiago, which included a 1½ hour rest.

The drive is a delightful one. The road mounts steadily till it overlooks a long narrow fiord. A railway bridge was being constructed here, I suppose for the new line to Ferrol. Looking back, there is a charming view of Coruña, crowned with its famous lighthouse.

We soon met one of the creaking carts, so common in Portugal, about which I had often read. First a sound like the distant whistle of a steamer was borne to our ears. As it approached it took more and more of the pureness of a sustained note of music, now and then adding the upper octave. But when it passed us it sounded like a saw mill at work, and how either the oxen who draw it or the peasants who walk by it can tolerate so ear-splitting a noise, I cannot understand. The wheels are nearly solid, and entirely of wood, keyed on to the axle, which itself revolves in wooden bearings; thus the sound is caused by the friction of wood on wood. We passed many little buildings, like tiny chapels, with a cross at one end and a miniature bell-cote at the other, as we drove along. The first we saw was of stone, and larger than most. I asked the driver if it was a chapel. He laughed until he nearly overbalanced. 'No,' he said, 'it is for storing the food for the animals.'

Great mimosa trees and camellias are seen here and there. By the road are the industrious road menders, a pleasant class to speak to. They wear a very smart costume, consisting of a black coat with violet facings and gilt buttons and a violet stripe down the trousers, a large felt hat, and a brass plate in front of the latter giving their number and occupation. The peasants are picturesquely attired about here. They are dressed in white coats braided with black and having gilt buttons, red waistcoats, white knee breeches and white stockings. All reply courteously to the 'good day' which it is a pleasure to wish them.

The road continues to rise. The vegetation becomes less southern. The hedges are lined with violets and primroses. We gallop up the shorter hills and go a steady pace on the level. A long ascent where it is pleasant to walk brings us over breezy downs to the highest point of our journey. Here the horses drink from a tank by the wayside. We halt a short time at a village further on. A tall and battered cross stands in a little plaza. Does it mark a resting-place of pilgrims to Santiago? Centuries ago they came barefoot over the hills from Coruña, and thousands and thousands of devout wayfarers must have wearily passed along the track. Now there is one of the finest roads in Europe, and a bicyclist looks on the run as an easy day's ride.

At half past three o'clock we halted at the village of Ordenes for lunch, and to rest the horses. A tiny inn with a pleasant balcony offered hospitality. We had brought our food from Coruña and ate it leisurely as we watched the life going forward in the street below. The landlady, a pretty, tall, slight woman, went backwards and forwards to the fountain. The buckets in which the peasants in this part of Spain carry water are curiously and very practically shaped. I got a photograph of the lady on one of her return journeys.

A tip for monopolising the balcony and for the use we had made of one of her rooms for tidying ourselves, brought a look of amazement to the face of our hostess. What could our money be for?

Pigs abound everywhere and are fat and well cared for. The children looked fresh and rosy, the people well clad. Where is this great poverty of Spain? We could not find it.

It was dark as we approached Santiago. We did not say much but I think no one can enter it without a feeling of awe.... Early the next morning we started off through the narrow streets for the great square. I know few Cathedrals which are so imposingly surrounded as this famous church, itself a most majestic monumental pile. Though the style of these buildings does not appeal to me personally, I feel I cannot criticise them. All is so overwhelmingly solemn. —

More typical of Elizabeth, however, is her writing about mountaineering, such as the following passage from *Adventures on the Roof of the World* (1904), which is illustrated by her own photographs.

She had set out from a little inn in the Trift Valley, above Zermatt, at 4 a.m. on 14th September, 1895:

— The party consisted of my two guides, Joseph and Roman Imboden, father and son, and myself, and our idea was to cross the fine peak of the Rothhorn, 13,855 feet high, from Zermatt to Zinal. I had been up that mountain before, and so, on many previous occasions, had Imboden, but, oddly enough, he had never been down the other side. Roman, however, had once or twice made the traverse, and, in any case, we knew quite enough about the route from hearsay to feel sure we could hit it off even without Roman's experience.

Some fresh snow had fallen a few days previously and the shabby part of the Rothhorn on the north side was unpleasantly white, besides which there was a strong and bitterly cold wind. We pretty well abandoned all idea of getting down on the other side when we saw how unfavourably things were turning out, and though I felt greatly disappointed I never have and never would urge a guide in whom I have confidence to undertake what he considers imprudent. We left the matter open till the last minute, however, and took both the knapsacks to the top, where we arrived at 9.15.

Warming ourselves in a sunny and sheltered corner of the by no means inhospitable summit, we had some food and a pleasant rest. I cannot say if the meal and the cheering effects of the sunshine made things look different, but it is a fact that after perhaps, an hour's halt, Imboden shouldered his knapsack and remarked to me, 'Come along, ma'am, as far as the end of the ridge; we will just have a look'. Hope awakened in me, and scrambling to my feet, I followed him. The wind was certainly high; I had difficulty even on those easy rocks in keeping my footing; how, I wondered, should we manage when the real climbing began? I had read of an *arête* of rock, little broader than one of the blunt knives we had used at breakfast, and the idea of passing along it with a shrieking gale trying to tear us from our perch was not alluring. Presently we reached the spot where one quits the gentle slope and comparatively broad ridge, and embarks on the profile of a slender and precipitous face of rock, with nearly vertical forehead and small and infrequent cracks for hands and feet. We were going to do more than look at it, apparently; we were about to descend it, for without any further remark Imboden began to get ready, letting Roman pass ahead. Taking hold of the rope between his son and himself he told me to stand aside while he gradually paid it out as Roman went down. The first yard or two consisted of slabs, set at a high angle. Then the ridge abruptly curved over and one saw nothing but air till the eye rested on the glacier thousands of feet below.

In a few minutes Roman had disappeared, and the steady paying out of the rope alone indicated that he was climbing downwards. After a time he reached almost the end of his tether of about 30 feet – for we were on a very long rope – and his father called out, 'Rope up!' 'Let the lady come to the edge and give me a little more,' came a voice from far down. Putting the final loop into my hand and bidding me sit down, Imboden held me hard by the cord behind until the tautness of the piece between Roman and me showed it was time to be moving. I then advanced very cautiously to what seemed like the edge of the world. Turning round with my face to the rock I had my first glance below. Far down was the top of Roman's hat, and as he saw the advancing soles of my boots he grinned with appreciation, feeling that now we really were embarked on the enterprise. 'There's a good place down here, ma'am, come along!' he called up, with one toe on a ledge three inches wide, two fingers thrust into a crack, and the rope held out of his way by being put, the remark concluded, between his teeth.

I had no doubt it was a nice place when one got there, but meanwhile I had to make the best use I could of my eyes to find a suitable assortment of hand and foot holes. Soon I, too, was clinging to the face of the precipice, and Imboden was left above out of sight and before long almost out of hearing.

The wind here was far less trying as we were sheltered by the topmost pinnacle of the mountain. To me the feeling of danger from a gale on a rock peak is due even more to the difficulty of hearing what one's companions are saying than to the risk of one's balance being upset. It is extremely disconcerting, when a climber, descending steep rocks and anxious to make a long but perhaps an easy step downwards to good footholds, calls for more rope, and is promptly swung clear out into space by an invisible guide above, who has misunderstood his orders. When a party is accustomed to work together, this sort of thing seldom happens, still it makes all the difference in the pleasure of negotiating difficult rocks if the air is calm.

Our only trouble now was owing to the fresh snow, but this had partially consolidated, and we got down steadily and safely, gradually leaving behind the cold wind which whistled amongst the crags above.

It was early in the day, and we went slowly, stopping once or twice to photograph where warm and sheltered resting places of comfortable proportions tempted us to linger. The rocky knife edge was unpleasantly sharp for the arms bent over it, but useful ledges down the side helped to distribute the weight and amuse and occupy the mind. When we finally reached the end of the rocks, and had nothing but snow between us and the Mountet Hut, we considered ourselves as good as there, and made a long halt on the last stones.

We were wrong, however. 'My boy, I will go ahead now,' remarked Imboden, stepping off into the snow. He went a few paces, and then looked first all round him and lastly at us. 'Blue ice,' he muttered, with intense disgust. 'Blue ice right down to the bottom!' We shrugged our shoulders; Imboden was ahead doing the work; we could afford to be philosophical. I should not like to say how many strokes of the axe each step required, but the slope was steep, a slip could not be risked, and Imboden hewed out great footholds in the slippery wall. After this had gone on for some time he paused. 'Upon my word,' remarked he, 'it will take us the rest of the day to get down at this rate! I shall try another way.' So we turned and remounted the slope, and sitting down once more on the stones, Imboden traced out a possible route down the face of the mountain, bearing diagonally across it. It looked dullish; besides, thought I, after all, we don't particularly want to go to Zinal. Roman put into words what, I think, sprang simultaneously into both our minds. 'Let us go back to Zermatt over the top of the Rotthorn again!' 'Yes, let us do that!' I exclaimed.

Imboden gazed from one to the other of us in amazement. 'Go back over the top of the Rotthorn?' he repeated, 'Why, we should simply be out all night!' Roman didn't answer, but his eyes wandered persistently up the *arête*. His father now began to calculate, and by some strange process of arithmetic he came to the conclusion that if we hurried very much it was just possible that we might get off the difficult part of the peak before night overtook us. Still, he was far from reconciled to the idea, while every moment Roman and I liked it better. Imboden saw how keen we were, and presently exclaimed; ''Well, I'll go if you both want it, but we must be quick; if we spend the night on the top of the Rotthorn and a storm comes on, we may simply lose our lives!'

There was no need, however, to tell Roman to be quick. He was told off to lead, and I followed, with Imboden last. The memory of that ascent has remained in my mind as a confused dream. Every scrap of my attention was given to holding on and pulling myself upwards, never pausing, except in the very worst places, to see what either of the guides was doing, and with every feet and handhold fresh in my memory, I was full of a delightful sense of security which muscles in first class condition and complete absence of any sensation of fatigue fully justified. We rose at an incredible pace, and after an hour and twenty-five minutes of splendid exercise, we threw ourselves once more on the flat little top of the Rotthorn. We had now only the descent by the ordinary route between us and Zermatt, and this seemed a small matter compared to what we had accomplished that day. —

In her autobiography *Day in, Day out* (1928), Elizabeth Le Blond gives advice from her later experience travelling in the United States:

— Hotel charges in New York are both higher and lower than in London. If one knows the ropes it is possible to obtain excellent accommodation in New York in a central position for considerably less than similar accommodation would cost in London. It is also easy to pay very much more than at home. But though I have stayed at various hotels in New York, on other occasions I have put up at the National Arts Club, thanks to an introduction from the late Mr John Lane. This Club is in Gramercy Park and several artists and others reside there permanently. The building looks out on a quiet, tree-filled square that might be in the heart of a sleepy Cathedral town in England and the atmosphere within the Club is full of repose.

I feel sure that there must be many who would like to pay at least one visit to the United States but who never entertain the idea because they are certain they could not afford it. There I think it may be helpful if I give some practical information derived from my own experience.

First of all, as to the best time of year to travel. Although steamer fares are higher, it is less expensive to tour in summer than in winter, for round railway tickets at exactly half fare may then be had. A good example of a round ticket was that which I took in 1926. It started at Quebec and followed the Canadian Pacific Railway to Vancouver, allowing halts everywhere without any formality. From Vancouver I crossed to Victoria and thence to Seattle. From there I went down the coast by train to San Francisco, which was my farthest southerly point, and I returned to the east via Salt Lake City, the Denver and Rio Grande line (the highest broad-gauge railway in the world), Colorado Springs and, finally, via Chicago to New York. With this ticket I covered 7000 miles or more and it cost £32. Sleeping berths were extra and about £1 a night must be estimated for them. In all I spent nine nights in the train. The inclusive cost of my trip, which lasted from July 27th when I sailed on 'The Empress of France' until October 4th when I landed in London from the 'Minnetonka', was £209. This included a trip to the Yosemite from San Francisco.

As my son's house in Southern California was let for the summer, I stayed in hotels all the time, and though some were quiet country hostelries, as at Santa Cruz, others were large hotels, the best available, such as the Château at Quebec and the Whitcomb at San Francisco. Rooms are usually expensive and food just the contrary. For instance, lunch at the Whitcomb was 50 cents, equivalent to about two shillings, and dinner 75 cents, or three shillings. Not many courses were supplied but the food was excellently cooked and abundant. If a traveller knows the ropes he can often have all he wants as regards board and lodging for considerably less in the Far West than similar accommodation and food in England. And above all he will find nearly always scrupulous cleanliness and the greatest civility. I feel sure that no woman who has travelled alone in the United States can feel anything but gratitude for all the kindness she is sure to meet with. —

KATHERINE EVERETT

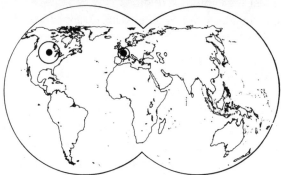

Encounters with bears in Canada, the honeymoon from Hell, and a glimpse of the demi-monde

Katherine Everett (née Herbert) (1872-1963), daughter of Henry Herbert of Cahirnane House, Killarney, who also owned Muckross, wrote an interesting autobiography, *Bricks and Flowers, Memoirs* (1949) which describes her travels.

As a young woman while studying at the Slade art school, Katherine was offered a six months trip to America by an aunt. After some hesitation as to whether she should interrupt her studies, in *Bricks and Flowers* she writes:

— A week later we were on the liner *Lusitania*. How my life does change! It seems to go suddenly from one extreme to another. So short a time ago I thought of little except of how to express the human form, and had Aurelia's muddled home as a background; now here I was with waiters and stewards rushing about, crowds everywhere, music playing, bugles sounding, lavish tasteless decoration all round, and much time spent in trying to eat quantities of food.

We could spend the daylight hours playing games or listening to an American reading 'Uncle Remus'. In the evening we were expected to attend dances, concerts or lectures, and finally on the last night sing 'Auld Lang Syne' while crossing hands with complete strangers.

Our stay in New York remains a confused blur in my mind. My aunt had many friends, who were so kind and hospitable they made us feel we would be welcome to spend the rest of our lives in their homes, but we both wanted to get away from this tiring, exciting town, where from luncheon time till the small hours we were taken from place to place. In one super-magnificent mansion I observed some little gilt chairs with box-like seats made of glass, through which you could see jewel-framed miniatures and gold ornaments. I pictured a heavy guest sitting on one of these chairs and finding his behind suddenly encrusted with splintered glass, diamonds, pearls and filigree gold.

I also remember with gratitude finding in my bedroom a large bunch of red roses with stems eighteen inches long, with a card attached on which was written, 'From one American in the name of many others who have seen and loved Killarney'.

After a final party we got away to Montreal, breaking the journey to see the Niagara Falls. There we behaved as tourists should, and allowed the determined attendant to dress us in mackintoshes and hand us over to a relentless guide, who insisted upon our being photographed, once under a wall of water and again emerging through a mist of spray. The resulting pictures made us both look slightly cretinous, but the guide, after a prolonged examination, remarked, 'Not as stoopefied as some'.

We reached Montreal in bitterly cold weather, and my dear aunt immediately fitted us both out in raccoon fur coats, in which we looked like the native bears and were just as well protected.

We had an introduction to Mr Hosmer, the head of the Cable Company, and made friends with him and with other people with whom we had a link and as usual met with much kindness and hospitality.

Montreal was our starting point for the long journey across Canada, and when we left we were seen off with flowers, fruit and chocolates ... The train felt like a temporary home, going slowly over that vast prairie, pausing every evening for twenty minutes to allow us to take exercise on the platform and see a rather theatrical Red Indian – or someone dressed like one – trying to sell souvenirs. The approach to the Rocky Mountains was inspiring after days of watching waving grass and flat plains, and I was allowed to travel over the pass in the cab of the engine-driver, who told me all the wonders of this line and the stupendous difficulties overcome in crossing so great a range of mountains. As one looked down the immense ravines below us, these difficulties were not hard to imagine.

On reaching British Columbia we left this train in order to see more of that most attractive country, and also to meet an old friend of my aunt's, who as the head of a large electrical engineering scheme was supervising the construction of a dam. First we had to take a sleigh and drive to a lake, a great sheet of water where we picked up a paddle-boat which went chuffing along from one primitive landing-place to another. Occasionally there would be a solitary passenger to take on board, more often a barrel of something or a package to be picked up. The lake was surrounded with snow mountains and pine-trees came down to the water's edge. It was a lovely scene, silent and empty and everything sparkled like a frosted Christmas card.

Katherine Everett and her son Henry

Towards evening we came to a slightly larger landing-place, from which a little mountain train was to take us up to the camp. It was a funny-looking little train. The engine was very small and could draw only two carriages, one open like a cattle-truck and the other, which we were to occupy, upholstered in faded red plush. We were told this train had been bought secondhand in three separate lots and that our carriage had been made originally for Brigham Young's wives. The engine would puff along for a few miles and then stop to be fed with wood, until finally it stopped intentionally for us to get out. It was a brilliant, moonlit night and we could hear the rushing river nearby and the sighing of the wind in the pine trees. Half a dozen men were waiting for us and helped us to scramble on to the rough verge ...

We spent ten wonderful days at the camp. The country was lovely and we picknicked out of door. I went about on snowshoes, often with a Scottish engineer and a sad man who told me tales of his hard life here. He was surveying the area and one day, when taking a sight, he clutched my arm saying, 'Quiet – look!' and just ahead of us was a big brown bear with a baby bear at her side.

'Don't move,' he whispered. 'I won't be long getting my rifle. She won't hurt you but if you move she'll take her cub away.'

The bear heard him as he went quickly down the hill and standing up on her hind legs and extending her front paw, she drew her baby to her side. It was such a maternal gesture, so like a fond human mother putting her arms round her child, that it seemed murder to shoot either of them, and though rather frightened to do so, I moved, and immediately the bear shuffled off, heading the baby in front of her. The engineer was disappointed and said in his pessimistic way, 'My luck always is out. I'd have made a fine rug of the old one and the young one would have been tender eating'.

Our next stay was at a mining camp where we put up at a primitive hotel, surrounded by shacks and huts, with snow mountains all round. Escorted by friendly guides, I went down mines, saw others now disused, their machinery rusting, and heard all the talk of the various assays of ore from the shafts that were being worked. The mining business seemed dishonest. A prospectus would be sent out with glowing acounts of the profits which might be expected from some mine which the men on the spot knew had no future, while some of the good ones were not put on the market, but held by groups in the know. To me it was a new adventure and full of excitement. Standing in a rough crate and holding on to a rope, I went down a mine, and was then allowed to work a compressed-air drill. The rock I cut was collected, and later on I was given a pin-point of gold and told I had mined it, which I doubted, but pretended to believe. —

When she married Herbert Everett the pair had an unusual honeymoon:

— Herbert loved the sea and believed he would do good work making a voyage in a sailing ship. I was sure he could and thought the idea exciting, so we arranged for a passage to Australia on a 700 ton barque.

I took with me a number of old-fashioned books, thinking that they would fill the many gaps in my education and that I should have plenty of time to master them. I also provided two large sacks of onions, with vague ideas of averting scurvy, a sack of wholemeal flour, a kettle and spirit lamp and plenty of tea. In addition, not realizing what sea-water and exposure would do to them, I took materials to make large embroidered curtains.

We went on board on a fine evening in early June, and a tug took us down the river, past barges and ships and past Greenwich, looking like an eighteenth-century print in a golden mist and backed by stately trees....At dusk, clear of the land, this tug cast off, and shouts of farewell were drowned in the rattle of the sheets as sails were hoisted and our small barque gently heeled over to the pull of the wind. Our journey had begun. We were to have one hundred and seventeen days of it with no possible hope of escape, no possibility of acquiring anything beyond what we had – not so much as a postage stamp - and with no sight of land but for a distant view of Tristan da Cunha, looking no large than a bee's wing on the horizon. Variety we had, but it came from the elements: storm, hurricane, rain – tropical or merely enveloping and penetrating – cold, heat and calm, which, in an unfortunate moment, I said I liked. The utter horror with which this avowal was received was genuine and when we stuck for a week, helpless and motionless, in the neighbourhood of the equator, in an atmosphere like hot porridge, I was not allowed to forget my expressed liking.

I had walked onto the ship carrying my kettle and spirit lamp, both of which the captain removed, saying, 'On my ship no lamps or lights are allowed'.

'What do you do when it gets dark?'

'Sit in it or go to bed.'

And so it turned out. We had our first meal with the captain and his wife, who was the only individual other than the crew on the ship. Both were elderly Liverpool people, and were not a nice couple. He had started before the mast, and was surly and gross. She was of the same type, and although she had voyaged in her husband's tramps to various parts of the world, she knew nothing but the quality of the fare at the nearest eating-house. Her large, red face would expand when speaking of chops and steaks and liver.

The food that first day, served by a barefoot boy, was just edible, but the mate, who came in as soon as the captain finished, explained, 'It's all first rate now, but wait till you get the condemned stuff. The Old Man puts the all right in front for the Inspector to see and the rest he gets on the cheap and makes his bit. You wait, you'll find out soon enough'.

I liked the mate, who was a middle-aged, small, dark working class man with a master's ticket, very efficient, having to serve for his living under an old man for whom he had the utmost contempt.

'Driving his ship on dead reckoning, the old blighter! Half the time he's out on her position,' he would explain.

The mate amused himself by trying to frighten me.

'She's a rotten old tub anyway, and you know he's out to lose her, for she's been through her third survey, and the owners reckon the insurance would pay them better than selling her abroad.'

'Really? How odd!'

'He's done it before for them, and that's why they employ him. He got his ticket suspended over that other one, and was a year ashore. He put her down nice and handy on a low reef off Tasmania, where he and the crew could get away while she broke up slowly.'

Whether the ship was really destined to this end I cannot say, but on the voyage subsequent to ours, under the same captain, she was lost with all hands off the coast of Tasmania. Evidently the spot was not so handy.

I had not long to wait before verifying the mate's warning about the food. It was revolting. The large tin of tea brought in at breakfast was a curious metallic black colour and tasted as I should imagine cuttle fish ink must taste. As it was made at five in the morning and served at eight, the pot seemed able to add its own tinny flavour. When I asked for hot water I sensed for the first time the old woman's antagonistic feelings towards me, for she snorted and said something that sounded like 'la-di-da'. Bacon, swimming with grease, was brought in, and Herbert whispered: 'I wouldn't take it, it's very rank' ...

The other meals were of the same character, the dishes having names I had not heard before. 'Strike-me-blind' was a rice pudding of a quality more suitable for ammunition than for eating. 'Dogsbody' was pale, greasy suet with bits of high meat inserted. 'Crackerjack' was ship's biscuits, freely seasoned with weevils, pounded in a canvas bag with a belaying pin and soaked with hot water and pea flour. 'Slathery Jack' was a mould of such glue-like consistency that once it was bitten into, one's teeth couldn't part. The mate ate little and abused the food, but the captain and his wife ate with gluttony and no manners. I gave up the contest and throughout those months lived on a little tinned milk and hot water, wholemeal bread and boiled onions, and occasionally some burnt and lumpy porridge.

Having vaguely thought of my voyage to America when agreeing to this one, I found the contrast painful....Thinking of apples made one's mouth water too much and once, longing for tea, scones and real butter and jam, I found myself on the verge of tears....

There were two bunks in my cabin, one narrow with high sides like a coffin, and the upper one wider, with no sides, like a large tea tray and unsafe in heavy weather. In the lower bunk not only was it difficult to bend one's knees or avoid being bruised, but there was a rat which I called Richard, who gnawed and gnawed close to my neck, and then I could hear him scurry down the side to start near my toes. I begged the mate to get rid of him, but he said he couldn't, adding, 'He'll get out all right, and if you're asleep he'll eat the soles of your feet'.

He lent me a sheath-knife, but I never used it on Richard. When he sounded too near I climbed to the tea tray, risking being flung to the floor. To add to this, when the ship rolled there was a frightening banging in the hold, then for a few seconds a rumble like distant thunder, and then thud against the side, pause, rumble and thud again. The mate explained that this was an agricultural machine that had broken loose in the hold.

'The Old Man won't let me try to fix it, and perhaps I couldn't. There's a lot of cargo down there, as like as not she'll get a hole stove in her side. Christ! I'll be glad to get out of this death-trap!' —

After their 117 days at sea, they continued from Hobart to Sydney on a liner. It did not sound a very auspicious honeymoon! And indeed Katherine's marriage broke up when the 1914 war began. She returned to Ireland to nurse in Mercer's Hospital, Dublin, after first being a VAD in London. With her two young sons she next worked as a gardener/companion to someone in the New Forest, Hampshire. After that she returned to Ireland to live in a house provided by Olive Ardilaun. Later in life she travelled on the Continent. Evidently speaking good French, she gives us an amusing vignette in *Bricks and Flowers* about a woman she met in France:

— On this second visit to Annecy with my grown-up son we stayed in a small hotel near the lake, which was filled with French families of humble class, among them being a tall, good-looking woman at whom they all looked askance, never speaking to her. One day as I walked alone in the woods on the hillside I came on a sunlit glade where this girl was lying full length, wearing no clothes except for a filmy scarf, making a picture Titian might have painted. Seeing I was not shocked, she drew herself up on her elbow, smiling, completely without self-consciousness.

'Madame would rest herself?' she indicated the mossy ground.

'You are on holiday?' I asked.

'Yes, I and my friend who has taken the villa on the other side of the lake and placed me here for a change from Paris. I visit him when he sends his auto for me. At this moment *je me tint les rhins*.'

I wondered what she was exactly, and as though reading my thoughts, she told me something of her story just as people will to complete strangers when they are lonely.

'I began life with nothing – no family, no money, hardly any education, nothing but work and poverty before me. And then I met my first friend. He was good and I belonged to him for five years.'

'You could not have married him?'

'But no, Madame, that could not enter at all. He was married with a family but he needed the solace I could give him, and he did so much for me, giving me lessons in literature and the art of dress and deportment. He also taught me to save, telling me that of all he gave me I was to put something away. "Just a little every week," he would say, "and it mounts and means safety for you, my child."

'Then his business took him to South America, and my next friend was different – young and gay, but not serious, wanting too much drinking, dancing and spending, so I left him. Now I am settled seven years with my present friend and all goes well. When we part I have a *dot* if I should choose marriage, or start business in lingerie and hats. For, you see, I am a serious business woman – not like those "cocottes", who have no thought for the future.'

'What happens to them in the end?' I asked.

'If they live, the "Commune" keeps them and makes them occupy themselves with the care of the public lavatories.' She spoke in a tone of contempt, adding, 'They pay for not having foresight and discretion'.

This odd interview has remained in my mind, partly I think because I had never known anyone so frank about her particular profession and so French in her view that her life had been fortunate, well-balanced and provident.

When we walked back to the hotel together I was amused on meeting a stout couple to notice the man's furtive, admiring glance at my companion in her smart clothes, and the malevolent, angry look in his wife's beady, dark eyes. Nor was I surprised when that afternoon, my sun-bathing friend having been called for in a fine motor car, this woman sidled up to me and said: 'Madame surely does not know how the person she was walking with occupies herself?' Her little eyes snapped avid enquiry.

'That is not my affair. I found her so well-mannered and so good-looking,' I answered and left her. —

(ETHEL) BEATRICE GRIMSHAW

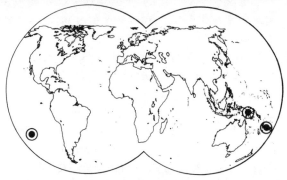

A woman who devoted her life to the South Sea islands of the Pacific

Books about adventurous women have all neglected Beatrice (1871-1953), third daughter of Nicholas Grimshaw, of Cloona, County Antrim, educated in Belfast, London and Caen. This remarkable Irishwoman deserves a biography. Being so little known she is considered at some length here.

In her early twenties Beatrice moved with her family to Dublin and lived on the ground floor of 6 Fitzgibbon Street, working as a journalist. She writes in her autobiography *Isles of Adventure* (1930) about her early dreams. Her early career consisted of teaching 'others and older people their jobs'. She was 'very young and rather brazen and full of the "beans" that go with a good muscular system,' for she soon, with five hours to spare, obtained the women's world 24 hour cycling record. Having no husband or brother to escort her she had to ride through the dark alone (no other man would have been respectable) with food, wearing an ankle length skirt. From 8 a.m. on she was paced by various friends.

As a result of this exploit she became sub-editor of a sporting paper, and later editor of Dublin's *Social Review*. Journalism in Dublin, she wrote, was then a 'gay scramble'. Female careerists, like herself, could be daring, but within 'iron limits'. Such women had bicycles and rode in bloomers. 'Much was made and said of latchkeys, but one lived with respectable widows, and the chaperon was never absent, even from bicycle clubs famous for hard riding. "Fast" was a word at which everyone trembled, unless it applied to the speed of your wheels,' but Beatrice did not care about being labelled a 'New Woman'.

From an early age Beatrice had dreamed of the South Sea islands. Life in Dublin was not challenging enough for her, and also being tired of being in the 'top drawer', she moved to London to work as a freelance journalist. She next had the excellent idea of offering press coverage to shipping companies in exchange for her passage. Various companies accepted her offer, though had they not she was still determined to travel as a stewardess, as a paid companion, or at her own expense third class.

She left for Tahiti in 1906 and the initial six months round the world expanded like 'the magic tent in the *Arabian Nights*' until in the end it covered all her life and she wrote eighteen books about it.

Beatrice describes the call of travel in her book, *In the Strange South Seas* (1907), illustrated by her own photographs: 'Love is not stronger than that call – let sweetheartless girls left alone, and the man of cities who has loved the woman of the wandering foot, give bitter witness. Death is not stronger – those who follow the call must defy him over and over again. Pride of country, love of home, delight in well-known faces and kindly hearts that understand, the ease of the old and well-tried ways, the prick of ordinary ambitions hungering for the showy prizes that every one may see – these are but as dead leaves blown before the wind, when the far-off countries cry across the seas,' and she dedicated the book to those who could not go, to the left behinds, also to those who will never forget while 'spiring masts stand thick against blue skies, and keen salt winds wake madness in the brain.'

Beatrice later travelled with a revolver round her waist in a decorous, but detachable, riding habit. The islands, she writes, 'are not for the weakling, for the lazy, the intemperate, the sensual. They are not for the man who dislikes civilisation because it asks too much of him. The islands will ask more; they will demand that he stand on his own feet, keep himself up without leaning on the shoulders of his neighbours, make his own code and stick to it without being forced to do so by anyone else. A man who cannot get on well in cities or in settled countries, will not get on in the Pacific world, unless his failure was due to being too big, not too small for his surroundings.'

In 1909 Beatrice was diving for pleasure in the Torres Straits. Later she ran a coffee plantation for several years in Papua New Guinea. She went diamond prospecting, and in 1923 and 1926 was the first white woman to go up the Sepik and Fly rivers.

Beatrice earned her living in two ways, by writing some thirty popular romantic novels, often with South Sea island or Papuan settings, and by her journalism, published by *Wide World Magazine, The National Geographic Magazine*, and in the house journals of shipping companies. She was also always on the lookout for opportunities for investment which she could recommend to would-be settlers. 'To find out, as far as possible, what were the prospects for settlers in some of the principal Pacific islands, was the main object of my journey,' for this practical side of Pacific life had received little attention from previous writers. She launched herself with *In the Strange South Seas*, describing visits to eight islands of the Cook archipelago, all annexed to New Zealand in 1900. She lists the products of the Cook islands and prices for leases of land. 'The young would-be planter should have at least £500 to start on, exclusive of passage money.' Copra was the safest investment. The cost of clearing and planting the land was about £5 an acre. In seven years returns would begin to come in and profits should be £5 for every acre of trees. Meantime bananas could be grown on the same land to yield a quicker return. Coconut trees bear for sixty years or more and a planter could live quite respectably on fifty pounds a year.

Her travelling was not comfortable. Beatrice complains of the cockroaches, which spoil her tea, eat her dresses, fly into her hair and climb into her berth at sea. She describes Raratonga, which then had a population of 1,900. Tuberculosis and other diseases were common. The queen of the island lives very simply with her pet turtle, she is over six feet tall, dignified and kindly. Though uncrowned she is as reverenced as in the old days before missions came, when the islanders had been cannibals. The queen was believed to still possess 'mana', the magic power of second sight, which brought good or evil luck, and could slay at will.

Beatrice was the first white woman to climb the 3,000 foot mountain on Raratonga. This took fourteen hours, with two others, 'working as hard as white ants'. She also went on bathing picnics with the native women. She describes housekeeping in the South Sea islands, not as practised by government officials, but how the settlers lived in all the islands she visited. Settlers dined at midday, kept few servants or none, and lived simply. Clothing was mostly handmade, the native girls married aged thirteen, so the only servants were boys or men, who got paid between five and ten shillings a week. Settlers grew their own food, taro and yam. They picked wild chillies, pineapples and paw-paw. Meat was usually tinned unless a turtle was caught which could feed a large household for a week, soup being made from the flippers. She describes the method of constructing houses, and insects, such as the stick insect, to be found on almost every coconut tree, which smells bad and squirts a fetid fluid into the eyes of a would-be handler.

Beatrice took passage in 'Duchess', a 175 ton three-masted topsail schooner with three white and eight islandmen crew. In this ship she visited the outer islands of the Cook group. The ship was her home for over four months. She does not advise the elderly tourist to emulate her, but the true traveller 'who wanders for the joy of wandering'. The cabin floor was the same size as her smallest flat box, and stank of oil and ancient copra. She was seasick for two days and then recovered. On Mitiaro island, with a population of over a thousand, no white woman had previously been seen.

They sailed on to Aitutaki, passing through a narrow passage in the reef in the ship's boat. Beatrice goes in a whale boat whose crew row out to some of the uninhabited islands within the lagoon several miles out:

— But the islets! If Raratonga was the realisation of a childish dream, this was the embodiment of a vision of fairyland. There can surely be nothing on earth more lovely than the islet constellation enclosed by Aitutaki reef. The water, shallow, sun-jewelled, and spread over a bed of spotless coral sand, is coloured with a brilliance that is simply incredible. Emerald and jade and sapphire – yes, one expects these, in the hues of the tropic seas. But when it comes to whole tracts of glancing heliotrope and hyacinth, shot with unnamable shades of melted turquoise and silver, and all a-quiver with pulsations of flashing greens, for which there is no name in any language under the pallid northern or burning southern sun – then, the thing becomes indescribable ...

In the midst of this magical sea, rise the islets themselves – fairyland every one. Their little beaches are sparkling white, as only a coral beach can be; palm-trees, heavy-headed with their loads of huge green nuts, cluster thick along the shores; coral-trees drop their blood-red flowers into the glass-like water of the lagoon; ripe oranges swing their glowing lamps among the darker green of the woods that rise behind. Big white clams with goffered shells, each holding meat enough for one man's dinner, gleam along the edges of the shore; large, long-legged crabs wander rustling and rattling among the stones. The murmur of the barrier reef is very far away; its thin white line of foam gleams out a long way off, under a low horizon, sky shot strangely with lilac blue – a lonely, lovely, exquisite place, the like of which one might seek the world all over, and never find again.

We landed on the sand, and I set about exploring, while the men knocked down coconuts, and squatted in the shade to drink them, and suck fresh oranges. The island on which we had landed was one of the smaller ones, not more than an acre or two in extent. It rose to a high point in the centre, and was so thickly wooded all over, that I could hardly make my way through. There was no sign of life or habitation, and the ripe fruit was everywhere rotting on the ground ...

We did not get to the other islands that day, partly because I wasted so much time looking for shells, and partly because the largest were still some miles away, and the wind was stronger than ever. One, I heard, had ground enough for a paying plantation, and was already fairly well supplied with coconuts. All are perfectly healthy and free from fevers of any kind, and though mosquitoes are present in rather large numbers, careful clearing of their breeding grounds would in time drive them away. —

The next island is Mangaia, surrounded by an unbroken reef which has to be jumped over in a dug-out canoe on the crest of a wave. The islanders, who used to be fierce cannibals, have become reserved and independent. There are 2,000 islanders, a handful of whites and no land for rent to settlers. On the following island, Atiu, the natives are less amiable, there is only one white man, and plenty of land to let, but there is no resident missionary and the people are primitive.

They sail on to three more islands, Mauke, Manuwai and Takutea. Beatrice sleeps 'with one eye open' and her revolver nearby, 'for there are incidents of my wanderings that I have not told, and only those who know the Eastern Pacific may guess at them'! She also feared shipwreck on a coral reef, but she accepted 'rough fare, hard lodging and long fatigue' for that is the rule of island life, 'the pungent taste of danger, now and then, gratefully slaking some deep, half-conscious thirst derived from fiercer centuries; the sight of many lands and many peoples – these, and other pictures, painted themselves among the little gold stars swept by the rocking masts, as I lay, remembering'.

So they sailed on to Mauke and then Manuwai, in 1904 a penal settlement and copra plantation. There were two islands within the same lagoon and 'Duchess' was the only ship that ever called there. Beatrice, the first white woman to see these islands, gives a description of the coconut crab, mostly found on barren coral islands where only coconut palms grow. Coloured red and blue, they have thirty inch long lobster-like bodies, one large and one small claw. The large claw can break a man's ankle bone, or a coconut. The crabs live in burrows and emerge at night. The natives had a special way of catching these crabs as they descend the trees.

From now on the captain gave Beatrice a trick at the wheel each day. 'At night, the smallest slatting of sail upon the mast would start me out of my sleep with an uneasy fear that I was steering, and had let her get too close to the wind...' She also learned to lower the boats, and manage a sixteen foot oar when they were becalmed. She went up and down the ratlines wearing the flannel gymnasium dress she had brought for mountaineering excursions, taking photographs aloft whenever possible. 150 miles off Niué (Savage

Island) they ran by Beveridge Reef, wrongly charted according to the captain, hence the number of wrecks. He went aloft to sight the reef in rather poor weather, then took the boat out to survey the reef, while eight sharks cruised round 'Duchess'. The boat overturned with the captain and three men in her. Beatrice writes:

— What happened during the next half-hour has never been very clear in my memory. The wind kept rising, and the afternoon grew late and dark. The overturned boat, with the four heads visible about her keel, drifted helplessly in the trough of the seas, at the mercy of waves and sharks.... The wind screamed in the rigging, and drifts of foam flew up on deck, and the Maoris ran about and shouted, and got in each other's way, and tried to heave ropes, and missed, and tried to launch a boat under the mate's direction, and somehow did not – I cannot tell why. And right in the middle of the play, when we seemed to be making some attempt to bear down upon the drifting wreck, a grey old man who had come on with us from the Cook Islands, but had kept to his berth through illness most of the time, burst out on deck with an astonishing explosion of sea language, and told us that we were nearly on to the reef, which it seems everyone had forgotten! —

Beatrice goes to the top of the deck house to get out of the way, the old man orders a leadsman to take soundings, and they get away by an unpleasantly close shave, bear down on the boat, righted by this time and the men in it baling constantly, and salvage the captain.

The island of Niué then had 5,000 inhabitants of whom twenty were white traders. It was approached by a mere crack in the reef, and 'Duchess' called there twice a year, a mission steamer and another trade steamer once a year each. The island owned nothing larger than a whaler, had no telephones or doctors, so, said Beatrice: 'If you want to die there during the intervals between ships, you may do so unopposed'.

Beatrice fell in love with Niué's winsome little capital Alofi, and rented a two-roomed house with a verandah for two months. At least a thousand of the island's menfolk worked as labourers in Samoan plantations or in the guano pits of Malden island, or went to sea. Women were in the majority, and worked as stevedores, doing all the heavy work. Beatrice became friendly with a number of the women, and went swimming with them.

— The reef was a good way off, so we all struck out for that, when we came up panting and blowing from the dive. The girls gave me a fine exhibition of underwater swimming now and then, slipping easily underneath the gleaming surface, and disappearing from view below, for so long a time that one became quite nervous ...

Under water among the coral reefs! It sounds romantic, but it was not pleasant. Five feet beneath the surface the light was as clear as day, and one could see all about one, far too much, for the things that were visible were disquieting. I knew extremely well that coral reefs are the haunt of every kind of unpleasant sea beast ... there were far too many fish also, and they were much too impertinent... then I saw a thing that as nearly as possible made me open my mouth and drown myself.

It was merely a bunch of black waving trailers, coming out of the dark of the rocks and spreading between me and the pale-green light of day.... I was on the top of the water, twenty yards away, and swimming at racing speed, when I realised the fact that I was still alive, some moments later. —

Soon after this a four foot snake, with a black and white banded skin, swam past, confronted calmly by the native women. Beatrice later saw snakes in large numbers basking on the rocks.

She never discovered exactly what it was she saw underwater, but a few days later she watched a native draw up a big devil-fish, with eight dangling arms over six feet long. 'It is the unpleasant habit of this fish, when attacked by a human being, to fling its hideous tentacles over his head and face and force them up into eyes, nostrils and mouth so as to suffocate him, if he cannot master the creature.'

Later, on another island, Beatrice had a narrow escape from a shark, after which she gave up bathing in unprotected tropical waters!

After two months on Niué food was becoming short. By the time 'Duchess' returned the natives were eating green bush parrots. Beatrice re-embarked to sail a thousand miles north to Penrhyn and Malden islands. Food on the ship was terrible. Tea tasted of cockroaches, copra bugs fell out of the biscuits, and bread was made with musty flour. Board of Trade lime juice was carried by law. On this long passage without landfall a gale carried away their lifeboat, topsail, topgallant and main gaff, and swamped the passengers' cabin. For almost seven weeks Beatrice was isolated from news. Native passengers slept in the hold on benzine tins, and explosives were carried for the Cook island reefs. Then:

— A giant waterspout suddenly formed out of the low-hanging, angry sky that had replaced the clear heat of the morning. First of all, a black trunk like an elephant's began to feel blindly about in mid-air, hanging from a cloud. It came nearer and nearer with uncanny speed, drawing up to itself as it came a colossal cone of turbulent sea, until the two joined together in one enormous black pillar, some quarter of a mile broad at the base, and probably a good thousand feet high, uniting as it did the clouds and the sea below. Across the darkening sea, against the threatening, copper-crimson sunset, came this gigantic horror, waltzing over leagues of torn-up water in a terrible dance of death, like something blind, but mad and cruel, trying to find and shatter our fragile little ship. —

Happily they were able to tack and avoid getting nearer than three hundred yards to the waterspout, which would otherwise have sucked them into its maw. As Beatrice remarks, life on a South Sea schooner is not all romance!

With brief stops at Manahiki and Rakahanga, the ship next took Beatrice to Samoa. The island of Tonga was then seldom visited by travellers, except for a few hours during a steamer's day in port. There was no hotel, but Beatrice rented a tiny bungalow for four weeks. It stood on white coral sand, close to the lagoon, shaded by flamboyant trees. It was simply furnished with pandanus leaf mats. Huge clam shells outside were filled with wild hibiscus, oleander or frangipane. Pineapples cost fourteen for a shilling, or could be picked wild. Beatrice lived on bread, fruit and tea. As sharks were seldom seen inside the reef she would float by night beneath a sea of stars. She visited the Bats' Wood in a buggy, driving mile after mile over uneven grass roads, along avenues of blossoming orange trees, where thousands of fruit-eating flying foxes, as big as cats, hung upside down waiting for the night, quarrelling and swearing. Taboo to the natives, they were never killed, for it was said that the prosperity of Tonga depended on them. But to Beatrice each evening when they took off they were like a screaming cloud of evil spirits.

Beatrice describes the brass bands and choral singing on Tonga. Women were respected here more than anywhere else in the Pacific, and men did the hard labour.

They sailed on via Vavau to Upolu, where the natives were Christianised and many were literate. For hygienic reasons and to bleach it the men plastered their hair with lime. Beatrice visited R.L. Stevenson's villa Vailima (subsequently restored as a museum by the Robert Louis Stevenson Preservation Society), then owned by a German merchant. According to Paul Theroux in *The Happy Isles of Oceania* (1992), the house is now occupied by paramount chief Malietoa Tanumafili. Beatrice did not climb to Stevenson's tomb on Mount Vasa, high above the harbour. When she grew tired of the civilised section of the island she took ship in an ugly little oil launch and went to a native village at Falepunu twenty miles away, beautiful with waterfalls,

outriggers 'skimming like long-limbed waterflies about the bay,' and winding, shady fiords. With two others, a half-caste Samoan lady and a New
Zealand girl, she landed on the beach and stayed for a week at the village
guest house a mile inland.

The guest house belonged to the village chief, and had a roof but no walls.
The roof was made of branches layered to form a lattice, the supporting
pillars being tree trunks. Every inch was laced and latticed with plaited
coconut fibre, or sinnet, stained black, red and yellow and woven into intri-
cate patterns. Beatrice was welcomed by the chief and his wife, and a feast
was prepared of fowl, baked bread-fruit and taro, and fruit. They addressed
her as 'Tamaite' but, like most women travellers of that time, she was given
the status of a man, so she was offered kava, the national drink, not normally
drunk by females. Beatrice writes of this week:

— Uneventful, yet very happy, was the little week that time allowed me among
the pleasant folk of Falepunu. When the low, yellow rays of the rising sun shot
under the wide eaves of the great guest-house, and striped the white coral floor
with gold, and the little green parrakeets began to twitter in the trees outside,
and the long sleepy murmur of the surf on the reef, blown landward by the
sunrise wind, swelled to a deep-throated choral song – then, I used to slip into
my clothes, come out from my mosquito tent, and see the beauty of the new
young day ...

Iva, Pulo-Ulu and Kafi would be awake also, and moving about. No minute
of daylight is ever wasted in these tropical islands; where all the year round the
dawn lingers till after five, and the dark comes down long before seven. None
of my house mates had much toilet to make. They simply got up from their
mats, hung up the pillows, put the mosquito nets away, and walked forth, clad
in the cotton lavas-lavas of yesterday, which they had not taken off when they
lay down. Taking soap and bundles of coconut fibre off the ever useful rafters,
they went to bathe in the nearest river ... the Samoan generally washes his
garments at the same time as himself. —

Afterwards they breakfasted together. Goods were held in common in
Samoa, so Beatrice's food was liberally distributed by Iva to her cronies, and
Beatrice could help herself to anything they owned. 'Such is the "faa Samoa".
That anyone continues to retain anything worth having, under such circumstances, speaks well for the natural unselfishness of the people. They may be
a little greedy with whites ... but among themselves they are wonderfully
self-restrained, and at the same time faultlessly generous.'

She describes many other customs and habits of the islanders and their social etiquette on the giving and receiving of presents.

At the end of her visit 'the pendulum of time held back for a whole, dreamy, lazy week,' she rode back the twenty miles to Apia. Being accepted so readily by the Samoans made it hard for Beatrice to tear herself away and sail on to New Zealand which then had a population of less than a million, including a few thousand Maoris and very few visitors. At this time when early Victorian coaches were the only means of transport, other than by water, except for a limited railway, Beatrice felt she had moved back a century. 'Brumbies' (wild horses) were still being hunted and once broken in fetched thirty shillings each.

At the end of this, her first book, Beatrice heads a final section 'Dangers'. She downplays cannibalism, extinct for two generations in all the principal groups of the central, East and South Pacific. The South Seas, she writes, are no more dangerous for a woman travelling alone than the Mediterranean, though there is some element of risk in a sailing ship voyage, some of the corners to which schooners, rather than steamers, penetrate being still somewhat lawless.

It was possible in 1905 for those young, single and able to rough it, to spend six months in the islands and return to the British Isles for £100. Luxury travel would cost £220-£300, and second class only £150. Travellers, Beatrice advises, should ask Messrs Thomas Cook, and start from Sydney or Auckland. From Marseilles the journey took five weeks. Ladies need plenty of 'washing blouses' and light underclothing, plus some muslins. Men can buy white drill suits in the colonies more cheaply. Sun umbrellas are necessary but not topis, also riding habits and side saddles. There are no fevers on any islands.

Beatrice warned against the Western Pacific, for the Solomons, New Hebrides and New Guinea are different and cannot be recommended to the ordinary tourist. The natives are dangerous and almost all cannibal. There are almost no hotels and steamship communication is limited. Fevers are common and in some islands crocodiles very numerous. Nevertheless it was to these dangerous areas that she next turned her attention.

Beatrice planned to travel alone, which meant with no other whites, from Fiji into the Western Pacific islands. No white woman had ever gone far from the capital in Fiji, nor travelled alone. Advised to take a revolver with her, she also bought a side saddle and a small tin trunk into which fitted her clothes, mosquito net, oilcloth covered pillow, billy for tea, tin cup and saucer, canvas shoes for rough walking, ship's biscuits, tinned meat, sugar and salt.

She started off with a great feeling of excitement, accompanied by three Fijans and a borrowed Australian horse. 'I rode all day with perfect safety, protecting myself from the scorching rays by a grass hat and a holland coat, worn over my thin cotton blouse,' but she could not help remembering that 'among these very peaks, and in this valley that we were traversing, countless murders and ambushes had taken place, and cannibal feasts been held, in the stormy seventies. I was going to sleep in a native village, far from any white people; I could speak hardly anything of the language ...' At first she slept with her revolver beneath her head. Later she decided that this was absurd.

When she reached a village she created a stir: 'The two great ends of a Fijian's existence are eating and talking ... Five pounds weight of solid yam is the minimum allowance for a single man's meal among all employers of Fijian labour'. The villagers sat up all night endlessly discussing her hair, teeth, clothes, manners, age, and even what she had been heard to say when she stepped on a nest of centipedes. Beatrice describes Sunday in this village. At daybreak a drum called all to church, then the rest of the day was devoted to cooking the pig killed in honour of her arrival. 'And the next morning, when the sun was just lifting above the hills, and the great, green banana leaves were crystallised all over with dew, and the plumes of the waving guinea grass were frosted glass and silver, I mounted and rode away for ever...'

But she found her men had over-eaten in the village to the point of making themselves ill.

As part of the purpose of her travels is to see where settlers might buy or rent good land, she mentions that on the Ba River there are 100,000 acres of native land rising six hundred feet above sea level available for sale and suitable for stock raising. Rent would be about a shilling an acre.

Her men continued to stop at more places in order to glut themselves on pig, yam, crayfish, fat river clams, stewed fowls cooked with native peppers and shallots. By this time she and the three Fijians are in a mbili-mbili being carried down river to the coast. Once there Beatrice stays at a white magistrate's house, and then hires a cutter to cover the seventy miles back to Suva, sleeping in a 'little dog kennel forward' for a wretched day and night.

After this Beatrice took a steamer to Vanua Levu, the second largest island in the Fiji group, and spent six weeks travelling in the the interior, through swamps, gullies and thick lianas, getting wet and very dirty. Reflecting upon what drives her to put up with this she concludes: 'Some need, so exceedingly deep down in the roots of humanity that one cannot even define or name it, seems to be satisfied by wanderings such as these. It is a need not felt by all (though lying latent in very many who never suspect its existence, until sudden changes of circumstances call it out), and those who do not experience it find it hard to understand. Yet it is one of the strongest forces in the world – hunger, love, the lust of battle, alone can rank with it in power over humanity.'

On this wild island, with few white residents, Beatrice saw Fiji in the rough. She noted that the native, or 'kaisi', though no longer subject to arbitrary execution by the chiefs, could still leave his village only with the chief's permission. Beatrice explains that the natives are descended from ancestors who were slain by the dozen and thrown into their chief's grave. War canoes used to be launched over hundreds of writhing bodies whose life-blood stained its keel. Living kaisi had been put in the holes that received the pillars of every chief's dwelling, and some also got eaten by their chief.

En route to the Ndreketi river on this island the terrain was particularly difficult, and Beatrice's horse, Somo-somo, gets stuck:

— I had just dismounted to let the men lead the horse down a gully that looked much like those we had passed, and was scrambling up the far side, after crossing on a log, when I heard a terrified yell from Gideon: 'Missi N-grim-shaw! Horsie lie down, by-n'-by he n-dead!' Turning round I saw poor Somo-somo, who had missed the jump at the bottom, plunging and struggling madly in the gully, which was filled with treacherous mud. He had already sunk half-way up his belly; his eyes were starting from his head, and he snorted fearfully through his dilated nostrils, in the very extremity of terror. The men hauled helplessly on the reins, screaming at each other, and shaking with nervousness.... The banks were hopelessly steep; it was not far off dusk; the nearest village where help might be obtained was two hours away – and all the time, poor Somo-somo, of whom I had really grown fond, was dying a horrible death, staring wildly at me in vain hope of help, and breathing now in long drawn, painful snores of agony....the sight was indescribably painful, and the feeling of helplessness still worse. But my three men were children of Nature, which meant three useless babies in trouble of any kind, and Somo-somo's life hung on me.

I told one of them to take a stick at once, and test the depth of the mud. The horse had now sunk to half-way up the shoulder. Fortunately the test revealed that he had touched bottom, and would go no further. The danger, however, was none the less. I knew that he might struggle himself to death, and guessed that his head would sink when he became exhausted. As for the men, they were squatting down to their eternal cigarettes, quite prepared to watch the horse die, and, with true savage cruelty, to laugh over its expiring struggles as an excellent show.

... Then I lost my manners. It does not matter what I said. There is a kind of English that every Fijian understands and obeys. I gave them that English, reproducing it phonographically from my recollections of the sort of thing the island mates used to say to the cargo-workers on the quays ... It seemed to touch the spot. They got up and went to work.

I told them to haul on the head-rope, and lift the horse's quarters with saplings. I made them cut down a considerable section of bush ... I worked them like mules for over an hour, and scolded like a turkey-hen all the time. At the last, a piece of fairly solid standing ground was manufactured, and Somo-somo, filthy, exhausted, terrified and trembling, got out with one final struggle, and stood on the bank, swaying on his feet, and looking like death. But he was saved. —

In September 1905 Beatrice was in Sydney from where she intended to visit the New Hebrides. The islands were largely unknown, though only four days away by the steamer which left once a month for this group of islands, extending over 700 miles of sea. Beatrice was told that the natives there were murderers and cannibals to a man. If she went there she would be shot and/or eaten, or else die of fever. The few travellers who had landed there only took short walks ashore. Intrigued by these islands in which 'the foot of the tourist does not tread, strange customs and old ways flourish undisturbed, and windows are opened into worlds far other than our own,' Beatrice set off in a slow steamer with two other passengers, both island traders.

Eight days later they reached Vila harbour. There are, Beatrice tells us, thirty-five islands in the New Hebridean group varying from a few acres in size up to a length of sixty miles or more. The entire population was then between sixty and one hundred thousand, which included three hundred French settlers and about two hundred British and colonials, mostly missionaries. Maize, coffee, millet and copra were the principal crops. An argument was then going between the British and French over the ownership of the islands, so administration was poor. The Anglo-French convention was signed in 1906, after Beatrice visited. In 1905 the natives carried rifles and tended to be trigger happy, so Beatrice did not advise British settlers to emigrate there at present. 'Business is certainly not on the up grade. Tenure of land is not too certain; tenure of life no better.' The islands also had a severe strain of malaria.

Beatrice wanders off from island to island, to Malekula, then Wala. 'Dates disappear, and times melt away, within sound of the lazy whispering coco palm.' The local men wear cartridge belts of woven pandanus fibre, a boar's tusk round their necks and a pig's tail in each ear.

Malekula island, sixty by thirty-five miles was still unexplored, the missionaries being on the coast. As interior tribes descended sometimes to burn, slay and destroy, no money would induce a guide to penetrate the interior, even if armed. In October 1905 the crews of the French and British warships *Meurthe* and *Pegasus* marched eleven miles inland and back again. This was to warn the natives rather than avenge their murders of several white traders.

Beatrice goes with one white man and two mission natives, carrying food but no arms, to a village six miles inland, up a narrow inlet, then four miles on foot, as riding was impossible. They met natives, all armed, who regarded them with 'sullen curiosity'. The women were terrified at the sight of Beatrice and would not come near. Beatrice knew that if women were there she was relatively safe, and she gave one woman a pink ribbon. The native women, used as breeders and beasts of burden, had a low place in island society.

The Makelulan settlement they come to is surrounded by a stockade. The houses are huts of reed and bamboo. There is a temple and drum idols with uncanny skull-like faces. As the drums are beaten the men rush round them, singing loudly: 'The wild, monotonous chant went on and on, as if it would never end'. The heavy heat, and perhaps a touch of fever added to the dream illusion, and Beatrice felt she was living in a nightmare, especially when watching the dance of Atamat and Fintimbus, in honour of a famous cannibal chief.

Beatrice does not fear ending up in the pot for 'if they had contemplated a bit of baked man as a treat' the natives would have indulged in this quietly, and deliberate killing for the sake of eating was uncommon.

Beatrice goes on to another village on the coast, and the locals were persuaded to bring their sacred mummies out of their 'hamal' in exchange for tobacco. It was sacrilege for a woman to go inside a hamal. Beatrice, nevertheless, managed to do this in another village where no one was around.

Mission stations in the New Hebrides, Beatrice writes, occupy much the same position as the monastery of the Middle Ages. Their hospitality is the traveller's only refuge from the hardships of camping amid land-crabs and mosquitoes on the beach. Beatrice travels on foot with a missionary, one of a dozen whites living on Tanna, for thirteen miles uphill to the cone of the island's volcano which was seldom visited. The natives had a deadly horror of it, so only a mission native would go. Tourists off the monthly Sydney boat never went as they feared the cannibals!

Beatrice, her companion and two mission natives, climbed 2,000 feet on a foot-wide bush track, past two mission villages. 'The tangled bush palm and pandanus, matted together at the roots with purple flowered shrubs and trailing pink convolvulus, and linked aloft by closely knitted lianas, thinned out by and by, and began to display a flooring of fine black sand.' Then the trees ended abruptly and they were out on a barren, desolate plain, 'painted crimson, buff and yellow, curdled and coiled like the scum on boiling milk, and looking as hot and molten as though the wicked black cone in the centre had only this morning cast it forth.' They cross the lava beds to the eight hundred foot cone top hidden by smoke:

... suddenly, as I stand on the edge looking over, and feeling rather giddy, without understanding why, the scale of the place bursts upon me. I realise what I am looking at. The sky-line of the crater shuts out so much of the surrounding world that there is little to compare with – but somehow the 'values' explain themselves all in a second, and the crater expands like a bursting red flower, while I, deprived of my lawful inches and comfortable self-importance, stand like a wretched little insect, a speck that does not count, on the verge of utter immensity. It was merely my eyes, accustomed to things of moderate size, that were in fault, not the crater. Eight hundred feet is the drop from where I am standing to the sulphurous gorges and canyons beneath; half a mile at the least is the distance from lip to lip of the great black cup. And as for the powers that sleep below.

... I did not mean to do it. I thought I had developed some nerve during the course of several months' solitary wanderings about the wild New Hebrides. I thought I could face a noise without losing head and presence of mind. But the fire fountain jumped a hundred feet higher into the air, and the crater, like a wild and wicked brute when you put your head into its den, suddenly bellowed right into my face with the voice of a dozen tropic thunderstorms and a thousand angry bulls, coupled to something that was entirely volcanic and indescribable – something that turned one's spine to ill-set jelly, and made one mysteriously understand the motions of the starfish that jerks off its arms and legs when terrified.

I wanted to jerk off mine, but instead I found myself running down the side of the cone hand in hand with two extremely frightened niggers, without an idea as to how I got there, or where I was going. It was not courage, for I had none left, but pride of race, that stopped me half a dozen yards below the crater lip. White people must not be frightened before blacks. So I went back and sat on the edge again – because the rush of hot wind from below, and the extreme straightness of the 800 feet drop inclined one to giddiness, and looked down once more.

By and by it bellowed a second time, and the very heavens shook, while the caky crumbled edge on which I sat trembled heart-shakingly. But I wanted to see this time, so I looked down, still feeling very much like the starfish, without its happy means of relief.

It was all over in a few seconds. The fire fountain rose halfway up the crater sides, and tossed a few glowing lumps of lava into the air. They did not reach within a hundred feet of the rim, but it was rather anxious work, seeing how far they meant to go. The red crack glowed scarlet, and from the dark wolf-mouth away down at the bottom of all things, burst once and again that terrifying bellow. It was impossible not to feel that there was something alive – alive and powerful and infinitely wicked – down there. —

Fascinated, Beatrice stayed on the summit for more than an hour as the lava grew pink in the setting sun and became spotted with holes of fire, and the gorge of fire beneath her roared and glowed.

At the end of her book *From Fiji to the Cannibal Islands* (1907), Beatrice includes an appendix in which she summarises practical details for would-be settlers. A second class ticket from Britain to Suva or Fiji cost £48, or £80 first class. It was a six and a half week voyage via France, Spain, Egypt, Arabia, Ceylon and Australia, then another steamer from Sydney. There was also, she explained, the Cunard-American route, the same price but shorter, with the Canadian Pacific Railway taking five days across the American continent; from Vancouver to Suva was only eighteen days by sea. She also recommended a round the world route out via New York, Chicago, the Sante Fe railroad to San Francisco, steamer to Tahiti, Union steamship to the Cook Islands and New Zealand, then on to Fiji. This route involved no 'roughing it' anywhere. A passage on a trading schooner from San Francisco or Tahiti, however, would introduce more hardship. The cheapest way was third class which cost about £20. 'This method is quite good enough for strong, enterprising young men, who do not object to steerage accommodation, but would hardly suit a pleasure tourist.'

Beatrice settled for some time on the island of Sariba, two miles from the Samarai islands, off the tip of Papua New Guinea. She designed her first house, built by a white man with a team of natives. It had sago leaf thatch, bush timber frame covered with sago sheath and black palm wood floors. She decorated the sitting room with a frieze of pearl shell, ornaments of shell and coral from the reef. She had a cutter and crew and sailed to and fro to Samarai. She lived there for two and a half years writing and then sold it to a missionary society, and built another house on the Papuan mainland. This second house, built of local materials, had three hundred acres of forest and was named Marana (daylight), as it faced east, looking through forest to the distant sea. Beatrice stayed there a year, clearing some of the rest with the help of Northern River headhunters. She had a cheap ninety-nine year lease of the land, and no rent to pay for ten years.

It was from this house that Beatrice adventured, as the first white woman, up the Sepik River in 1923. She writes enthusiastically about this trip in her autobiography *Isles of Adventure* (1930):

— There is not a more wonderful river in the world than the Sepik, the largest river of the island-continent of New Guinea.

It is wider, longer, deeper than most of the great European rivers. Large ocean liners can – or could, since they have never done so – travel up the first sixty miles; and steamers drawing ten to fifteen feet would find plenty of water for three hundred. Above that there are rapids, but the Sepik still remains a big river for another three hundred miles, back towards the mountains of Dutch New Guinea. Above this point, nearing its source, it dwindles to a tiny stream.

There is oil somewhere along its course – not yet located; there is gold; there is a seventy-mile stretch of sago, and hundreds of miles of wild sugar cane. Tobacco is grown by the headhunters of the middle river in such quantities that stray traders buy it by the ton, the quality of the leaf being good enough for white men to make into cigars. There is much swamp country, but there is also flat land suitable for cotton, tobacco, or sugar; and even the swamplands are naturally rich for they grow sago and nipa, the latter now known to be one of best sources of commercial alcohol. —

No other woman travel writer explored the Sepik until Christina Dodwell wrote about her solo trip by dugout canoe in 1979, *In Papua New Guinea* (Oxford Illustrated Press, 1983). Dodwell seems unaware of Grimshaw having been there before her, though not alone. Beatrice travelled in a Catholic Mission launch of ninety tons, which went two hundred miles up the Sepik for the first time, and stayed a week in head-hunting country, seeing many sights that hardly any white person, and certainly no white woman, had ever seen before.

— The heat, with every mile, grew worse and worse – it was already bad at the mouth of the river – and mosquitoes increased in a sort of geometrical progression, till one began to wonder how human life continued to exist any farther up. —

They passed thirty foot plumes of nipa palm, and miles of sago. Beatrice explains that an eight year old sago palm, cut down at the limit of its natural life, will provide starchy food for a family for six months.

— The pith is chopped out and washed in bark troughs; the resulting starch is collected and made into cakes. On the Sepik sago is boiled into a pale jelly, and sometimes cooked into thin flexible cakes, rather like oatcakes in appearance. This fine nourishing starch is entirely different from the grained stuff – mostly made from potatoes – sold in shops under the name of sago. —

Beatrice is interesting on the subject of the native tribes she meets, in those days little known:

— These people are not supposed to belong to the same race as the common, unenterprising cannibals of the upper and lower river, who merely enjoy an occasional fight, and devour an enemy once in a way. It is thought that they came across country to the Sepik from the sea countless generations ago, armed with a little more knowledge, a trifle more civilisation than the other tribes, and immediately proceeded to make themselves unquestioned masters. 'Romans of the Sepik', they might well be called. They are better, bigger, stronger than anyone else on the river. They hold the others in subjection, make them grow tobacco for the conquerors' needs, and exact tribute of yams and sago as they please. They are much cleaner than the other natives; they have not a bad idea of art; their houses are well built and their towns, some of which number nearly two thousand people, are kept in good order.

What they know of white people is not much. One or two explorers, a few recruiting schooners, the tiny mission pinnace creeping up and down the river, a Government canoe once in a long while – that is all the headhunters see of the white people who own the land. —

Head hunting was openly practised, for there was a display of them in every village men's communal house, and the canoes clustering about their launch offered heads for sale. Many of the natives had learned pidgin English working on plantations. Some of these, returning to their villages, were carried up river by the mission steamer.

The following episode shows that Beatrice certainly did not lack courage:

— Later we stopped at a village renowned for its friendliness. Here, it was said, the white man was in no danger at all of losing his head; here everyone had always been civilised and well behaved. Crowds met the launch; men clad in a handful of fur and an armful of shell beads, their hair trained into long wiry curls, their eyes painted horribly with black, their noses and cheeks reddened. They jumped about, wild with excitement, as the two missionaries and myself came ashore. They had never seen a white woman; they expressed their astonishment, somewhat unflatteringly, by yelping like dogs. No doubt they were friendly, but they had not brought their women out, and everyone who knows New Guinea knows that suggests distrust.

One of them, who spoke pidgin English, proposed a sort of confidence trick – they had their women away back in the bush, he said, and if I would leave the white men on the bank and go with the natives, they would take me to their women – and then, apparently, everyone would trust everyone else. The offer was accepted. —

Beatrice goes a few hundred yards with the men into a deeply shaded village, with well built houses and a fine assembly hall inside which were a number of high stools carved from tree trunks and finely carved with four outward-curving legs: 'And now, out of the high-up door of the women's house, small, brown faces began peeping. The men roared to their wives to come down; and very timidly they came, pattering down the high ladder, staring and laughing nervously. Most of them would not even approach until the men, shouting with laughter, dragged them up to me. They were rather superior to the usual type of savage women, not nearly so hideous, nor so crushed looking. One inferred that the wives of the headhunters were not ill-treated, and enjoyed some position in the community.'

As there was no interpreter Beatrice found communication difficult. She remarks that the mission work of the Fathers seems rather hopeless! Her description of the physical discomfort of her trip adds to the atmosphere she creates:

— It was a typical Sepik River afternoon; over huge open lagoons, steely and livid, under a sky that was black with terrible heat, the launch panted on her way; through narrower reaches, less than half a mile in width, where the silent dark green trees on either bank stirred not a leaf, but stood like gloomy soldiers, still at attention. The boat was full of mosquitoes now. Whenever we approached the bank they came on board in thousands, and if one walked about in the villages one had to fight them off ceaselessly with branches of trees. All the natives carried long brooms made of cassowary feather or coconut fibre, and used them continually. And with every mile of our advance up the river the mosquitoes and the heat increased.

Everyone was streaming from every pore; clothes remained saturated night and day. Sleep within airless, close mosquito nets became almost impossible; rest at any time of the day was hopeless. Two thoughts dominated the mind above all other – mosquitoes and heat, heat and mosquitoes.

And yet – how lovely the waterways that we passed; the tributaries running far back into lagoons set with silvery sugar cane and gemmed with secret, exquisite islands. Sometimes the tops of coconuts, rising above apparently untouched brakes of cane, told of the existence of hidden towns in the centre of natural island fortresses. The Sepik has many villages that are thus half hidden, and many more entirely concealed, kept jealously guarded from any white who may stray into the wild interior of the forgotten land. —

Three years later, in 1926, after eighteen years in Papua, Beatrice was also the first white woman to go up the Fly River, named by a Captain Blackwood of HMS *Fly* in 1842. She went with Sir Hubert Murray, the Lieutenant Governor, two other white men, and armed Papuan native police, in a 180 ton government oil launch. Nothing larger than a forty ton launch had previously gone three hundred miles up this huge river. The tidal influence extended some hundred and sixty miles, and there were many shoals so they used a leadline. Even eighty miles up the Fly is more than a mile wide. They saw hundreds of huge crocodiles, and the hard to see five foot tall cassowary bird. The Fly River preserved heads were famous at this time.

At one point they almost ran aground in Lake Murray. The women of local tribes, never before seen, now appeared because of Beatrice's presence, but all of them were terrified. Beatrice bought human jaw bones, coloured dark red and hung like lockets on native string.

Beatrice now lived in a cottage of timber and iron with four rooms on the edge of a precipice overlooking the three hundred foot Rona waterfall, twenty miles from the Papuan coast. It was built by half-caste carpenters under her orders. Pale eucalyptus and grasses surrounded the house. By the time she wrote her autobiography, however, in her late fifties, she lived in Port Moresby in the house in which she said she hoped to end her days, a house which stood above the sea in 'peaceful loveliness'.

This was not to be, however, for Beatrice died over twenty years later and for her last fourteen years lived in Australia still writing novels.

Beatrice is still remembered in Papua and by some Australians who have lived there, but the rest of the world seems to have forgotten this intrepid Irishwoman, explorer of the South Seas and author of forty books including her novels. She has a gift for description. This passage comes from *Lost Child* (1940) set in 1916:

The dull-gold coasts of Queensland within the colossal lake of the Barrier Reef; league-long breakers, pearling to starboard of her, empty lands lying to port; beneath her keel the kingfisher coloured seas. Summer lived here; Summer never ending, with few to savour it, only when ships went by... and rarely, a yacht, did men's eyes rest upon the loveliest and loneliest coast in the southern world.

A coast now sprouting high-rise blocks, hotels and many golf courses!

BEATRICE EDITH GUBBINS

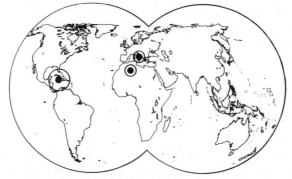

Europe between the wars, including a picture of peaceful Sarajevo

Beatrice (1878-1944) was the youngest of Thomas Wise Gubbins' seven children. The family moved from County Limerick in 1883 when her father inherited Wise's distillery in Cork, which he decided to manage. He then bought Dunkathel at Glanmire, a few miles outside the city, where Beatrice grew up. When her eldest brother Joe inherited the house he decided to live mostly in Somerset so she remained there with her mother and sisters. As her two brothers' children died young, Dunkathel was eventually inherited by Russell cousins, who live there to this day.

During the earlier part of this century the five Gubbins sisters, only one of whom married, efficiently managed the Dunkathel estate. Beatrice became a talented artist studying in Cork at the Crawford School of Art, travelling widely both in Ireland and on the Continent from her late teens, as she recorded in her diaries. When the motor car appeared she became a motorist, sketching wherever she went. Beatrice and her sister Kate were also keen photographers. All five sisters suffered to some degree from the handicap of congenital deafness, but this did not prevent Beatrice working as a nurse during the 1914 war in Cork and Exeter, when, sketching Dartmoor, she found it 'not a patch on Connemara'.

Beatrice travelled as much as she could throughout her life. She had an endless thirst for the cultural riches and scenic beauties of Europe and her artistic eye is evident in the following extracts from her unpublished diaries.

In spring 1922 she was in Corsica for two months with her friend Con Hughes:

— April 10th. Left Ajaccio at 7.15 am in motorbus for Piana. At the starting place we met an American girl (Miss Latrobe), who was going to Bonifaccio and persuaded her to come with us and then to Bonifaccio with us afterwards, and so make the No. 3 for whom we have long been searching. So she persuaded the office people to change her ticket.

Such a beautiful drive, by Calcaloggio, Sagone and Cargèse winding along valleys, through mountains, over some of the passes, then going right down to the coast with snow mountains in the distance at times ... on turning the last corner you come on a vision of beauty – Piana with the Rodur Ranges behind it, the purple mountains behind them and the snow-capped mountains behind them again, a magnificent sight.

We stopped at an excellent inn, the 'Arret d'Omnibus', clean, comfortable and good food. We strolled down the Calanche road. These huge masses of rock are truly wonderful, the colour and grotesque shapes. Piana itself is a most quaint and paintable village. A quick sketch was all I had time for this evening.

April 11th. This morning, after some difficulty, we managed to get hold of a carriage and a pair of mules with a Russian to drive us to Porto, a village about six miles away. The road runs through the Calanche and then winds down the mountain through the luxuriant 'maquis' with beautiful views below of the coast, while the peaks tower above one on the right, some with snow. A really lovely drive.

The village itself is pretty. Got back for lunch. We took our tea on the coast walk. Con was tired so Miss Latrobe and I went on nearly to the point. Perfectly lovely coming towards Piana in the evening light, just in nice time for dinner. The inhabitants seem rather excited this evening, letting off bombs every few minutes in honour of the elections, which do not take place until May!

April 13th. At 8 am we started off in the motor for Bonifaccio, picking up Miss Latrobe at Hotel Continental. A perfect day for the expedition. We went by Cauro, and after a long climb over the Col de Calaccia, with a 'coast' down of about fourteen miles (the hairpin turns taken at an alarming speed) to Olmeto and the old Port of Propriano, from there up to Sartène, an old, old town built on a rock surmounting a valley and most picturesque. We lunched there and had a stroll around. On by a twisting road round mountains and down to the coast, up and down.

Shortly before getting to Bonifaccio the road becomes white in the glare of the sun. Bonifaccio itself is a quaint ancient town packed on a rocky promontory which is worn away by the sea, leaving it very overhanging. The streets are narrow with arches across, and very steep stairs, almost like ladders. We saw three churches, St Dominique, St Francis and Ste Marie, and then took a boat, rowed by the two chief men of the lifeboat crew, and very charming they both were, to see the Dragonette cave. The water is beautifully clear, real emerald green, and the stones beneath, with masses of different colours, look like an Axminster carpet, while overhead is an opening, the exact shape of the map of Corsica!

Back to dinner at Hotel des Etrangers, outside the town (rooms 7F), fairly clean and comfy ... —

In later years Beatrice travelled farther afield to the West Indies with her friend Helen, sailing in *Ariquani* (7,000 tons) for her first long sea passage. They went to Barbados, then Trinidad where the day trip cost twenty-two shillings and was too short, then to Costa Rica, where they saw splendid virgin forest from the train on an overnight trip, while the ship loaded up with bananas and grapefruit. Beatrice mentions the gaily painted bullock carts with solid wooden wheels. *Ariquani* took them on to Port Royal and Kingston, Jamaica. Here the island looked so inviting that Beatrice arranged to transfer to the *Camito* sailing five days later. The two women hired a Buick and drove 62 miles to a quiet hotel in Mandeville where they dined on the verandah amidst fireflies.

— March 20th. Very sorry to say goodbye to Mandeville at 10.30. Had a lovely drive by cave valley, Brown's Town and Runaway Bay on the north coast, through St Anne's Bay and Roaring River Falls where we had lunch, so cool and delicious among the palms, bananas and the roar of the cascade. A little summer house and not a soul anywhere near. On by Ocho Rios and Dun's Bay, a charming palm-fringed bathing beach, with the wonderful emerald water inside the breakers. —

By the end of the day they had driven 95 miles. The next morning there was an earthquake, 'the house shook and proprietor and daughter rushed out. They called it a sharp shock. Sketched humming birds and fireflies.' In Kingston's Hope gardens Beatrice saw a humming bird sitting on its tiny nest. She left Jamaica with 'great regret'.

Some of Beatrice's diaries are illustrated with thumbnail sketches made on the spot, to be enlarged later. Her paintings, displayed at Dunkathel, may be visited by the public. Her subject matter is varied, from some excellent portraits of people who worked on the estate, to watercolours of scenery from misty Ireland, to the clear light and evocative atmosphere she recreated in her North African work. She had already been to Morocco when in January and February 1931, accompanied by her brother Joe, his wife Elma, and Helen, she set off for almost six weeks to tour Algeria and Tunisia.

Croydon to Le Bourget was Beatrice's first flight. She found it 'wonderful but very noisy – visibility bad, foggy, so flew mostly at about 200 instead of 2,000 feet'. The next day they took the train to Marseilles, then ship to Algiers. The passage was 'grey, cold and very rolly, managed all meals, but parted with tea and very nearly with teeth!'

In a fifteen seater car with chauffeur and guide they saw the sights of Algiers, then two days later drove along the coast and into the Atlas mountains to Michelet, from which prominence French guns then commanded surrounding villages.

— 19th January. At 9 am we walked with our guide (a Kabyle man) down to his house, very primitive but clean, one room, no furniture but a sort of mud bench against one wall. A two foot wall divided the animals at a level 2' lower than the dwelling room. There were two very pretty young women (sister and wife), two children and the old mother. This is a place one would like to stop at, but we had to start off at 10.15 for Bougie [now Begaia], 94 miles through magnificent scenery and over four cols to Azaga, where we lunched. Afterwards through cork forests and finally winding down to Bougie, a French town, well situated on a hill facing west over the sea. —

They drove on to Constantine, then to the ruined Roman town of Tingad [or Thamugadi] 'with "pictures" the whole way, first streams and trees, after tilled land which reminded me of Kerry bogs, taking on much the same purples, browns and oranges with the blue mountains.'

The next stop was the gorge of El Kantara, which they walked through, then on to Biskra, toured by Beatrice on a camel's back. She includes photographs in her diary of the double-wheeled desert car (a light truck) and of their group picnicking in the desert en route to Touggurt and El Oued 'the city of 1000 domes, all sand-coloured, not walled in, but just squat in the desert of dunes and palms.' There they took mint tea with the marabout, visited the half-finished mosque and watched the sun set from its minaret.

Their tour continued through Tunisia. In the end Beatrice got neuralgia from the open-sided desert car on top of a heavy cold, and arrived back at Marseilles 'rather miserable'.

Beatrice's last foreign trip, when aged sixty, was to spend April 1938 in Yugoslavia. She travelled with two women friends via Venice on Palm Sunday, then by boat to Split and down the Adriatic coast to Dubrovnik, which was overflowing with visitors for Easter, the locals all in national dress.

Beatrice and her friend Honor next go to Sarajevo by rail:

— a beautiful journey, winding practically all the way by the river. First through rocky mountains, a narrow fertile valley with the most ethereal delicate colouring I've ever seen – probably due to the early morning light. The river sometimes vanishes, then reappears in a rather lovely light green colour.

From about Mostar the people are mostly Moslem. The women wear cream flannel knicks and bright yellow hankeys on their heads. The river runs through a magnificent gorge after Mostar for miles and miles with snow-topped mountains, while the banks change to grey overhanging rocks. Masses of wild laburnum and primroses. The houses have wooden tiles. Towards Sarajevo it is much cultivated with flocks, herds and shepherds. Arrived Sarajevo 5.30 where Hotel Central's bus met us.

29th April. Wandered round Sarajevo. Saw them making carpets, both knotted and woven, some of them very fine. Then saw the mosque of which there are several, but they don't compare with those of Morocco. Wandered round the town and bazaar which is fascinating. Fez and black yashmaks are much worn here. Saw over a small Greek church and tried pencil sketching.

30th April. Left early by train and change at Lasra for Jaiça, such a quaint old town with fortress and catacombs, beautifully situated on the river. We saw the fine falls where two rivers meet. From there by bus winding through gorge after gorge along the rushing river, wonderful scenery. The local women wear mostly white with red aprons and sometimes red or black coats. They look quite charming tending their herds, or helping plough. The men's dress is also very picturesque ... —

Ending their tour of Yugoslavia their route home was via Trieste, Venice, and the night train to Calais. Viewed from the perspective of the 1990s, Beatrice's diary gives us a touch of traveller's nostalgia!

KATE O'BRIEN

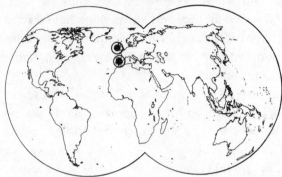

One of Ireland's best-loved writers, on Spain and on Galway during changing times

Kate O'Brien (1897-1974), the distinguished Irish writer best known for her novels, could be called the first modern Irish woman writer, being ahead of her time in her attitudes, especially towards feminine conventions. Born in Limerick, she was educated there and at University College, Dublin.

Deeply interested in Spain and Spanish literature, from the time when she had worked as a governess in Bilbao in the 1920s, she later published *Farewell Spain* (1937) during that country's civil war. Her journey round Spain is a personal journey, about all she can remember about Spain and wishes to see again. 'The route will be a plaiting together of many routes; seasons and cities will succeed each other here in reminiscence as almost certainly they did not in fact ...' Here she is near Santander at Santillana del Mar:

— It stands in a green, wet valley. The hills about it are not impressive and the sea which it claims in its full name is invisible and some kilometres away. It consists of two narrow streets and a bedraggled square. There cannot be in the whole town more than seventy houses, but they are all *palacios*. It is built of that pale buff sandstone which gives Spain such an unfair advantage architecturally. No stone could be more beautiful or more felicitously suited to the romanesque manner which France sent over the Pyrenees in the twelfth century and which achieved indigenous perfection in its new place. Three or four of the *palacios* were still kept up, when I was last there, by wealthy Spanish families who come there sometimes – I suppose to shoot. I cannot think of any other recreation they could find for miles around. One house is owned by an Austrian Archduchess, a relation of Alfonso XIII, and very comfortable she has made it for herself. The other *palacios* are tenanted by villagers, whose mules and oxen are very well stabled in the great stone entrance halls. I do not know who their landlord is, or if there is, or was, a twentieth century Marqués de Santillana.

The Renaissance laid gracious hands on this curious feudal settlement of grandees. It caressed the strength it found, coaxed and embellished it. For all its creativeness it chose here mainly to conserve, to carry on, to add without senselessly taking away. A lesson another vigorous age might ponder with advantage.

It found almost nothing to improve in the Colegiata, which stands out clear and simple at the bottom of the hilly longer street.

The descent may be difficult. If it has been raining the cobbles will be slippery as well as bumpy. The children will all accost you if you look foreign. They'll ask for cigarettes and for two pins they'll make fun of you. You may meet a team of oxen coming up, and have to sidle against them like a brave bullfighter. A mule may unexpectedly swish his tail in your face out of a magnificent front door. But you will descend and long before you do you will see the façade of the parish church. It is of the same stone as the *palacios*, it is 'románico puro' and if you don't like it – then there is exactly nothing to be said. But if you do like it you will agree with me that here – more demonstrably than almost anywhere – functional rightness is beauty, beauty is functional rightness. In the old, wide, regional sense. For this is a church, but not for Baptists or for Irish Catholics, or for a Cardinal Archbishop. It is the parish church of a small feudal town and it was built in the days of faith, not many hundred years after Pelayo, nearby at Covadonga, had driven the Arabs back for ever over the Cantabrian mountains and had begun the history of a Christian race. It is founded on simple theology, on the Catechism – not on hysteria or inquisitorial fanaticism. It is a church for men's daily use, designed neither to inflame nor to alarm them. Its architectural mode suggests patience and mercy.

Within it is dark, and its arches have each an individual irregularity which puzzles modern builders, I believe. The proportions are without flaw. It has a dim but good-seeming retablo and another altar piece which the sacristan holds in such high regard that he keeps it covered, except to show to tourists. It was the gift to his hometown of a local boy who made good in Mexico in the late nineteenth century. It is a low relief of religious figures done in beaten Mexican silver and is atrociously ugly....

It is an easy walk here from feudalism to neolithic life. The caves of Altamira are not much more than a kilometre away. But it is uphill, so we'll take the bus.

There are two caves. You pay three pesetas, I think, to be shown through them and to visit the little museum. The guide has by now shown me through them so often – I have taken this one and that one to see them – that he begins to suspect I am a formidable authority on neolithic man....

The first, which he takes you to second, on the principle of reserving the better thing, is a vast display of stalactites. Very drippy and dank. The state or someone has illuminated this dwarf forest here and there with coy little red and green lights. Everyone loves this cave and tells the guide that it is just like fairyland ... On my last three visits to Altamira I refused to go into the fairyland cave, much to the distress of the guide. But I really detest it and as I'm not a geologist I don't see why I need induce geological nightmares. I prefer to sit on the one little bench on the top of the hill and think up theories about the twenty-thousand-years-dead painter of the other cave.

That is dimly and cautiously lighted, because if the Neolithic Leonardo, going one better than the Florentine, managed to mix his three colours so that they would endure for twenty thousand years on the wet walls of the inner earth, his fame may well have been helped, the experts think, by the chance that his frescoes have lain a small eternity in unventilated darkness. So they are not floodlighted – there is only one small bulb in the inner cave where they are – and you must peer and grope until you are used to the dimness, and must follow the guide's flashlight accurately – he moves it about at rather too great a speed, I think – if you are to see the animal pictures decently.

As far as I remember there are six animal forms painted on the low ceiling and uneven wall of the cave. They are done in three colours, black, red-ochre and brown, cleverly combined with the lovely buff of the surface. The figures, bisons, stags and horses are approximately life-size, and are painted recumbent and in action. They are full of individuality and the technique is of elimination – observation whittled down to record essentials. Experts cannot decide whether they are the work of one man or of many, but intuition apprehends a personal, isolated inspiration in the idea and its execution. No one knows how the colours were made. But there they are – the beginning of painting, and setting for a high standard indeed, but hidden ironically, and perhaps for immortality's sake fortunately, from all the eras of painting, and all the schools, until now. —

Today Santillana remains the same, an architectural gem, but gone are the oxen and mules. The beautiful *palacios* are restored, a few are now hotels, and there are many tourists. At Altamira the 'fairyland' cave is still open, but the cave with drawings is only accessible upon special request. Access is limited and one has to reserve a visit a year ahead!

Later in the book Kate returns to Bilbao, which she knows so well:

— Bilbao is the first Spanish town I ever knew. I lived and earned a living there

for nearly a year when I was young and Alphonse XIII was still a merry monarch.... It is a town of solid vulgarity and great melancholy. Although founded as a city in the early fourteenth century, it seems to have played little part in Spanish history until the nineteenth and so is architecturally un-dramatic, unatmospheric....Steeped in local pride, in Basque nationalism, deeply and irrevocably Catholic and believing, Vizcaya is passionately demo-cratic, passionately for justice and common sense....

The river Nervión is navigable here for fourteen kilometres from its mouth, that is right to the heart of the city. And as Bilbao, surrounded by great mountains, is the centre of very rich iron-mining and steel-founding indus-tries, the port is busy and important. French, Belgian, English and German exploiters have had their lucky dip at this source of wealth, and their directors, engineers and imposing offices and banks swell the population and the osten-tatious luxury of the new part of the town...

The mining villages nearby from which all this fatness comes are worth observation....I have walked through these villages, on pleasant afternoons of summer, and in winter too, through streaming mud. The one weather seemed of as little consequence as the other, as little use. The houses are always high, for it is a Spanish fashion to build tall and live apartment-life even in loneliest townships. They climb after each other, as a rule, these houses, along a steep gully of mud and stones which is the street. They are filthy, and almost empty of furniture. They have electric light and no other decency. In the dark wine-shop which is also the general store, there is almost nothing to be bought, but if you drink a glass of the local red wine, the harsh, good *chacoli*, and talk with the men about the doorway, you will hear little from them about life as it looks from where you and they stand....

These villages are awful in their stillness and despair. The crumbling Ren-aissance church, very filthy inside but recklessly *churrigueresco* of décor, the dilapidated girl at the brothel door, boys, pale and stooped, coming up the lane from their shift, a little way off heavily loaded trolleys rattling down the hill. And in the valley the pricking lights of Bilbao, outlines of banks and moving ships, softly sounding horns of Hispano-Suiza ...

The bulls are always very big in Bilbao. So is the bull-ring, almost as big as the new ring in Madrid, I'd guess. And round its painted parapet, behind the audience's heads, the names of all the great toreros of history are written up, reminding one of the writers' names in the British Museum Reading Room. One afternoon there I saw a young matador, fair-haired, pretty, greedy for fame, fight his dangerous bull with a display of graceful audacity which made me uncomfortable – as certain quite good-seeming actors sometimes make one feel. I could not assess his performance, which had an allure of brilliance. But the expert I was with said in sudden disgust: 'This fellow's a vulgarian. He'll get the horn in a minute and serve him right'. And he did. He was carried out with blood streaming down his new pink silk. It was a bad *cornada*, but he recovered.

But why drag in this controversial bloodiness? Bilbao has other amusements than *corridas*. You can see the Basque pelota game played there at its best. There are two fine frontónes, or courts, and you pay very little to go in and can sit for hours watching long professional programmes. You can make bets on the players, too. The bookies stand in front of the graded seats and yell their odds all through the games. It is, as you know, a form of rackets, played in a very big court with a hard ball driven by *palas* or *cestas*, strapped to the players' wrists. The former are flat wooden bats, the latter wickerwork scoops, long and curved. The game, which is of the Pyrenees, is very much liked all over Spain now and in most towns of any size there are frontónes where professionals play every evening ... —

In 1946 Kate wrote her best-known novel, banned in Spain, *That Lady*, about the cast-off and imprisoned mistress of Phillip II, entitled *For One Sweet Grape* in the US and adapted for the stage in New York. Kate O'Brien's novels often show women struggling for opportunities to travel and educate themselves.

Kate's other travel book is *My Ireland* (1962). This book too is digressive, a book of memories, opinions and imagination, for instance:

— The lighthouse of Loop Head, at the south-west point where the Shannon becomes a part of the Atlantic, is the exile's last glimpse of Erin – it must be, by the map, whatever Kerry and Sligo have to say. And it is a fine, severe last glimpse – to stiffen backbones and upper lips of unnerved emigrants, one must hope....The exile might wonder, gazing aft, why indeed he had to leave a land so arrogant and self-sufficient, and yet feel momentarily glad of the compactness of a mere ship within which to hide and be small and safe. —

Galway is her favourite city, next to her native Limerick, reminding us that travel includes appreciating the homeland:

— Galway without its seaboard and its bay, without its country people in and out, without its Irish-English talk, torn away from its Corrib, its fishermen, its Blazers, its whiskey, its wonderful tall stories and its west wind – would be a ghost indeed, a pitiable and haggard refugee. But in her place, where she lives, she is of famous and unfadeable charm. For my part, I suppose that I met her too late in my life – for age does not wither *her*, but only us – to fall outright in love with her. Be that as it may, I faithfully love one city in Ireland and that is enough of such feeling here at home, where promiscuity would be out of order. But Galway is attractive, it is seductive and frivolous, of a character odd, deeply formed, inviting curiosity and bright acquaintance. So that I often wonder, as I see strangers enjoy and study the place, as I mark the old stones and the dignified and now shabby façades, doorways and towers, the traces everywhere of merchant princedom and of former traffic with France and Spain, as I pick up the legends of the tribal families, and of their feuds with the original princes, the Rourkes and Flahertys and O'Connors, as I sense the good breeding, the calm good humour and self-respect all about, in newspaper-sellers and Sisters of Mercy and tipsy clubmen – observe the liveliness, worldliness even to cynicism which informs the modern town, I marvel sadly that the children of the marshy hinterland, Connemara, are still compelled to go so far away, who have this real city of their own wherein to find an urban life.

It is in general a shame that the Irish young, sick of lonely farmlands, will not make the lives they desire in Irish towns. And in Galway the pity of this strikes sharply. For her, potentially, in our now so wonderfully mechanised and minimised world, is everything that the nineteen-sixties-seventies are going to have to show. And here too are the educational facilities required by any who will want to take part in these sixties-seventies. Galway has good schools and technical schools, and is a University city. And for the last it is a perfect place. To be a student in Galway is a true felicity nowadays, I am inclined to think. The city is small, and conditioned to the leisure that students like; also it is a city where talk, youth and extravagance, of idea as of purse, are taken for granted; and it holds in gift the natural pleasures that the young rush after. To swim at Salthill, to row in the Corrib, to climb the Bens, to walk from Spiddal to Carraroe, talking Irish there and back; to play camógie or gaelic or rugby or any known game; to fool about friendly streets, drink coke and play far-out jazz; to read and fight and blaspheme; to find things out, to make mistakes, to explore every dark thing known up to date from Los Angeles to Shanghai – to have in fact what used to be called a gentleman's education, my belief is that a maid or a man has only to sign on at UCG ...

So why do the children stray?

The world has narrowed; mere mechanics have brought it all into one habit, and a transistor or a tube of Pepsodent in Ballyhaunis is indistinguishable from its equivalent in Mexico City. But scenery, to use an old-fashioned word, keeps its distinctions from place to place; as do such things as weather, climate, manners – and faces. Admittedly, all of these, from scenery on through the list, are worth investigating in their earthly variations, but excess of curiosity about them can be wasteful, disappointing. Anyhow, all are good, exceptionally good, in Galway. So it is a place to invite individualism and the young should not turn from that invitation, for there are few cities in the world that tender it so certainly, I think, or with so much charm. —

PAMELA HINKSON

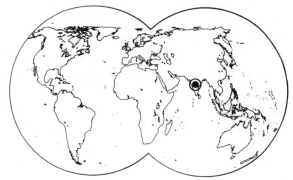

India in the 1930s

Pamela (1900-1982), born in London, daughter of H.A. Hinkson, Mayo Resident Magistrate, and Katharine Tynan the writer, was educated privately in Ireland and on the Continent. As an established journalist she travelled widely in Europe and America. Her most successful book was *The Ladies' Road* (1932). During World War II she lectured in the US for the British Ministry of Information and worked at the Shamrock Club in London for Irish in the services. She returned to live in Ireland in 1959.

Her 1938 first visit to India, as guest of the Viceroy in these final years of the British Raj, resulted in *Indian Harvest* (1941). During a stay of over four months Pamela travelled widely and was impressed by the immensity, beauty and cultural variety of India, the boundaries of which then included what are now Pakistan and Bangladesh. Her visit aroused her concern at the *purdah* restrictions of India's women, only three years after women had become enfranchised.

In those days it took twenty-four hours to travel from Bombay to Delhi. This passage comes from her train journey from Bombay to Peshawar.

— The long journey and the immense width of the plains as we crawled across them made me think of the size of India. And I thought again of those first-comers who had made this journey and similar other journeys into the heart of India by such different means. The slow miles of those journeys, with each mile taking the travellers farther and farther away from the harbour and the ship which was their connection with home. I marvelled afresh at the race that had established itself in India in such conditions. I was to marvel more after a brief experience of the hot weather. Now we travel in what would have seemed inconceivable luxury and security to those first-comers. We have electricity to keep the punkahs moving and ice – a block of it in your railway carriage when you travel in Indian summer makes the hours between eleven and five a still endurable interval of existence before you live again with the dropping of the sun – where, without it, those long hours would be almost unbearable. And we have in the British houses sanitation and clean water and mosquito nets. And some mosquito-breeding swamps have been cleared at least. And we have medical supplies and all the defences against disease which were then non-existent.

Those first pioneers, crossing these plains in their bullock wagons or on horseback or even on foot, faced more powerful enemies – India's defences against their establishment of Empire – than any hostile army that could have assembled to meet them and bar their way....Reading the history of India, that is one of the things that amazes one – the distances travelled, not only by the British rulers of comparatively recent times, but by all those earlier invaders from the North who established the Mogul Empires ...

We passed villages – some a collection of thatched-roofed mud huts. Others of a superior kind, with houses built of stone. Those houses turned their backs to us and had each a small backyard with a high wall about it, for the *purdah* women. I was to learn the true significance and the terrible results of those walls later.

'In April,' my companion said, 'all these hills will be one mass of scarlet with the Flame of the Forest out.'

The bare branches of the Flame of the Forest trees are awkward and unbeautiful, hiding the loveliness which they are to show in the flowering time. There is something symbolical in that. That first day I had experienced none of the weariness of India – although it was in the faces of the sad little sweepers who appeared with their whisking brushes by the carriage door at every station. I could not know yet how the flaming beauty that was to break from those clumsy branches was to lift my heart, three months later, when I saw it at the end of a day of hot weather travelling across a parched and lifeless land. —

Later she visited the State of Alwar in Rajputana (now Rajasthan):

— The colour of a town in Rajputana makes British India colourless by comparison. Surely the sun does burn there with a fiercer, rosier heat. At midday we reached our destination and drove through the wide streets of the rose-coloured city. It should be 'half as old as time'. But it was only built in the last century, hence the width of its streets, which the Maharaja who built it designed with the space of some he had seen in Europe. In those wide streets the crowds come and go. And all the colour of the *pugris* [turbans] I had seen at Horse Shows and polo matches in Delhi were dim by this blaze of scarlet and orange and green and pink and yellow that men wore on their heads. It was as if they had a natural need of that brightness of colour and here, in a country of their own rule and custom, they could express themselves fully. The dresses of the women, the full skirts, the printed veils of gauze and silk were equally brilliant and varied....

It was now too hot to do anything but sleep after lunch. I retired under my mosquito net, which was still a novelty. Within its white draperies I felt safe from the giant hornets that came in and buzzed about the rooms by day, the mosquitoes that sang by night. Awaking from one's afternoon sleep in Indian hot weather, life seems so intolerable that one can hardly rise to face it. Tea brought to one's bedside washes one's mouth and enables one to make the effort of living again. Up and dressed, one recovers.

'What do you want to see?' my kind host asked.

But after a day's knowledge of me he had said, when we set out to visit a palace; 'From what I know of you as a sightseer, we shall be back in a quarter of an hour!' He had added: 'I can see that you are much more interested in people than in buildings'. He was perfectly right in his perception. I liked to meander through the country, among the people, better than seeing things with guides. That is the way one traps the elusive atmosphere and the colour of a country, to remember it for ever. —

Pamela had an attack of neuritis so she consulted the IMS Colonel who ran the State hospital. He happened to be an Irishman, and they got on well. She visited his hospital frequently, learning about local medical problems.

— We drove one evening to see the new State hospital at the edge of the town, built but as yet uncompleted. When it is finished it will be as up-to-date as any in Europe. Everything has been thought of – green inside walls to make rest and coolness for the eyes, in that climate most necessary, provision for washing and disinfecting the clothes of the patients when they come in. The small private rooms for richer patients with bathrooms attached, and each a balcony outside, would tempt anyone to be ill in them. The house to hold the nursing staff stood beyond an open space that would presently be a garden between it and the hospital. Negotiations were in progress for the service of nursing nuns of an order comprising nuns of various European nationalities but with a Mother House in Paris.

I asked questions. What, from a doctor's experience, were the results of the *purdah* system? He answered at once, as I had been told already, osteomalacia – softening and inadequate growth of the bones, due to lack of sun and light and air, particularly in the growing years of young girls and girl children. This, he added, especially with the poorer *purdah* women, who have only backyards to walk in which the sun never reaches, as it may reach the gardens in which the *purdah* Maharanis and rich women walk. Osteomalacia is the cause of much malformation and resultant terrible suffering of many Indian women in childbirth, and following inevitable weakness or malformation of the children born of them....

He told me many other things about *purdah* and its results, as we stood on that balcony in the evening coolness that had come after the burning day....After our visit to the new hospital we drove out of the town to see the new tuberculosis settlement, a group of white houses designed to catch all the sun and air for those who lived in them. But even these houses had to be made with the backyard for the women to walk in, hidden. The reformer in India has to accept such things which directly oppose his effort and undo much of his work... —

Pamela Hinkson, the experienced journalist, well conveys the atmosphere of India in the 1930s. Her book is a historical as well as a personal record of a perceptive European woman's first visit to this fascinating sub-continent.

ANITA LESLIE

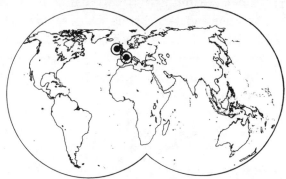

Ambulance-driving during the Second World War, and a rat in the Shelbourne

Anita (1914-1985) was the daughter of the writer Sir John Randolph Shane Leslie of Glaslough, Co. Monaghan, Winston Churchill's cousin. Her mother was American. Educated privately, she at first led the life of a society socialite, marrying an older man in her early twenties. Dissatisfied with this life, in 1940 she joined the British Mechanised Transport Corps as an ambulance driver. Later, having transferred to the French army because it alone allowed women to work in the front line, she crossed the Rhine with the 1st French Armoured Division in one of twelve ambulances driven by women. She was awarded the Croix de Guerre, and her war memoirs *Train to Nowhere* (1946) were highly praised. After her second marriage to Bill King she wrote *Love in a Nutshell* (1951) about sailing in *Galway Blazer* through the Caribbean with Bill and their baby.

Anita wrote many biographies from her first *Life of Rodin* (1939) to her last *Cousin Randolph* (1985). Some of her other subjects were Mrs Fitzherbert (the famous Dublin-born actress, mistress to the Prince of Wales, by whom he had ten children before becoming George IV); Winston Churchill's American mother, and his grandfather; Francis Chichester and Madame Tussaud.

Anita's witty autobiography of her lush pre-war youth, *The Gilt and the Gingerbread* (1981), was summed up thus by an *Irish Times* reviewer: 'If Somerville and Ross, J.P. Donleavy and Caroline Blackwood all sat down together to write the Great Irish Novel, they might evoke something very like the world of Anita Leslie'. Her second autobiography, *A Story Half Told* (1983), deals with her adventurous war years during which she really grew up, and makes fascinating reading. Subsequent quotes all come from this book.

From 1940-1945 Anita wore uniform and forgot what it was like to choose a dress or carry a handbag. Until 1944 she served in South Africa briefly, then Egypt, Palestine, Lebanon and Syria, before being sent to Italy. 'The hospitals of the Naples area were overflowing. Day and night two streams of wounded arrived by sea from Anzio beyond Cassino' and later about three hundred wounded arrived daily at Capochino Airport outside Naples. 'All day long my face wore a grey dust mask and my hair stood out stiffly.' Then came D-Day in Normandy. 'The wounded forgot to drink their tea and only wanted news.' That July Anita applied for permission to join the French army.

In France General Soudre told her, 'We are in full attack and there's plenty of work for the ambulances. Nice to have *une irlandaise* in the Division'.

Anita relates the following episode:

— After Mass I was temporarily given an ambulance and told to drive three wounded soldiers and a small boy called Ramon back to the Brigade hospital. I climbed into my driver's seat glad to get back to the job I knew so well, but everything went wrong during that first evacuation. A Bailey bridge had sunk below a river and we had to turn round and do an eight-mile detour over bad tracks. The little boy was eight or nine, he began to beg for air. 'Vite, vite,' were his last words and I poured with sweat as we bumped over the rough road. We carried him straight to the operating theatre but he died on the table. For a long time the surgeon kept pulling his tongue. It was no good. I had to go back disconsolate to the soldiers lying on their stretchers. 'They could not save le petit?' The men minded terribly when a child died. It was different to a soldier getting killed. — The next day Anita had to tell the child's mother.

She describes the difficult physical conditions that rainy autumn. The weary, sodden French soldiers, the even wearier disarmed German prisoners.

— The village of Saulxures where we ambulance drivers were allotted a room in which to dry our clothes, had been bombarded for two weeks and shells continued to whistle overhead, but as our troops advanced through the narrow mountain passes gaunt-faced inhabitants began to creep out of cellars. This was the world in which I found myself – I who had once been an idiotic London debutante.

One morning we came upon something rather extraordinary. The body of a woman in German uniform was brought down from the mountain. French parachute troops had found her and several other women snipers tied in trees. Their bodies were bound so securely that they did not fall even after they were dead. *Blitz Mädchen* they were called. —

In March 1945 Anita hears that her mother, whom she has not seen for almost five years, is dangerously ill with pneumonia in Dublin, so she is given compassionate leave. As no French soldier has ever wanted to travel to Ireland she has to make her own way, hitch-hiking by truck and plane. In London a V2 rocket awakens her at 7 a.m. 'After the last months of cannon noise the possible need for a rush for cover pervaded one's dreams.'

'Hundreds of Irish volunteers were perpetually going home on leave. One had to don a mackintosh on the boat – and military caps were put in pockets. The Irish were then no longer considered to be in uniform! However, I was unique in wearing French insignia!' They reached the Dublin docks late, in heavy fog. The horse-drawn cabs had gone to bed. She arrived at the Shelbourne Hotel near midnight.

— My heavy sleep was disturbed by strange dreams. I woke with a start several times thinking that some animal was digging into my hair and jumping on and off the bed. Then I dreamed I was in a saw-mill. I woke up in the dark and could swear I *heard* the sound of sawing. It was light when I finally woke and looked at my wrist watch. It said exactly eight o'clock. Then something moved under the eiderdown. I lifted it up and saw a huge rat curled up in the crutch of my knees. He must have been in the room when I arrived. When I shut the bottom window he could not get out so he had very sensibly tried to gnaw his way through the wainscotting – a heap of sawdust showed that my dreams of a saw-mill had not been completely imaginary. Then he must have dug into my hair for his traces showed on the pillow ...I uttered a yell and ran out into the corridor ... —

At St Vincent's Hospital she finds her mother:

— I went back to the hotel for meals and enjoyed the wondrous silence of Dublin streets, broken only by the clip-clop of an occasional horse-drawn cab. In England and France one always heard military vehicles roaring around. In Ireland there was no petrol whatever. The country had just slipped back to the eighteenth century. I loved it. —

After three days she goes to Castle Leslie, eighty miles north of Dublin. This took six hours instead of four by train, as the engines were stoked with turf. Her father, normally on duty as a Home Guard in London, had returned to Ireland during her mother's illness and was 'alone' in the castle with six servants, cook and kitchenmaid, butler, parlourmaid and two housemaids.

The house was freezing, and there had been no electricity for three years. 'Outside on the front door steps the local boys' brass-bugle band stood playing in my honour. I wished the French army could see them.' Back in London for three days she is invited to lunch by Winston Churchill at Chequers, just back from watching the second airdrop on Arnhem. After that she flies back to Paris and takes the night train to Alsace.

At dawn on 6th June, 1945, three ambulances were ordered to drive three hundred miles across Germany to collect sick French prisoners from a place called Nordhausen in the Hartz mountains. When they arrived they found the American army in charge: 'We stared at what appeared to be a factory yard covered with small aeroplanes' which turned out to be parts for V2 rockets. Nearby were the huts used as SS barracks, and a huge gibbet from which twenty to forty corpses at a time had once dangled. A French doctor shows them the large swimming pool. 'Starving men would be given hot soup and then thrown in on an icy night to see if they contracted pneumonia or died of heart failure.'

In this camp 15,000 prisoners had lived surrounded by electrified barbed wire, and worked twelve-hour shifts in vast underground V-weapon factories. 1,000 a month died from starvation and exhaustion. 'No one had ever escaped from Nordhausen and no one was intended to survive. A few of the young and strong lived two years, but most died within twelve months.'

The Americans were now using Nordhausen as a transit camp for various released prisoners and deported workers brought in from the area. The ambulances first transported some TB cases to a nearby sanatorium, then took sixteen prisoners released from Buchenwald (40 miles away). These men were all in a deplorable state:

— After fifteen hours on the road with our poor fellows we felt we had known them all their lives. They could only talk in whispers, their lungs were gone, they were light as birds when we stopped to give them a drink or to pass the urine bottle but how well we grew to know them. Several were Frenchmen who had been refusing to do agricultural work in Germany because the BBC gave them to understand the invasion was imminent and they could help by refusing to work ... These men had a look in their eyes I had never seen. My heart ached as I held them up to cough.

What a journey. Yet it was worthwhile, they were going home, going back to France; even while spitting blood, this long day's drive filled them with wonder. Two men had TB of the intestines which gave them diarrhoea and, having no bed pans, we had to stop the ambulances, lift out the stretchers and roll them into the grass while holding them gasping with weakness. American soldiers came up to gape and stayed to help, silent and gentle when they saw hip bones protruding through the skin ...

That night, as the sun set with unusual beauty and the fields glowed in golden light, such nausea came over us that we could hardly drive. It was not the inelegance of these dying men but the cruelty of humanity that hurt. —

DERVLA MURPHY

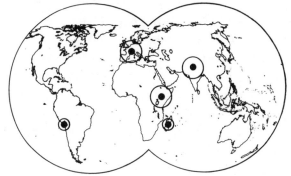

Our most celebrated woman traveller, illustrated here by accounts of Tibet, Uganda and Zambia

Dervla Murphy (born Co. Waterford 1931) is Ireland's most intrepid woman traveller, and needs no introduction, for many of her books are still in print. Her early life, how she left school at fourteen and spent her twenties caring for her ageing parents, is related in her autobiography *Wheels within wheels* (1979). Dervla was only free to travel after the death of both parents, then she set off on her bicycle Roz in the bitter winter of 1963, subsequently writing *Full Tilt: Ireland to India on a bicycle* (1965) (still in print). The journey took her six months.

Since then she has travelled on foot with a mule, donkey or pony, or by bicycle in ways never before attempted by any lone woman, producing books about Tibet, Ethiopia, Nepal, South India, Baltistan, the Andes, Madagascar, Cameroon, Rumania and various parts of Africa. Several of her journeys were undertaken with her young daughter Rachel. She has, in addition, written two books of social discussion, on Northern Ireland in *A Place Apart* and on nuclear armaments proliferation in *Race to the Finish?*

Dervla has by now acquired an immense fund of knowledge about peoples, their customs and histories. She has had some narrow escapes from death, as well as the inevitable attempted rape, accidents, illness, sunburn and exhaustion. Her period of travelling dates from before mass tourism had begun. Nowadays she carries a map with her to avoid what she calls 'tourist sodden' areas.

Her first long journey, as described in *Full Tilt*, tells us why Dervla travels: 'I regard this sort of life, with just Roz and me and the sky and the earth, as sheer bliss'. Travel for her is a therapeutic escape, but one which in the end always becomes more than that as she gets involved with the people she meets. In Kabul she remarks of a young American she considers typical of back-packing westerners: 'To them, travel is more a *going away from* rather than a *going towards*, and they seem empty and unhappy and bewildered and pathetically anxious for companionship...', young people without an aim, who hold themselves apart from the people they travel among. Dervla asks: 'Is this something else our age does – on the one hand make communication easier than ever before, while on the other hand widening the gulf between those who are "developed" and those who are not?'

Dervla has also become accustomed, over the years, to being considered 'a goddam nut-case,' as a passing American names her in *Full Tilt* after she has refused to take a lift. Her philosophy of travel has not changed over the years. She tells us in *Full Tilt*:

— When Stern toured France and Italy he needed more guts and initiative than the contemporary traveller needs to tour the five continents; people now use less than half their potential forces because 'Progress' has deprived them of the incentive to live fully. All this has been brought to the surface of my mind by the general attitude to my conception of travelling, which I once took for granted as normal behaviour but which strikes most people as wild eccentricity, merely because it involves a certain amount of what is now regarded as hardship but was to all our ancestors a feature of everyday life – using physical energy to get from point A to point B. I don't know what the end result of all this 'progress' will be – something dire, I should think. We remain *part of Nature*, however startling our scientific advances, and the more successfully we forget or ignore this fact, the less we can be proud of being men. —

By integrating wherever she travels Dervla has become an expert communicator:

— When you ask for fried eggs by making noises like a hen after laying, followed by noises like something sizzling in fat, the whole household is convulsed with laughter and not only are fried eggs served, but you are unanimously elected as one of the family. —

In between the trials of non-cooperative customs officials and climatic extremes, Dervla has been attacked by wild dogs, stoned by youths, stung by a scorpion, invaded by bed-bugs, suffered from dysentery, heatstroke and malaria, broken three ribs in Afghanistan and a leg in Rumania, to mention only a few of her vicissitudes. On the other hand she sometimes reaches a state of elation brought about by her surroundings, which makes up for all the rest. In Pakistan, on a pony, for Roz was useless in the mountains, she writes in *Full Tilt*:

— We covered about thirty-five miles today through the wildest landscape I've ever seen. This Gilgit region really does something quite extraordinary to one's mind. The completely unbroken solitude and the absence of anything recalling the rest of humanity produce a unique feeling of liberation as one moves slowly through these tremendous gorges. Today the outside world and my own life – past and future – as part of that world seemed so utterly unreal that for a time I ceased to be aware of it and existed only in the present, acutely conscious of my surroundings and of physical sensation, but removed, in a dreamlike way, from myself as a person. It was a strangely relaxing experience – though in retrospect slightly eerie. —

Dervla's list of kit for her journey to India included a .25 revolver, and the most terrifying happening en route was being attacked on a snowy track in the Yugoslav mountains by three wild dogs. She shot one dead, wounded a second and the third ran off. After eventually reaching Delhi, Dervla next became involved with Tibetan refugee children in Dharamsala, then several months later bicycled up the Kulu valley in the Himalayas.

One day, as she describes in *Tibetan Foothold*, having already pushed Roz up 8,800 feet that day, she arrives by 7 pm at 9,500 feet dripping with sweat in her thin clothing. It was dark but she knew a full moon would rise over the mountains. At this point memories of the previous attack in Yugoslavia return to her:

— During the next two and a half hours I struggled against the soft snow and the preposterous gradient ... and by nine o'clock I had begun to feel really scared. Apart from the unbeatable hell of our June trek through the Indus Gorge this was the most frightening experience of my life. Since last winter's unfortunate encounter in Serbia, forest, snow and moonlight ring only one bell for me – *wolves* – and every time I heard a rustle I would have jumped a foot if I'd had the energy. —

Eventually she finds a house and collapses on the floor in front of the fire, to fall asleep immediately. This poor family welcome her with great consideration, rescue Roz and unstrapping the saddle bag lay it beside her head, 'typical of the thoughtfulness I have experienced everywhere among allegedly uncouth peasants.'

To Dervla's communication skills must be added her tenacity, ability to go without food for long periods, her tolerance and her sense of humour. Her latest book, *The Ukimwi Road; from Kenya to Zimbabwe*, is the fruit of a 3,000 mile bicycle ride on Lear, a mountain bike, undertaken in 1992 as a four month therapeutic mystery tour. Soon, however, Dervla gets involved with the major human problem she meets en route, Ukimwi or what Africans call 'the slim disease' – AIDS.

As she expects her journey is greeted with surprise. An African asks, 'What is your *mission*, what are you working for? Who is funding you, or are you sponsored, cycling for charity?' Dervla writes:

— To Africans the concept of unsubsidized solo travelling seems a weird aberration. Sometimes I tried to explain that Westerners can save money on Third World journeys. This four-month 'African Experience' was to cost me less than £420, plus £470 for my air-fare; and the days have long gone when one could survive in Ireland for four months on less than £900. —

In a Ugandan hotel which costs £2 her room has a bath but no water.

— I supped off more soggy rice and an extraordinarily nasty fish stew. Then I fell into bed and had a unique experience.

Switching off the light, I was resigned to the inevitable; one learns to live – even to sleep – with mosquitoes. Moments later the fleas became apparent: several fleas, simultaneously settled down to their evening meal. I resigned myself to those, too. Given their way fleas soon become replete and desist; to interrupt them merely wastes energy and prolongs the agony. And anyway the mosquitoes were going to give me an itchy night. Then something else made itself felt, something unfamiliar and dreadfully numerous. Switching on the light, I found the bed swarming with mites – creatures much too small to be lice, so minuscule that one could see them only because they were moving. I looked at my naked body; they were swarming on it, too. Then another movement caught my eye: truly this room was an insect game-park. Down the wall from the wooden ceiling scores of red-brown bedbugs, the size and shape of a little fingernail, had been marching – until the light went on. Bedbugs are allergic to light and now they were in disarray, scuttling to and fro instead of

proceeding in an orderly fashion to their destination. Experienced travellers maintain that bedbugs and fleas cannot co-exist; this fallacy I am now in a positive to disprove. Having rid myself of the mites (that took time) I slept in the bath with the light on. Only the mosquitoes followed me. —

In Uganda Dervla meets Jill and Helen, African feminists happy to meet a liberated Irish woman cyclist. Wherever she goes AIDS comes up in the conversation and Dervla gets into yet another discussion about the disease. Helen explains that African men have gone weak under westernisation.

— Before they were important, now there's no warriors, no hunters, just lying around drinking. Then hunting girls to prove they're still *men*! But for us nothing's changed – work and more work, from before dawn till after dark. Our only change is a bad one – more children, when men only have one wife. —

In Tanzania an expatriate tells Dervla that if Africans persist in their happy-go-fucky life style, and refuse to use condoms, the rest of the world will soon lose sympathy:

— I commented that this would not displease some of the Africans I'd met on my way. Nor can the West afford to be censorious; we too use sex as a commodity, in more convoluted but no less degrading ways – and without extenuating circumstances. —

In Zambia, while in the Zambezi game reserve, Dervla is suddenly struck down by her first ever attack of malaria. Feeling utterly lethargic she thinks:

— Thomson didn't react like this, he just bashed on regardless up the next escarpment...I recalled Mary Livingstone, lying dying of fever on a mattress spread on three tea-chests – that was at Shupanga, not far from here, during the ill-fated Zambezi Expedition. Then I thought, 'Must move, must take Halfan'...I looked at Lear, leaning against a baobab tree eight yards away. He seemed virtually inaccessible. Four baboons loped past, then paused to survey me. In game reserves they don't feel threatened by humans. —

As the nearest town is forty miles away she takes two Halfan and sleeps through the noon silence of the bush:

— One knows that nearby are many living creatures: insects, reptiles, birds, monkeys, antelope, elephants, hyenas, leopards, lions – all now utterly still, under a sky pallid with heat. —

When she awakes her mild delirium has gone, and leaning on Lear she crawls along the road and finds a game warden in a thatched hut. She sleeps on his floor and for the next thirty-six hours drifts in and out of fever with no sense of time, while the warden plies her with jugs of hot, black tea.

Weakened by malaria Dervla is forced to give up her plan to cycle round Zimbabwe and leave her bike near the South African border. South African travel is planned for her next adventure.

Dervla's style of travel is for the hardy few, but it makes fascinating reading!

~

And what of Ireland's travelling nuns?

Edmund M. Hogan's historical survey, *The Irish Missionary Movement 1830-1980* (1990), points out that the early missions were to the Irish diaspora, as 50-70,000 people left Ireland annually in the second half of the nineteenth century. Sisters of Charity, Loreto, Presentation, Mercy, Dominican, St. Columban, Ursulines and other Orders, travelled to distant places, often lived there under difficult conditions and had all kinds of adventures.

Mary Purcell in her *To Africa with Love* (1987) gives us a biography of Mother Mary Martin (1892-1975), founder of the Medical Missionaries of Mary in 1937, who travelled to USA, Africa, China and Japan for her work, in spite of indifferent health. The author draws on the Order's archives, on letters from Sisters in the missions, on diaries from other nuns who worked with Mary Martin, and from the files of their magazines.

There are also two biographies of Catherine McAuley, who founded the Sisters of Mercy in 1831, by M. Bertrand Degnan (1957) and Angela Bolster (1990).

Nuns are usually reticent people, though some, like the charismatic healer Sister Briege McKenna of the Congregation of the Sisters of St Clare, who has a worldwide ministry of evangelism and healing, write at length about their work. Much could still be gleaned about the travels of nuns and many nuns could no doubt write about this, had they the encouragement and the time.

SISTER HILARY LYONS

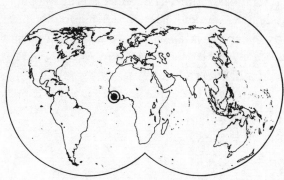

A missionary in Sierra Leone

Hilary (born into a Co. Mayo farming family, 1924), eldest of nine, has for forty years been a Holy Rosary mission doctor in Sierra Leone. She writes as follows:

— Was it the urge to travel that took me out of Mayo at the age of nineteen, or was it a 'call to help people who have not our opportunities', which is what I told my mother at the time. It was probably a bit of both. Whatever it was I have been happy in Africa and travelled much more than I dreamed of then, in Africa, America, Europe and once, before their war, for two lovely weeks in Lebanon.

My most recent work in Sierra Leone, West Africa, where I have spent forty years, was supervising Peripheral Health Units. Someone commented 'this is a good job for you as you like going places anyway,' and it is true. There is a get-up-and-go inside me. It is only too sad that so many beginnings are the endings of something else. I always cry at partings and see death as the great parting. Indeed I cry so readily at every funeral that in the days of the 'keeners' I could have been hired!

When I entered the Convent in 1943 the rule was that we would never return home. That was changed, though I was not to know it then. Mission work was something I wanted to do and had struggled to get permission for, yet when the blues, greens and amethysts of my native mountains pulled away behind me the tears came down – as they do to this day each time I leave home for my two years stint in Africa. Once the mountains are gone I lift my head and anticipation takes over.

Back in 1953 we travelled by sea in m.v. *Tamele*, a cargo boat with three bunks to a cabin. You could stand and lie down but there was no place to sit. The owners were not obliged to provide much comfort for passengers. We

were satisfied. We had not chosen Africa for comfort.

We sailed down the Mersey on a grey January day wide-eyed at the fuss and bustle of Merseyside, agog with the excitement of being en route for Africa. Two of us were new to the West Coast and soon excitement gave way to trepidation at the magnitude of the step we were taking plus a grinding loneliness for home, the familiar, the loved. Surreptitiously we crept to a deck where only deck chairs were stored, to sing the songs of Ireland and cry a little, hidden from the three mature missionaries on board with us.

We arrived on February 10th, 1953. Land was sighted at two a.m. and we were up at first light. Africa! What shall I say? The heat, hot sticky humid heat! We wore full old-style habits in those days.

The ship anchored off-shore as there was then no deepwater quay. We were let down the side in a sort of chair to the waiting craft below, our drapery notwithstanding. Passengers threw coins from the ship to Sierra Leoneans in small dugout canoes who dived to the sea-bed for them. I did not like that. We are not in a zoo, I fumed secretly. Neither did I like it when I saw my tin trunk (the Gucci luggage par excellence in those days) on a young man's head, as he scurried with incredible agility up the stone steps of the water front.

Strange that I have no impression of the great natural beauty of Freetown from those first days. I can only recapture the strangeness, so many black people talking, arguing, loading and unloading, their backs glistening with perspiration in the heat. And my own mounting anxiety as to whether I could cope in this seemingly other planet. How did I not see the Lion (Leone) mountains, lordly palms, sparkling water, rioting bourgainvillea, the impressive scarlet hibiscus? It was too early in the year for blooms of frangipani, lagostrimia and the flame trees. All the above have sustained my soul with a magic sense of God's presence throughout the subsequent years. Ah that first day! I saw only dimly.

We travelled from Freetown to Bo, the second largest town, by train. The one hundred and sixty miles took fourteen hours. The train started off so slowly that we were overtaken by a cyclist on East Street. This was subject matter for my first letter home.

Thus began my travelling in Sierra Leone. Since then I have covered the country by car, jeep, truck, canoe and on foot in the rain forest. I have also had one trip in a hammock, as chiefs are carried, to honour my first twenty-five years there.

Tips for travellers are to remember the potholes in the dirt roads, wear a snug cotton bra and always carry water. As for food, villagers give hospitality if they are expecting you, but bring some non-perishable supplies, just in case. Do not drink too much, or looking for a secluded patch in the bush may be difficult! Poor organisation in these matters can lead to the trekker's syndrome, a full bladder and an empty stomach. Traversing swamps on foot is inevitable. Wear plastic sandals as they do not become soggy. There are water snakes, so *pray*! Schistosomes and amoebae are other occupational hazards.

I travel alone with an African driver and sometimes I am the only white woman in the village. I have never felt afraid. Once you check in with the chief, state who you are and what is your business, you are accepted. The best room will be found for you and all your needs provided for. Nothing will, however, protect you from mosquitoes. Hordes of hungry, whining, little demons bear down on arms and legs. One or many may be carrying the malaria parasite. If your name is on it you will go down ten days from now. Rats are occasional visitors, but have never come nearer than eating my soap. Villages have no electricity so if you need to use the pit latrine in the night watch out for a cobra, who make be taking a night's lodging and will defend his territory!

Though I have never feared humans in Africa I have sometimes been fear-frozen. Once when travelling in a small dugout canoe I was told to sit on a small box, face forward and not move. I asked if there were alligators and was told there were, but we were unlikely to see any. I thanked the Lord for that and proceeded to enjoy the scenery. Rich film stars, I told myself, pay a fortune for less. Suddenly they shout: 'Look! There!' I sat immobilised. Nothing to say or do. This is *it*. But all they were looking at was a deer. He had fallen off the bank and was swimming to safety. Relief made me feel faint. After a few moments of canoe-hunting the poor animal, out-numbered and out-manoeuvred, was caught and killed. We pulled in at the next village to share the venison. Such a diversion is, of course, unscheduled, so a laid back attitude to time is essential. A reflection that punctuality as a virtue does not appear in the Gospels is a help.

I love the village women. There is a traditional secret society among women in which girls are initiated into adulthood at puberty. This is the Sande or Bundo society, and officials are called Sowui's, who have graduated by virtue of their excellence in maintaining Mende culture, their skills and their age, to this exalted position. These senior women are keepers of the dream, for not to be initiated is not to be a true Mende woman.

The core rites, which include circumcision, are kept secret. Apart from that there is intense training for a woman's role in Mende society, and within this training dimension I work with them. They transfer knowledge through song and dance. Shrewdly perceiving the eroding influence of Western ways on their lives they are quite willing to augment their knowledge and skills. I am able to incorporate health promotive messages into their songs and dances. They now have songs about immunisation and child nutrition, and above all how to protect themselves from the high maternal mortality that is their greatest present affliction. Change is slow and though I often tangle with them on harmful taboos, my admiration is unbounded. They and their sisters survive incredible workloads while breast feeding or lactating, poor diets and the agony of high child and maternal mortality rates. These nurturers of life not only survive, they grow.

While travelling in Europe or North America I am usually alone, fundraising or visiting friends. I have had my share of experiences. I worked one hot Summer in Brooklyn's naval dockyard alongside two young black Americans, on two ships fitted out for action 1945, but too late for the war. The contents of their operating rooms finished up in Sierra Leone!

In Lebanon I was fortunate enough to visit a former residence of a Saladin or Sultan at Biet-e-Dien. Here the clothes worn by the harem women were on show, including high heeled shoes with bells. The harem bathroom was large and circular, ringed by cushions. Beneath were furnaces which kept the room warm. The women bathed in hot water, then reclined on cushions to be oiled and perfumed by their maids. Women of noble family, as members of the prince's harem they wore elaborately jewelled silks and satins, had sumptuous food, a lavish life-style and if they produced children, the respect of his Highness. What more could a woman want?

Travel expands the mind to a realisation that there are other ways of living rather than our own. And there are surprises when travelling! Once I checked into a small hotel in Amsterdam. The second evening my friend and I came into the foyer, where the desk clerk asked if we would like a drink. We began to talk. He asked. 'Would you be a nun, Ma'am?'

Surprised, as I was not wearing a veil, I asked how he had guessed.

'The suit you're wearing is the same as my Auntie Marie wears. She's a Mercy nun in Sydney. You've a ring on the right hand. Married women in the English-speaking world wear wedding rings on the left hand.'

I congratulated him on his perspicacity. Then he said: 'I hope you don't mind my asking, Sister, but did you know this is a gay hotel?'

Well, I nearly dropped my teeth!

Travelling with a veil or without makes a difference. The veil represents respect. Without it you are on your own. Once in a Cologne hotel a receptionist gave me a quick, but rude, once over, modest clothes, shabby luggage, and only snapped into, 'Madam, can I help you?' when I produced travellers cheques. We are judged so readily by external appearance.

I ask myself if my contentment while on the move is an Irish trait. Have not the Irish, from Brendan the navigator onwards, and for different reasons according to their circumstances, always had this drive to burst out of their island? But did they not migrate there in the first place? —

MARY RUSSELL

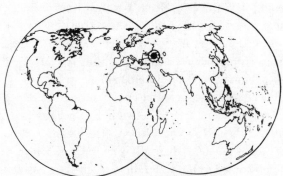

A traveller in modern Georgia

Mary (born Dublin 1937), holds an MA in Peace Studies and is a freelance journalist, writing for Irish, British, African and Middle East publications. Since her three children have grown up, she has been based in Ireland, sometimes working from Oxford when not travelling for her work. Her fascinating book *The Blessings of a Good Thick Skirt: Women travellers and their world* (1986) has been reprinted frequently. The idea for the book came from a series of articles on women travellers commissioned by *The Guardian*. The only Irish women discussed in this book are Elizabeth Le Blond, about whom Mary is very amusing, and Dervla Murphy.

Mary Russell is interesting on attitudes women may have towards travelling on their own versus family responsibilities. She believes that the women travel-explorers, such as Mary Kingsley and Freya Stark, are people certain of their priorities: 'A man, however, companionable, would always come second and it is perhaps this attitude, so different from that of many women, conditioned as they are to finding fulfilment in marriage, that sets the woman traveller apart' because, 'The need for separateness is an important element in her make-up, a need which would be threatened by marriage.' It is true that the few Irish women travel-explorers confirm this, for Daisy Bates left her husband and son, Beatrice Grimshaw never married, and Dervla Murphy, a single parent, took her daughter with her.

Mary Russell's next book was *Please don't call it Soviet Georgia*, a journey through a troubled paradise (1991). She had considerable difficulty in obtaining permission to go and in the end her route was closely monitored, solo women travellers being frowned upon. She sent her mountain bike from London to Tbilisi, via Moscow, in advance, her idea being to cycle down the least frequented routes. In the end her Georgian hosts, who were held responsible for her, would not hear of her going off on her own, though they knew she had led an adventurous life as a journalist in the Middle East and had bicycled alone 1,000 kilometers from Le Havre to Marseilles and on to Algeria. Reluctantly they agree to take her and the bike by jeep to the valley of the Alazani:

— The day was passing on and I wondered when we were going to be able to take out the bikes and get going. First, said Alec, we have to collect an old college friend – Soso. Soso was small and worried-looking, with curly hair and a five o'clock shadow. He was an environmental health inspector, an administrator who, like many Georgians, seemed to have unlimited free time. We went to Ikalto, the ruined monastery where the poet Rustaveli had studied in the twelfth century. The church was cold and unfriendly even though there were lots of candles burning. Outside, in the grounds, were the remains of two huge wine-trampling baths which helped to dispel the grimness of the church. In the porch an old woman sat finger knitting, and to one side of the church stood a semi-circle of trees. Seven trees. I felt more at home now. Seven was a sacred number in the old pre-christian religion here, for they worshipped the moon, the sun and the five terrestrial planets.

There were more churches to visit: Shuamta – a medieval monastic settlement for nuns. The long quiet track led to a cluster of red-pantiled roofs, each leaning on a different plane, the stones beneath them sun-warmed and glowing. Solitude. Shrouded by trees, the Shuamta church sat high on a hill, looking down on a whole range of hills, wooded with poplars. Georgia is a country of woods and forest. Maple, ash and alder lie on hillsides thick as moss on a stone and the trunks of ancient beech trees can sometimes measure 35 feet in circumference. The most sacred of trees was the oak – nearly every village had one and so powerful was its aura that the feudal lords would occasionally dare to cut them down in order to weaken the heart of the villagers.

The nuns of Shuamta lived here at the end of the track, far from human contact. No one around but themselves and their god. Further back down the track, the monastery for men was still inhabited. A young monk, robed in black, black bearded and with black hair, was doing something leisurely with a paint brush. A huge satin-black hound growled and prowled around us and was eventually called to heel by a tiny old woman, also in black....

It was the next day before we got going with the bikes. I had hoped for a seven o'clock start. By ten, the doldrums had settled on the household. Alec sat in the garden coughing his way through his first cigarette while Soso read the paper and Nono, his small son, stalked birds in the garden, taking pot shots at them with his father's air-gun.

It had been decided the previous night that we would not, after all, camp out in the hills, that Soso's generous hospitality being offered, he would be offended if we didn't stay with him. Reluctantly, I'd patted my tent bag goodnight and given in with what I hoped was a decent display of grace. Marina, Soso's wife, had prepared a huge meal and Soso's wine graced the table ...

My original plan of spending a week or two cycling in the foothills of the Caucasus had dwindled to this one weekend which itself was shrinking fast and now I wanted to be off. Awkwardly and pigheadedly, I held out for a day's cycling by the river and eventually we set off – myself, Alec, Soso and his son, Nono.

The bikes were unloaded a mile or two from the river, the event witnessed by a sizeable crowd. Alec's bike was not at all in good trim. The tyres were bald, the saddle the wrong height. The brakes didn't work and the chain kept slipping. It had not had any maintenance work done on it for some time, if

Mary Russell in Lesotho, Southern Africa, (top),
Dominican Republic (centre), and the Northern Transvaal (bottom)

indeed ever, and I wondered when it had last been ridden. I unloaded my own bike and had a few experimental spins round on it. Then I noticed something odd on the wheel. There was an ominous bulge in the tyre, like a blue-black boil. I bent down to examine it and wished I hadn't. A section of the wall of the tyre, a piece at the side about an inch square, had been worn down to the tread – probably by the continual bouncing on the back of the jeep yesterday. Through the wall of the tyre protruded a shiny blue blister of inner tubing. It looked horrible. At any moment it could burst and it was at that moment that I realized I had forgotten to bring my spare tubes and tyres with me. They were back in Tbilisi. We stared in silence at the boil.

'You can't ride it,' said Alec with what I thought was relief in his voice.

'Yes I can. I'll just have to go carefully, that's all. Very carefully.' I was not going to abandon the ride now at this stage.

I was all for leaving then and there, wanting above all to get going, but Soso insisted on attempting a repair job by binding the boil with sellotape.

And then we're off, the two of them taking it in turns to herd me along. Soso goes first in the jeep, keeping a few feet ahead of me so that my eyes are blinded with dust. I try riding with my eyes shut for a while but it's too nerve-racking. Then, to my relief, he gets impatient and shoots on ahead. Alec stays with me, bumping along on a frame that must be as uncomfortable as a bone-shaker. At one point, flamboyantly, he overtakes me, waving, and then falls off, for no apparent reason. Diplomatically, I look the other way. Next time I look back at him, he's holding the handlebars with one hand and smoking a cigarette with the other.

When we catch up with Soso, the two change over and I manage to lose them for a bit. After a morning's cycling we reach the Alazani river ...

We stand on the bank, discussing where to go next. Soso and Alec are all for going home. I'm not. I want to go on and on, now that I've got my freedom. For the first time for weeks, I've got to a place where there are no people, no cars, no sound. It's still Georgia but a different Georgia. I've got a bottle of wine, some cheese and some bread in my saddle bag. We can carry on and picnic somewhere along the river. The two men smile weakly. It's tough on Soso, cycling. His legs are short and riding that rickety bike must be hell. But I harden myself and set off, giving them the lead.

We turn away from the river and cross a ford where Alec and I wash some of the mud off our bikes. My shoes are so muddy that there's nothing for it but to wade through the water in them to get them clean. Nono watches me with envy, standing at the bank where he has been told to stand. I wash out my socks and hang them on the handlebars to dry. There are quite a few fords to get across. At one a man in a hammock swings quietly in the heat.

The trick with fording is to take a run at it and then keep going. The jeep goes first to test the depth. The problem, however, is that while I can throw my legs out sideways to avoid the worst of the spray, my saddle-bags can't and I'd forgotten my camera was in one of them. We load them into the jeep and Alec puts the other bike in as well. He's had enough. The jeep crashes on ahead and I'm alone again. Riding alongside an irrigation canal, I can get a good view of the river valley and the great plain of the Alazani running far out towards the mountains, across a plain occupied by huge, collective vineyards and neatly spaced walnut groves.

With the midday heat abating, clusters of people are starting to come back into the fields and vineyards. The canal runs straight and true and I could carry on forever. I pass a truck drawing water from the canal and the men all stop to stare as I wobble past. The track is rutted and scattered with large stones but the grass is velvet smooth, nibbled down by sheep. If I were on my own, I would lie down on it for ten minutes. Have a glass of wine, perhaps.

I suggested earlier that we might do this but the response was puzzling. Both Alec and Soso declined, even though it was time for a midday break. Was it too spontaneous a decision? Meals here can't happen suddenly. Hours of preparation must go into them. An ad hoc bottle of wine and a loaf of bread wouldn't measure up anyway. Even a picnic must be a feast. There was also the problem of receiving. Georgians, like Arab people, are great at giving. At receiving, less so. Receiving puts you at a disadvantage, makes you weak, beholden to your giver. Giving is a subtle form of power which disarms the recipient. Force-fed with kindness, I found my critical faculties often sapped. Cosseted with care, I was imprisoned by the anxieties of others.

'A woman alone, here in Georgia?' they said. 'Well, you won't be killed, of course, but it will not be pleasant. Better not to go alone.'

Grateful for their shelter and companionship, I had to take on also their protective mantle which weighed far too heavily on my shoulders, slowing me down, making me stumble, forcing me to struggle ungraciously against their good intentions, fearful of hurting their feelings. —

Mary Russell's next travel book will be about Antigua, Dominica and the Caribbean Windward Islands.

MONICA CONNELL

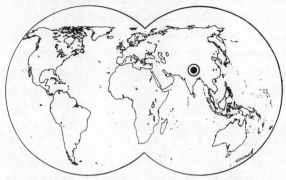

Anthropological studies in Nepal

Monica, born 1952 in Oxford of Irish parents, was raised and educated in Belfast, then studied sociology at London University, followed by social anthropology at Oxford. Her travel book *Against a Peacock Sky* (1991) was shortlisted for the *Yorkshire Post* best first work award for that year. A subsequent book, *Gathering Carrigheen*, about a Donegal community is not yet published. Monica is now married and lives in Bristol, after six months in Moscow. She is working on a novel.

Monica does not like the process of travel. She prefers to stay in one place and study the community and the culture. Her journey to Nepal was undertaken for her doctorate fieldwork in social anthropology. She and Peter, her assistant and photographer, took Nepali classes before leaving. Arriving at Kathmandu it took four months for her research project to be approved by Tirbhuvan University. Once approval was obtained, in October they flew to Jumla, a remote area of Nepal ten days' walk from the nearest motorable road. After four days in Jumla Bazaar settlement, they set out with their sleeping bags to look for a village where they could live and work, and arrived in Talphi.

— As soon as we were inside the village I felt a rush of panic. The paths were littered with heaps of excrement, and the houses were very close together, so there was a sense of being trapped, with people shouting and staring from all sides. A pack of dogs ran after us, barking and snarling and we had to stop and fend them off with stones. —

They got into contact with the villagers without much success and Monica felt 'appalled by the sheer arrogance of anthropology'.

Sitting, discouraged, beneath a tree outside the village and wondering what to do next, two boys come running up and tell them their father Kalchu has agreed that they can stay with the family for six months. In the end they spent a year in the village, slowly assembling, 'like a jig-saw puzzle', research on the life they see going on around them, without knowing what the final result will be.

Thinking back over her year in Talphi, it was the close relationship eventually built up with Kalchu and his family, and what Monica learned from the people as communication became easier, which remained most vividly in her mind. Monica learned, for instance, how to husk rice, grind grain, make *rotis*, dress in local clothes and replaster the floor of the house with a mixture of clay and cow-dung. She was taught not to fetch water, cook or touch any man when menstruating. Learning was part of the process by which she and Peter were 'humbled and then re-socialised'.

Monica never got used to the smoke from the fire in the centre of the room. 'In the end Kalchu let us cut a hole in the roof to serve as a chimney. We sacrificed a chicken first to stop the hole being used for access to the house by evil spirits. But the chimney only worked on windless days. At other times the smoke would still be blown hither and thither and we continued to suffer from headaches and coughs along with everyone else.' She also hated being permanently ingrained with soot. Several times when she had lice, fleas, worms and diarrhoea all at once, she dreamed of a bathroom.

One of the women with whom Monica becomes friendly is Jakali:

— One autumn, when Jakali's husband had gone on a trading trip to the south, the two of us harvested her millet crop. We spent five days wading through the sea of grain, slicing heavy brown heads from their flimsy stalks with sickles and tossing them onto baskets on our backs. Another time, in early summer, I helped her pick the purple *dantelo* berries that she used for making oil. The *dantelo* bushes grew wild around the village, between the fields and all along the river banks, and we wandered from one clump to another, scratching the backs of our hands on thorns as we rummaged for berries among the thick green foliage. When our baskets were full we took them to the stream and trod the mass of berries underwater so the fleshy pulp was washed away. Two of Jakali's daughters came rushing over when they saw what we were doing. She took off their clothes so they could play naked and they shrieked with delight as they flopped and splashed in the swirling purple water.

During the monsoon I didn't see Jakali for several weeks. She and her family had left the village, locking up their house with its beautiful carved window frame, and taking their cows, dogs and chickens to the monsoon settlements on the south-facing slopes of Jimale. Then one evening, when the rain had stopped for the first time since morning and the wind had swept the sky with watery blue and orange, she came to see me. I knew at once that there was something wrong; her face was strained and she was breathing hard as though she'd hurried. She sat down and carefully unwound the shawl that held the baby on her back. I gasped – the baby's head was covered in blisters; in places the film of skin had peeled away and the flesh beneath was red and angry. —

The baby had fallen into the fire. Monica offers to walk to the hospital with Jakali and the baby, but Jakali refuses, for outside the village evil spirits might enter the baby's body through the wound on her head. So Monica gets iodine, and dressings and boils water to treat the baby. She does her best with the struggling infant. Three days later Monica goes up the steep hillside to change the dressing and finds Jakali's wooden hut.

'Inside, a fire was burning in the central hearth. Jakali was sitting on the pine-needle floor, tapping out the dough for *rotis* between her palms and tossing the finished discs on to a heavy iron pan. The baby was lying across her lap, asleep.' Jakali says the baby is all right, though she cries a lot at night. After sharing the *rotis* with Jakali, Monica changes the baby's dressing, but Jakali still refuses to seek outside help. Monica gives Jakali some ampicillin capsules for the baby.

Three days later Monica returns and finds the baby lying face down on a shawl in the sun. The bandage is filthy and has slipped down over both eyes, but the wound has scabbed over, and the antibiotic has cleared the infection. This episode draws Monica and Jakali together.

Jakali now always brings Monica some little gift, eggs or potatoes. One evening Monica is invited for another meal. 'It was the night before her husband was to go on his annual trading trip to the southern border. All evening people dropped in to say goodbye, Jakali poured out bowls of beer and *raksi* for them and the night dissolved into laughter and stories until, quite unexpectedly, it was dawn.'

— After he'd gone I helped Jakali make some beer that would ferment, to be ready for his return in three weeks time. We sat on the roof to avoid the smoke in the house while the vat of barley boiled and boiled. Occasionally one or other of us would go inside to check that it hadn't boiled dry and to add some more wood to the fire. When at last it was soft Jakali tipped it on to the newly-plastered floor to let it cool. We crumbled the yeast and then crammed it all back into the vat, covering it with a sheet of birch bark. After three days

the fermentation had begun and we transferred it into a clay jar which Jakali sealed with cow-dung. Every day she put the jar out in the warmth of the sun; every night she brought it in. —

One evening, sitting by the fire carding wood together, Jakali tells Monica her husband is going to take a second wife, for she has only given him daughters and he wants a son, for only a real son who is flesh and blood can perform his funeral rites.

— Jakali had been married before – an arranged marriage to a man in Chaura. When she met her present husband they'd fallen in love; he'd paid adultery money to her first husband after she'd run away to live with him. I could tell from her voice and the sadness in her face that she loved him still. The real tragedy, however, was that in her first marriage she'd given birth to two sons, but their father had kept them both. Now she wasn't sure she could conceive again. —

Jakali has learned to accept that life is like this, 'for sometimes we laugh and sometimes we cry'.

Since leaving Talphi Peter has been back three times to see their friends, but Monica has never returned. 'For the time being, the memory is as much as my senses can process.'

ROSITA BOLAND

Hitching around the coastline of Ireland

Rosita (born Ennis 1965, but has lived mostly in Dublin), hitch-hiked round the coastline of Ireland alone in winter. This took almost three months, starting from her home town, staying mostly in hostels, occasionally in bed and breakfasts or with friends and relatives, and her book *Sea Legs* (1992) was the result. Rosita, who has also published *Muscle Creek* (1991), a collection of poems, at present lives in London and is writing a novel. Her previous continental travel includes East Europe and Turkey. In 1988 she spent a year hitch-hiking, camping and hostelling in Australia during which she crossed the three thousand kilometres of the Nullarbor.

Rosita writes, 'a hitch-hiker repays in kind by talking to the driver, who will often pick someone up precisely for that reason,' and *Sea Legs* is full of conversations with a multitude of different characters met on the road or in pubs. Rosita travels primarily to meet people.

Staying at Leon's Hostel in Clifden, Co. Galway Rosita goes into Mannion's pub to meet the locals who were, as usual, all men:

— I found myself in this situation many, many times. As a single woman, I had two choices. I could either sit quietly and read a book or newspaper while having a drink, or I could talk to people. Mostly, I chose to talk. There was absolutely no point in making this journey unless I talked to people in the places I went through. In pubs, I ended up speaking almost exclusively to men, since they were nearly always the only other customers. Sometimes I started the conversation, sometimes they did.

I ordered a Guinness in Mannion's and sat down. The barman looked like a sort of Celtic Woody Allen, with flaming red hair and thick-lensed spectacles, the frames of which were sellotaped together. A poker session was going on in one corner of the room, with plenty of ten and twenty pound notes on the table. A game of pool in another corner was being watched intently by a dozen or so people.

A very, very drunk man lurched over to me. His eyes had gone so far back in his head that they were practically slits. His face was paper-white. He was enormous.

'I'm a bogman and I'm a tramp!' he said, slapping me on the back with a hand the size of a steak. 'Would a woman like yourself be interested in a bed with a man like myself?'

I was not, to be mild about it.

The bogman and tramp introduced himself as being from Ballyconneely. My name provided him with great difficulty. He couldn't get his tongue around it.

'Are ye going to be long in Clifden, Movita? Is it Movita that's yer name?'

I nodded. His face was centimetres from mine. His arm was firmly round my shoulders. I was not enjoying my Guinness.

'You wouldn't think of changing your mind at all about my offer, Movita?'

The steak was applied once more to my back. Sick of this, I drank up and went down the street in search of Vaughan's.

Vaughan's was much more subdued. There were only a handful of customers, all of them engrossed in watching *The Late Late Show*. I talked to the barman about fish farms.

At closing time, I went to find the party at the Alcock and Brown. It was the twenty-first birthday of a local girl called Mercedes. There was no mistaking Mercedes, as she was resplendent in black ankle boots and a black cocktail mini.

'Do you know Mercedes well?' a few people inquired politely.

'Not *terribly* well.'

I was asked to dance by a drunk boy. He worked in the fishing, but was currently unemployed. He fixed his arms around me and wheeled me furiously about the floor, under the impression that he was waltzing with me. We bashed into the real waltzing couples. We tripped over flexes. We trod on sandwiches. I could see Mercedes' mother looking at us with a concerned expression on her face. All this time, I was desperately trying to extract myself from his arms.

When the music stopped, I tore myself away and fled to a dark corner. I took the opportunity to sample the birthday cake, which was very good.

The music started again. Someone was planting kisses on my neck. It was the drunk boy, who had appeared out of nowhere and who was loudly declaring that he loved me. People began to stare.

I pleaded a need to go to the loo, and bolted. There was an unlocked door in the kitchen and I let myself out into the street. The curtains in the ground floor function room had not yet been drawn. I could see Mercedes making a speech at the microphone; and my admirer, who was still prowling around; and Deirdre, still looking cool and unruffled, collecting up the trays of food.

I left them to it and went to bed.

If there were fireworks going off in my head next morning, I consoled myself with the thought that there must have been cannons in the heads of others in the town. I armed myself with the newspaper and went to have a quiet coffee in My Teashop while I was waiting for the firework display to burn itself out.

The Clifden shops had some wonderful names. Humanity Dick, Destry Rides Again, Fire and Fleece, An Spailpín Fánach. There were several craft shops, coffee shops, old-fashioned pubs; many of them with beautifully-kept shop fronts. I could well imagine it being crammed with people in the summer months, as everyone told me it was. It was clear that Clifden survived mainly on income from the holiday influx of people, and that the charming, carefully-painted shop fronts were tended and cultivated with the same care as prize garden produce, but the town itself remained vital. It did not seem to me to have traded its soul to the tourists and become spoilt, as has happened elsewhere.

The fireworks were now damp squibs. I put my boots on and started walking out the small peninsula west of Clifden, which has a name straight from a child's storybook; Bóthar na Spéire, or, the Sky Road.

The road was built high up on a peninsula, so that at times it seemed to be literally disappearing into the sky. And for once the sky was a wide and miraculous shade of blue, making it possible to see for great distances. Peninsulas unfolded themselves on the horizon, each new turn in the road revealed another bright-rimmed beach, another cove or island.

And tacked to every second tree were signs, some hand-painted, some commercially produced. All carried the message; 'No Fin Fish Farming here'. All the way through Connemara I had been noticing these signs, tacked to gable walls, to trees, gates and telegraph poles. About halfway round the Sky Road, I saw a hand-painted sign nailed to a tree: 'The West Awake/No Fish Farms/Nuvan Kills', with a black skull and crossbones daubed beneath it. The salmon cages were clearly visible in the bay beneath me.

So far I had not met anyone in Connemara who had a good word to say about fish farming. That weekend, there was an annual conference of the Irish Salmon Growers Association in Furbo. The use of the controversial insecticide, Nuvan, was one of the foremost issues under discussion. Nuvan is used in fish farming to kill sea lice, which feed on the flesh of young salmon. It succeeds in killing off the sea lice, but the side-effects connected with the use of this chemical are still a shadowy area. It is feared that the use of Nuvan on fish farms has an adverse effect on the surrounding environment, particularly on wild sea trout and wild salmon. It has not been scientifically proven that this is so.

There is no denying that the angular cages scattered in bays around the coast of Ireland are ugly eyesores which detract from spectacular views. Neither can it be denied that fish farms in Ireland – most of which have started up in the last decade – provide employment in remote coastal areas where, outside the boom summer months of July and August, unemployment is very high. The process of feeding the smoults, maintaining the cages, harvesting the fish and packing them all provide jobs. My brother David was working for Salmara, a fish farm off Derrynane Bay in southwest Kerry, where the same controversy was going on. Visiting him the previous summer, I had been told not to discuss Salmara in public. 'You could get yourself into a fierce argument.'

By the time I had walked almost the entire loop of the Sky Road, the blue sky had dissolved. There were huge clouds, constantly melting into each other and changing colour. The mountains became insubstantial-looking, the faintest wash of bluish-grey on a liquid horizon. I could see banks of rain rushing over the sea.

I began hitching and as the first drops of rain began to pelt down out of a black sky, a car stopped. The lift back into Clifden was on a road that was literally more pot-hole than road. The car bucked and leaped. The woman driver had had a blown tyre that morning on this same stretch of road.

'It's said,' she told me grimly, 'that there's a Clifden garage which survives solely on the income from fixing cars that have to travel this road.'

At Clifden, I left a note for Deirdre at the reception desk of the Alcock and Brown, returned to Leo's Hostel to pack my rucksack and waited for Pat O'Connell to collect me. Pat was the mother of one of my exiled London friends, Toni, and had invited me to stay the night at Errislannan, near Clifden.

Seal Cottage was a peaceful place, overlooking Mannin Bay, with a garden that ran down to the sea. The two dogs, Bruno and Sam, gave me a noisy welcome and then stretched out in front of the fire. We had gin and tonics and a leisurely supper, while outside the rain and wind lashed the windows.

Next morning when I went into the living room, Pat was looking through a pair of binoculars at seals on the rocks at the end of her garden. 'I see them clearly every morning,' she told me, and pointed out the seals to me. She was so used to seeing them that the slightest flicker of a fin revealed the seals to her, whereas I searched for a long time with the binoculars before I could distinguish seals from the seal-coloured rocks.

'And there is an otter in my garden,' she said, and went with me in her dressing gown into the windswept garden to point out where she saw her otter in the evenings.

I was getting the boat from Cleggan to Inishbofin at ten o'clock that morning. Pat would not hear of me hitching, so I said goodbye to Bruno and Sam, the seals and the otter's garden and we set off for Cleggan. —

Ireland of the 1990s is still still safe for the lone woman hitch-hiker, and a suitable country in which to end this volume.

SELECT BIBLIOGRAPHY

AITKEN, Maria. *'A Girdle round the earth', Women Travellers and Adventurers*, London: Robinson, 1988.

BATES, Daisy. *The Passing of the Aborigines*, London: John Murray, 1938. Elizabeth Salter, *Daisy Bates*. Sydney: Angus & Robertson, 1971. Julia Blackburn, *Daisy Bates in the Desert*. London: Secker & Warburg, 1994.

BIRKETT, Dea. *Spinsters Abroad, Victorian Lady Explorers*, Oxford: Blackwell, 1989 [mentions Flora Shaw].

BLACKWOOD, Hariot G. (Lady Dufferin). *My Canadian Journal 1872-78*, London: John Murray, 1891; *My Russian & Turkish Journals*, London: John Murray, 1916.

BLESSINGTON, Marguerite, (Countess of). *The Idler in Italy*, Paris: Baudry's European Library, 1841.

Michael Sadleir, *The Strange Life of Lady Blessington-D'Orsay*. London: Constable, 1933. Elizabeth Owens Blackburne, *Illustrious Irishwomen*, London: Tinsley Brothers, 1877.

BOLAND, Rosita. *Sea-Legs: Hitch-hiking the coast of Ireland alone*, Dublin: New Island Books, 1992.

BUNBURY, Selina. *A Visit to the Catacombs etc.*, London: W.W. Robinson, 1849.

CONNELL, Monica. *Against a Peacock Sky*, London: Viking, 1991.

COSTELLO, Louise Stuart. *A Pilgrimage to Auvergne from Picardy to Le Velay*, London: Richard Bentley, 1842.

CROMMELIN, May (Maria Henrietta de la Cherois). *Over the Andes from Chile to Peru*, London: Richard Bentley, 1896. *'I Little Knew'*, London: John Milne, 1908.

CUSACK, Margaret Anna, (Mother Clare). *The Story of My Life*, London: Hodder & Stoughton, 1891. Irene ffrench Eagar, *The Nun of Kenmare*, Dublin: The Women's Press, 1979. Margaret Rose O'Neill, *The Life of Mother Clare*, Seattle: Sisters of St Joseph of Peace, 1990.

DALY, Emily Lucy De Burgh. *An Irishwoman in China*, London: T. Werner Laurie, 1915.

DUFFERIN, Lady Helen Selina. *Lispings from Low Latitudes, or, Extracts from the Journal of the Hon. Impulsia Gushington*, London: John Murray, 1863.

EVERETT, Katherine. *Bricks & Flowers, Memoirs*, London: Constable, 1949.

FUSSELL, Paul. 'Travel, Tourism and "International Understanding" ', from *Killing in Verse & Prose and other essays*, London: Bellew, 1990.

GRIMSHAW, Ethel Beatrice. *In the Strange South Seas*, London: Hutchinson and New York: Doubleday Page, 1907. *From Fiji to the Cannibal Islands*, London: Everleigh Nash, 1907; *Isles of Adventure*, London: Herbert Jenkins, 1930.

HAMISH, Maureen (Mary Loughran). *Adventures of an Irish girl at home & abroad*, Dublin: J.K. Mitchell,1906.

HECKFORD, Sarah. *A Lady Trader in the Transvaal*, London: Sampson Low, Marston, 1882. Vivien Allen, *Lady Trader*, London: Collins, 1979.

HINKSON, Pamela. *Indian Harvest*, London: Collins, 1941.

JAMESON, Anna Brownell. *Winter Studies & Summer Rambles in Canada*, London: Saunders & Otley, 1838. Clara Thomas, *Love and work enough: the life of Anna Jameson*, 1967.

LE BLOND, Mrs Aubrey (Elizabeth Hawkins-Whitshed). *Adventures on the roof of the world*, London: T. Fisher Unwin, 1904. *Day in, Day out*, London: John Lane, 1928.

LESLIE, Anita. *A Story half told: a wartime autobiography*, London: Hutchinson, 1983.

LYNCH, Hannah. *French Life in Town & Country*, London: George Newnes, 1901.

MacCANNELL, Dean. *The Tourist: a new theory of the leisure class*, New York, Schocken Books, 1989.

MELCHETT, Sonia. *Passionate Quests: five modern women travellers*, London: Heinemann, 1991. [Includes Dervla Murphy].

MIDDLETON, Dorothy. *Victorian Lady Travellers*, New York: Dutton, 1965, London: Routledge, 1965.

MORGAN, Lady (Sydney Owenson). *France*, London: Henry Colburn 1818. Elizabeth Suddaby & P. Yarrow, *Lady Morgan in France*, London: Oriel Press 1971; Mary Campbell, *Lady Morgan – The Life and Times of Sydney Owenson*, *London: Pandora, 1988.*

MORRIS, Mary (editor), in collaboration with Larry O'Connor. *Maiden Voyages: writings of women travellers*, New York: Random House, 1993, [includes Kate O'Brien and Dervla Murphy].

MURPHY, Dervla. *Full Tilt*, London: John Murray 1965; *Tibetan Foothold*, London: John Murray, 1966; *The Ukimwi Road*, London: John Murray, 1993. *Wheels within Wheels* [autobiography], London: John Murray, 1979.

O'BRIEN, Charlotte Grace. *Selections from her writings and correspondence and a memoir by her nephew Stephen Gwynne*, Dublin: Maunsel, 1909.

O'BRIEN, Kate. *Farewell Spain*, London: Heinemann, 1937, ed. used Virago, 1985; *My Ireland*, London: Batsford, 1962.

ROBINSON, Jane. *Wayward Women: a guide to women travellers*, Oxford University Press, 1990.

RUSSELL, Mary. *The Blessings of a good thick skirt, women travellers and their world*, London: Collins, 1986, [includes Mrs A. Le Blond and D. Murphy]; *Please don't call it Soviet Georgia*, London: Serpent's Tail, 1991.

SHARE, Bernard (ed.). *Far Green Fields, fifteen hundred years of Irish Travel Writing*, Belfast: Blackstaff Press, 1992, [includes B. Grimshaw, P. Hinkson, A. Leslie, H. Lynch, D. Murphy, K. Wilmot].

SHAW, Flora Louise (Lady Lugard). *Letters from South Africa, Letters from Queensland*, both by *The Times* special correspondent, London: Macmillan, 1893. E. Moberley Bell, *Flora Shaw (Lady Lugard DBE)*, London: Constable, 1947.

SOMERVILLE, Edith OE. (With Martin Ross) *In the Vine Country*, London: W.H. Allen, 1893; *Strayaways*, London: Longmans, Green, 1920; *The States through Irish eyes*, Boston & New York, Houghton Mifflin, 1930, London: Heinemann, 1931.

THORNTON, Anna Jane. *The Female Sailor. Interesting and Wonderful Adventurers of that Extraordinary Woman Anna Jane Thornton, the female sailor; disclosing important secrets, unknown to the public, written by herself*, London: J. Thompson, 1835.

TRANT, Clarissa. *The Journal of Clarissa Trant 1800-1832*, ed. C.S. Luard, London: John Lane, 1925.

TRENCH, Melasina. *Journal kept during a visit to Germany in 1799,1800*, London: 1861.

WILDE, (Lady) Jane Francesca. *Driftwood from Scandinavia*, London: Richard Bentley, 1884. Horace Wyndham, *Speranza: a biography of Lady Wilde*, London & New York: T.V. Boardman, 1951. Joy Melville, *Mother of Oscar: the life of Jane Francesca Wilde*, London: John Murray, 1994.

WILMOT, Katherine and Martha. ed. Thomas U. Sadleir, *An Irish Peer on the Continent 1801-1803*, London: Williams & Norgate, 1920; ed. H.M. Hyde, *The Russian Journals of Martha and Catherine Wilmot*, London: Macmillan, 1934; ed. Elizabeth Mavor, *The Grand Tours of Katherine Wilmot, France 1801-3 & Russia 1805-7*, London: Weidenfeld & Nicolson, 1992.

Acknowledgements:

The author and publishers are grateful to the following for permission to quote from the works mentioned: The estate of Daisy Bates and John Murray (Publishers) Ltd for permission to quote from *The Passing of the Aborigines* (John Murray, 1938) / Rosita Boland and New Island Books, Dublin for permission to quote from *Sea Legs* (1992) / Monica Connell and the Penguin Group for permission to quote from *Against a Peacock Sky* (Viking, 1991) / Constable and the estate of Katherine Everett for permission to quote from *Bricks & Flowers, Memoirs* (1949) / Aitken & Stone Limited and the estate of Beatrice Grimshaw for permission to quote from *In the Strange South Seas* (Hutchinson, 1907); *From Fiji to the Cannibal Islands* (Everleigh Nash, 1907); *Isles of Adventure* (Herbert Jenkins, 1930) / The Russell family at Dunkathel for permission to quote from the unpublished diaries of Beatrice Gubbins / The estate of Pamela Hinkson for permission to quote from *Indian Harvest* (Collins, 1941) / The estate of Anita Leslie and her publisher Hutchinson for permission to quote from *A Story Half Told: a wartime autobiography* (1983) / Sister Hilary Lyons for her personal contribution / Dervla Murphy and her publisher John Murray for permission to quote from *Full Tilt* (1965); *Tibetan Foothold* (1966); *The Ukimwi Road* (1993) / Donough O'Brien and David Higham Associates for permission to quote from *Farewell Spain* (Virago, 1985); *My Ireland* (Batsford, 1962), both by Kate O'Brien / Mary Russell and Serpent's Tail for permission to quote from *Please Don't Call it Soviet Georgia* (1991).

Photo credits:

The author and publishers are grateful to the following who supplied photographs for reproduction in this book: page 39 courtesy of the National Gallery of Ireland / page 58 'Miss Gushington experiences a new sensation,' from *Lispings from Low Latitudes: Extracts from the Journal of The Hon Impulsia Gushington*, (London: John Murray, 1863) / page 69 by kind permission of St Clare's Convent, Kenmare / page 109 courtesy of Sir Toby Coghill / page 105 from *An Irishwoman in China* (London: T. Werner Laurie, 1915) / page 106 by kind permission of A.S.J. O'Neill, Belfast and the Percy French Society / page 121 from *Daisy Bates* by Elizabeth Salter (Angus and Robertson Publishers, Sydney, 1971) / page 134 from *Girdle Round the Earth: Women Travellers and Adventurers,* by Maria Aitken (Robinson Publishing, London, 1988) / page 143 courtesy of Caroline Everett, Sussex / page 177 courtesy of Bord Fáilte / page 193 courtesy of Dervla Murphy, photograph by Tara Heinemann / page 197 courtesy of Sister Hilary Lyons / page 203 courtesy of Mary Russell / page 209 courtesy of Monica Connell / page 212 courtesy of Rosita Boland, photograph by Vincent McGroary.

Pillars of the House
An Anthology of Verse by Irish Women

Edited by A.A. Kelly

Pillars of the House is the first anthology of Irishwomen's verse ever to be published. Arranged chronologically, it allows the reader to trace poetic developments from the seventeenth century to the work of some of Ireland's leading contemporary poets. Eavan Boland, Máire Mhac an tSaoi andMedbh McGuckian are among the eighty contributors. 'Social history through verse - what an entertaining way to learn more about ourselves.' *Women's Clubs Magazine*. Paperback £7.99

Women in Early Modern Ireland

Margaret Mac Curtain and Mary O'Dowd

The lives of our ancestors in a period of turbulence, change and shifting fortunes. Covering domestic, political and religious issues, this unique study covers the period 1500-1800. Contributors include Kenneth Nicholls, Prof P.J. Corish, Dr Jo Murphy-Lawless, Dr K. Simms, Dr Ciaran Brady and others. Paperback £14.95/ Hardback £27.50

As Wicked a Woman
Eleanor, Countess of Desmond (1545-1638)

Anne Chambers

'*As wicked a woman as ever was bred in Ireland*', her enemies declared. Eleanor, wife of the rebel Earl of Desmond played a part in the struggle of Gaelic Ireland at the beginning of a new era of English rule. A struggle that destroyed her home, scattered her children, killed her husband and left her in abject poverty but could not break her spirit.

'Anne Chambers is one of the rare exceptions. She has that quality, even in historians rare, of seeing, feeling and understanding the periods she writes about as if she were a contemporary.' *Irish Independent*
Hardback £8.95

Granuaile:
The Life and Times of Grace O'Malley
(c. 1530-1603)

Anne Chambers

The standard biography of this woman chieftain of the O'Malley clan. Granuaile, a notorious captain and pirate, was, even by today's standards, a woman of extraordinary power and character. 'Anne Chambers' portrait of Grace is detached, authoritative... a delightful book.' *Image*

'While Granuaile is a well-established legendary figure it was left to Ms Chambers to present us with an historical reality which is equally if not more compelling than the legend.' Garry Hynes, *Sunday Tribune*. Paperback £5.99

The English Traveller in Ireland

John P. Harrington

Absorbing, amusing and original, these illustrated accounts of Ireland cover 3 centuries of superb prose stylists including Edmund Spenser, William Thackeray, Robert Payne et al. Enlightening, educational, sometimes funny, often exasperating but always interesting. Hardback £22.95

Alexis de Tocqueville's Journey in Ireland
July/August, 1835

Emmet Larkin, Translator & Editor

A famous travel writer's sharply observed account of Irish society. Alexis de Tocqueville visited Ireland in July and August of 1835. He was welcome everywhere, in the mansions of the Protestant bishops and in the simple homes of priests whom he accompanied on their parish rounds. The diary and letters that he wrote provide a rare insight into one of the seminal minds of the nineteenth century. 'A more interesting picture of the poverty, minority domination and popular religion in action not long before the Famine years could not be imagined.' *Books Ireland*. Paperback £9.95